The Pilot's
Air Traffic Control
Handbook

TAB
PRACTICAL
FLYING SERIES

No. 2435
$24.95

The Pilot's Air Traffic Control Handbook

Paul E. Illman

TAB BOOKS Inc.
Blue Ridge Summit, PA

Notice Excerpts from aeronautical charts and other publications, included in this book, are for illustration purposes only and are *not for use in navigation*.

FIRST EDITION
FIRST PRINTING

Library of Congress Cataloging in Publication Data

Illman, Paul E.
    The pilot's air traffic control handbook / by Paul E. Illman.
      p.   cm.
    Includes index.
    ISBN 0-8306-9435-8 ISBN 0-8306-0435-9 (pbk.)
    1. Air traffic control—United States. I. Title.
TL725.3.T7I35 1989
629.136′6—dc20   89-31857
                                    CIP

TAB BOOKS Inc. offers software for sale. For information and a catalog, please contact TAB Software Department, Blue Ridge Summit, PA 17294-0850.

Questions regarding the content of this book should be addressed to:

    Reader Inquiry Branch
    TAB BOOKS Inc.
    Blue Ridge Summit, PA 17294-0214

Edited by Carl H. Silverman

Contents

Acknowledgments

To the many people in the Federal Aviation Administration who contributed their time and their expertise to help me prepare the chapters that follow, I am deeply indebted. Without their cooperation, it would have been very difficult to gather the information necessary to achieve the purpose of the book. Being able to go behind the scenes, for technical information as well as advice to pilots from experienced controllers, was essential. Accordingly, I must acknowledge the contributions of the following individuals, along with my thanks for their assistance.

Before anything was put on paper, I asked for a meeting with Bob Raynesford, the public affairs officer for FAA's Central Region. The intent was to seek his guidance as to people to see who could contribute to the various chapters. Bob not only suggested names, but along with his assistant, Sandy Campbell, gave me reference materials that proved very important as I moved into the actual writing.

Three people were critical to the validity of Chapter 1, "The Early Days—A Brief Review." They were: Stewart Morris, John Knoell, and Nick Komons. Stu Morris, at the time an area manager in the Kansas City Air Route Traffic Control Center, is currently the assistant manager for training. A veteran controller, he first loaned me a suitcase full of old magazines, articles, charts, and manuals he had accumulated over the years. He then put me in touch with John Knoell, one of the early controllers. John had names and events of the '20s and '30s at his fingertips, which, coupled with Stu's memorabilia, were valuable contributions to the chapter.

Acknowledgments

Nick A. Komons is the FAA's agency historian and author of *Bonfires to Beacons*, a book given to me by Bob Raynesford and to which I referred frequently in the chapter. To ensure further validity, Nick willingly agreed to edit the completed chapter, and, in the process, made several important factual corrections. John also edited the chapter, and their combined comments were major contributions to this brief look into history.

For the airspace and Special Use Airspace chapters, I turned to four authorities: Dick Mitby, airspace and plans specialist, and Roger Wingert, military operations specialist—both at the Kansas City Center. Dick and Roger were of great assistance in providing technical data and procedural information, and in reviewing the two chapters. Lt. Col. John Williams and Lt. Col. Bob Woolley, Air Force representatives to the FAA's Central Region, were especially helpful in clarifying many issues related to the Special Use Airspace. They, along with Roger, edited that chapter for its accuracy. Despite several meetings and phone calls with these four gentlemen, each continually responded with patience and courtesy. Their help was invaluable.

Another important source was Dale Carnine, airspace and procedures specialist, for the Central Region. Dale reviewed with me many of the FAA policies relative to the airspace system and proposed Terminal Control Area reconfigurations. He also saw to it that I had a copy of the 1988 issue of the *National Airspace System Plan*, much of which constitutes Chapter 11.

For the chapters on control towers and Approach/Departure Control, I sought the help of George Short, air traffic manager at the Kansas City Downtown Airport tower, and Ivan Hunt, air traffic manager at the Kansas City International Airport tower. George introduced me to Hal Roberts, the quality assurance and training specialist, who spent hours with me discussing tower cab operations and what VFR pilots should know about operating in a controlled environment. Many of his observations are incorporated throughout the book, and his editing of the chapter was a further contribution to the effort.

Ivan Hunt introduced me to Dave McNay, air traffic specialist, who is both tower cab- and radar-certified. Dave answered innumerable questions about the workings of Approach Control, walked me through the facility, sketched the floor plan reproduced in Chapter 7, took photographs, and edited the chapter. He and Hal assisted in any way they could, by phone or in person, and I am indebted to both for their patience and the assistance they so willingly offered.

Two visits to the consolidated Automated Flight Service Station (AFSS) in Columbia, Missouri, were made extremely valuable through the help of Norm Baker, assistant manager of the facility, and Walt Roberts, area manager. Norm reviewed with me the consolidated FSS concept, how it functions, and its advantages to IFR and VFR pilots. Walt then took me through the facility, explaining the various positions, and answering countless questions. Both he and

Norm also gave of their time to review the final chapter draft, which, without their complete cooperation, would have been a difficult chapter to write.

Back at Center, and again with Stu Morris' help, I met Dale Carrison, a veteran controller and active pilot. Dale was the ideal person to take me behind the scenes and explain the inner workings of the traffic controlling function. Whether at home or work, by phone or in person, he did his best to be sure that I had no unanswered questions. He and Stu edited the Center chapter, and both have my sincere thanks for their many contributions.

Bob Belinke, training specialist and active controller, was another important source of assistance. Bob not only tied several loose technical ends together for me but also edited Chapter 10, "ATC Specialists." His corrections were much to the point and were incorporated in the final product.

Others deserving recognition are Irv Hoffman, plans and programs specialist, who provided the floor plan of the Center that is reproduced in Chapter 9, and explained the physical organization of the facility and the functions within it. Another is Joe Doerr, a specialist in the Traffic Management Unit (TMU), who helped me gain some understanding of the traffic metering system and its role in spacing traffic into major airport areas. And then there was Bob Fousek, an area manager, who escorted me through the facility as I tried to take a few photographs. His patience with me at the time of a shift change (a critical period) was admirable.

Finally, four others deserve recognition: Don Hulsey, a veteran controller; Mark Hauser, another experienced controller; Nicole Dickey, one who is called a "developmental," and Scott Haney, an air traffic assistant. We all met to explore some of their feelings about being a controller, and their observations are incorporated in Chapter 10. I am grateful to them for their willingness to share their thoughts and for editing the completed chapter.

To each of the facility managers—Felton Lancaster, the Center's air traffic manager; Jim Jones, air traffic manager at the Columbia AFSS; George Short; and Ivan Hunt—I am indebted for allowing members of their staffs to contribute to this project. And to those who did participate, I can only reiterate my thanks for helping me construct what I hope will be a meaningful series of chapters—meaningful to both the users of the airspace system and to those behind the scenes who so professionally provide its many services.

Introduction

As we move into the last decade of the century, publishing a book on the national airspace and air traffic control systems has a certain element of risk—risk because what is fact today may be false tomorrow. Changes and new regulations are flowing out the FAA headquarters in an almost unprecedented volume, and the end doesn't seem in sight. Despite this period of revolution or evolution, three reasons compelled me to accept the risk.

For one, there are two constants that will probably always exist—controlled airspace and uncontrolled airspace. Changes proposed or adopted may enlarge the first and diminish the second, but the basic rules for operating in either are likely to remain essentially as they are today. I'll discuss some of the proposed revisions, but, again, they should not drastically alter the pilot's—primarily the VFR pilot's—responsibilities. It thus seems logical that, regardless of rating, we should know the regulations and procedures related to operating in both bodies of air.

A second reason for pursuing this effort is that new hardware may increase safety and enhance aircraft traffic flow, but another constant remains—the human element. Modern technology has been able to automate a multitude of mechanical operations, but it has not yet found a substitute for the mind and judgment of man. People are still piloting airplanes, and people on the ground are still directing and communicating with those whose well-being they are guarding.

It is this human element that I address primarily but not exclusively. From the pilot's point of view, particularly the VFR general aviation pilot's, what should he or she know about the functions and operations of those who staff the Flight Service Stations (FSSs), the control towers, the Air Route Traffic Control Centers ("Center" or "ARTCC," for short), and the other ATC facilities? What responsibilities does the pilot have when flying in controlled airspace? What do those on the ground expect of him or her?

In the same context, it seems that we who fly should have an understanding of what goes on behind the scenes in the various FSSs and traffic control facilities—again, from the human element aspect. For example, what happens in an FSS when you call for a weather briefing? What information does the specialist need from you at the outset so that he or she can render a thorough briefing in the minimum amount of time? What takes place when you file a flight plan or fail to close it within 30 minutes of your estimated arrival? How does Departure Control "hand" you off to Center when you've requested cross-country VFR advisories? How does the tower keep track of a sky full of arriving and departing aircraft at 5:00 o'clock in the afternoon? If you enter a Terminal Control Area (TCA) without clearance, how does ATC track your aircraft so that the FAA can have a little chat with you after you've landed? What happens when an ATC facility is alerted to an emergency or a pilot reports that he's lost? What are some of the things pilots do or not do, say or not say, that bug controllers or create potentially dangerous situations? From the controller's point of view, what advice would he (or she) give to the pilot that would help in the overall process of radio communications and traffic control?

These are a few examples of the areas the book addresses, coupled with direct quotes and suggestions from ATC personnel. Yes, some of the current hardware is described and pictured, but this is not a technical treatise on radar or state-of-the-art electronics. That privilege is reserved for others far more qualified. In the same vein, illustrations of the correct radio communications procedures are kept to a minimum. This is not because the subject is unimportant, but proper radio usage is covered in depth in the TAB book I co-authored with Jay F. Pouzar, *The Pilot's Radio Communications Handbook (#2445), Third Edition*, April 1989.

A third reason for undertaking this project was the desire to produce a single source to which pilots could refer for basic airspace and air traffic control information. Simply put, I wanted a non-technical publication that would answer most of the VFR pilot's questions while, at the same time, contributing to a better understanding of what takes place behind the scenes in various ATC facilities. To my knowledge, no current publication addresses the subject from both the pilot's and controller's points of view. To ensure the accuracy (not necessarily the detailed thoroughness) of what I said, every chapter, except Chapter 12, was reviewed, corrected, and edited by at least one authority in each facility. Chapter 12, on the National Airspace System Plan, was taken directly from the 1988 edition of FAA's Congressionally-requested *National Airspace System Plan.*

That said, we must recognize the limits of the written word. Skill in any undertaking is the product of *knowledge* plus *understanding* plus *practice*. A book—yes, this book—can contribute to the first two, but practice, and thus the development of *skill*, is the province of the reader. Admittedly, for some, skill in the areas the book addresses may not be necessary. Yes, we can fly around for a lifetime in and out of uncontrolled airports; it's possible never to file a flight plan, contact a tower, enter a TCA, or ask a Center for cross-country traffic advisories. Depending on where we are and our level of knowledge, we can avoid any or all of the ATC facilities available to us, which, parenthetically, we've already paid for with our tax donations to Uncle Sam.

Such self-imposed limitations, however, vastly limit the pleasures and benefits of flight. With only a few exceptions, the national airspace is there for student pilot to airline captain. But its use does demand a certain level of competence, founded on knowledge and understanding. Call it "professionalism" if you will—a professionalism that all pilots can attain—even those for whom flying is merely a weekend avocation.

In effect, that observation sums up the fundamental objective of the book and why it was written. It was the desire, within the scope of the subject matter, to contribute directly to the VFR pilot's knowledge and, ultimately, to the level of professionalism that aviation demands. If the chapters that follow in any way make such a contribution, the principal objective will have been achieved.

1

The Early Days:
A Brief Review

A COUPLE OF COMMENTS ABOUT THIS CHAPTER: FIRST, THE INTENT OF THE book is to look at our national airspace system as it is today—not to trace its chronological development over the past 60 or 70 years. Others have done that in infinite and precise detail. How we got to where we are is indeed a fascinating story of experimentation, trials, successes, failures, delays, government bickering, politicking, philosophical differences, and economic inadequacies. As far as the matter of regulation was concerned, aviation was developing faster than the bureaucracy would or could react.

From all of the delays and the debating, however, we have evolved to the airspace system we know today. Understanding the system does not demand a historical recitation. That we admit. But a look back at the process of evolvement does seem compatible with what I'm trying to accomplish in the balance of the book.

Second, unless one has lived through the period, any historical review requires the availability of sources and resources. In this case, perhaps the most valuable resource was the 1978 FAA publication, *Bonfires to Beacons*, by Nick A. Komons. In minute detail, Mr. Komons has traced the evolvement of the airspace system and civil aviation policy from 1926 to 1938. Without his in-depth research, reconstructing that period of aviation in this country would have been an infinitely more difficult task.

Two other publications were also valuable. One, *International Air Traffic Control* (Pergamon Press, 1985) by Arnold Field, provided past and current insight into worldwide ATC practices. The second was Glen A. Gilbert's *Air Traffic Control—The Uncrowded Sky* (Smithsonian Institution, 1973). Gilbert was one of the first traffic controllers, and his book recounts knowledgeably the maturing of ATC from the early days up to the 70's.

With these resources, as well as business and trade publication articles that appeared in the 1930s, it was possible to capsulize some of the principal events that contributed to the airspace system we have today.

****

In certain respects, flying around in the truly uncrowded skies back in the early 1920s must have been quite an experience. With only a few minor requirements, freedom of the air was just that—freedom. Rules and restrictions were practically nonexistent. Go where you want to go; fly where you want to fly; do as you please. Great—for those with the derring-do to trust the wood and wire crates powered by untrustworthy powerplants.

In those days, anyone could start up a flying school, "train" an eager would-be airman, and send him forth without tests or requirements to meet any standards. A wartime licensing regulation was cancelled in 1919. If you wanted to build your own aircraft, you went ahead. If it flew, fine; if it didn't, it was your neck. Aircraft standards were as nonexistent as those for pilots.

Those same freedoms, however, were fraught with negatives. Airports were primitive grass or gravel strips; lighting for night operations was still in the future; aids to navigating between two points were unheard of; and radio was little more than an experiment. Aviation was for the daredevils and the barnstormers who hoped to make a few bucks by thrilling a gawking ground-bound populace.

This is not to say that attempts to establish some modicum of regulation were never made. They were, but opponents, for the most part, were more vociferous and more successful than the proponents. In the process of debate between the pros and the cons, the United States trailed the European countries in trying to bring reasonable order to a fledgling industry—if aviation could be called an industry in those start-up years.

THE AIRSPACE—WHO OWNS IT?

One of the most disputed questions in the early days of aviation—and, in fact, in the development of air law was, who owns the airspace above privately-held property? The cities? The states? The nations?

The ancient Roman maxim, *cujus est solum, ejus usque ad coelum* (who owns the land, owns it up to the sky) is generally considered the first air law. Accepting that as fact, the law and its enforcers went to work in the earliest days of flying, attempting to limit free access to the airspace.

Probably the first enforcement effort was in April 1784 when a French police lieutenant issued an ordinance banning balloon flights over Paris without a special permit. This was in reaction to such a flight several months before.

Particularly in Europe, this was a question of concern and debate. The size and number of countries abutting each other made the space above their boundaries—and whether it was indeed theirs—a matter of security as well as national sovereignty.

At the start of this century, three divergent concepts prevailed:

- The skies, like the high seas, were free and the common property of mankind.

- The skies above the nations were an integral part of each and of their territory.

- A combination of freedom of the air, while recognizing that each nation had certain rights to its own airspace.

Resolution of this issue was critically important to the future of aviation, both in Europe and in the United States. A beginning was made following the end of World War I.

1919: THE INTERNATIONAL CONVENTION FOR AIR NAVIGATION

The war in Europe was over, and the airplane had clearly demonstrated its destructive capabilities while giving hints of its potential as a vehicle of commerce and peace. The legal and philosophical questions had to be resolved, however, as well as the rules and regulations that would govern aviation, particularly international aviation.

In 1919, the International Convention on Air Navigation met in Paris to attack the key issues. Emerging from the Convention was the International Commission for Air Navigation (ICAN). The Convention, adopting the third concept listed above, recognized the sovereignty of the airspace above each state, but it also provided for the freedom of passage of civil aircraft over state territories. ICAN, then, was created to enforce the legislative, administrative, and judicial functions established by the Convention. Further, ICAN had the power to require member states to develop local regulations that would conform to those of the Convention. It also adopted the "General Rules for Air Traffic", which would be applicable to the various states.

The United States, although an original member of ICAN, did not ratify the agreements reached by the Convention. As a consequence, the absence of uniformity here continued. ICAN made sense when small countries abutted each other. Flights between them demanded uniform regulation, but international traffic in those days was hardly a matter of concern to us. Consequently, federal inaction persisted.

Such was not the case, however, in several states in the U.S. Particularly along the eastern seaboard, some of the states, as well as the local municipalities, wrote their own rules—rules that only created confusion and did little to advance aviation during the early postwar days.

Failure to adopt even ICAN's simple regulations had other adverse effects as well. Without any semblance of federal control over pilot licensing, aircraft production, maintenance standards, or operating rules, capital investment in the industry was hard to come by. Investors with money to spend were more than reluctant to put spare funds into an industry which had no laws to govern it.

By the same token, insurance was difficult or impossible to obtain. The absence of control encouraged irresponsibility on the ground and in the air. With high underwriter losses and undefined legal principles relative to liability claims, insurance was as elusive as investment capital. Only some degree of order would salvage the infant industry from the chaos that was choking it.

There were those, however, who wanted no part of regulation. To quote a few examples that Nick Komons cites:

- A flier from Cincinnati: "What we want is progress—not red tape!"

- A fixed-base operator: "I think regulation will put the average commercial aviator out of business."

- A Philadelphia pilot: "As sure as the sun rises and sets, strict government regulations will retard commercial aviation ten to fifteen years, if not kill it entirely."

- And the reaction of a typical commercial operator: "It seems somewhat absurd to have all this hullabaloo and endeavor to set the massive and ponderous machinery of the law on a measly 120 [commercial] airplanes."

THE BEGINNINGS OF A U.S. AIRSPACE SYSTEM

If there was any single impetus that forced the development of an airspace system in the United States it was the advent of air mail. Using Army aircraft and pilots, the Post Office Department began flying the mail in 1918. A few months after the start of service, the Department hired its own pilots, bought its own aircraft, and took over the operation, initially providing service between Washington, D.C., and New York. The service was then expanded in 1919 from

New York to Cleveland and Chicago, and a year later from Chicago to San Francisco.

The saga of flying day and night over nonexistent airways in all sorts of weather and in open-cockpit aircraft has been well-documented. Only with help of a few bonfires thoughtfully ignited by concerned citizens was any sort of an "airway" visible to the pilots. It was primitive, at its best. That, however, was the airmail pilot's lot.

Yes, the Post Office Department was part of the government, but that didn't mean that aviation was under government control. During the first half of the 1920s, there was much activity, but agreements relative to federal regulations were elusive goals. The matter of states' rights was one issue, as was intrastate versus interstate commerce. Then came legal questions, not the least of which, again, was who owns the airspace. Progress was slow, but it was coming.

The Air Mail Act of 1925 allowed the Post Office Department to let contracts to private operators for the transportation of mail by air. This was followed in 1926 by the Air Commerce Act, which was the first organized attempt to regulate the growing industry. Emerging from the Act was the Aeronautics Branch as part of the Department of Commerce. It was the Branch's responsibility to license pilots and planes, develop rules, regulations, and operating standards, establish airways, enforce air traffic rules, conduct aeronautical research, and, in general, ensure the safety of aviation through federal regulation. The ancestor of the Federal Aviation Administration that we know today had been born.

THE BEACON SYSTEM

Backtracking momentarily to the early 1920s, relying on occasional bonfires while plowing through the skies at night was hardly a sophisticated means of navigating. By the same token, those bonfires, plus hefty doses of good luck, were anything but conducive to the development of an economic, dependable airmail service.

One solution, obvious to only a few, was the ability to navigate and fly safely at night. That was hardly an easy solution because it meant that aircraft landing, navigation, and instrument lighting systems had to be engineered almost from scratch. This would require extensive testing and experimentation to develop the most efficient lights for each purpose, followed by determining the best location of the lights on the aircraft for maximum effect. Another step was the need to identify the airport perimeters with a system of boundary lights, illuminate the wind sock or tee, and develop a rotating beacon or searchlight that would guide pilots to the field from many miles away. Plus, a beacon system had to be developed to provide a lighted "highway" for navigation.

An article titled "Out of the Darkness . . .", by Colonels Eldon W. Downs and Albert P. Sights, Jr. in the Autumn 1969 issue of *Aerospace Historian*, detailed the difficulty of the task. It was one obscure Army lieutenant, Donald L. Bruner, who, against all odds, took up the challenge. Not only was the necessary hardware nonexistent, but, in 1919 and 1920, most people, including Army pilots, thought night flying either too dangerous or unnecessary, or both. When the sun went down, airplanes should be in their hangars. Bruner thought otherwise.

Eventually overcoming resistance from even his own commanding officer, to say nothing of that of his fellow pilots, Bruner led a small task force assigned to him through the testing and experimental stages. And it was Bruner who, in 1923, spearheaded the first lighted airway—a 72-mile stretch from McCook Field in Dayton, Ohio, (where he was stationed) to Norton Field in Columbus. Between July 2 and August 13, 1923, pilots, flying one DeHaviland DH-4B, completed 25 of 29 scheduled flights. Bruner flew about a third of those himself.

Simply described, the system, as it grew, consisted of a series of towers erected on concrete slabs. Each tower had a flashing rotating beacon and two course lights, one pointing forward to the next beacon ahead, the other backward to the previous one. Each course light flashed alternatively, providing coded signals of the particular beacon, thus identifying its position along the airway (FIG. 1-1). The site number was also painted on the beacon's shed. Spaced approximately 15 to 25 miles apart, the beacons were of such candlepower that they could be seen up to 40 miles away in clear weather.

In addition to the lights, auxiliary or emergency landing fields were constructed along the airways. Hardly "airports" in the accepted sense, they were merely strips of gravel or sod set on leveled land leased from local farmers or municipalities. At the sites where a field existed, the beacon lights were green; at all others, they were red.

Based on Bruner's work, the Post Office Department began lighting the Chicago-Cheyenne airway segment in 1923. By 1926, the entire airway from New York to San Francisco was beacon-equipped.

The eventual feat of lighting 18,000 miles of airway with some 1500 beacon towers was a herculean accomplishment, especially considering the plains, mountains, and swamps that had to be conquered in the process. It was achieved by 1933, however, along with the construction of 263 lighted landing fields that offered welcome havens for pilots encountering bad weather or the all-too-frequent mechanical failures.

While the beacon system was indeed a step forward, it was obviously of little or no value in instrument conditions. Of course, in one respect, that wasn't of much concern because instrument flight—planned instrument flight, that is—was nonexistent in those days. Also, if not flying an airway, there were no aids to

---

Fig. 1-1. *A typical airway beacon, with the site number painted on the beacon's shed. Note the directional marker (arrow) on the ground.* (National Air and Space Museum, Smithsonian Institution)

guide or direct the pilot, other than city lights and dead reckoning. The system, however, was not designed for the casual pilot or the barnstormer; it was constructed for those flying the mail over routes designated by the Post Office, and eventually for commercial aviation. But even with its limitations, it was an important start.

RADIO COMMUNICATION IN ITS INFANCY

Almost concurrent with the development of the beacon system were the experiments with radio communication. In 1926 and 1927, successful two-way, air-to-ground communication was conducted, and the first transmitter/receiver went into production in 1928.

About the same time, teletype circuits came into being. These made it possible to transmit local weather conditions over leased landlines between stations. How the system worked was basically simple. Weather conditions, as collected by the U.S. Weather Bureau, were transmitted to airway communication stations. Then, over a given route and at prescribed times, Station A would teletype its local weather to all stations on the circuit. When the transmission was completed, the operator would ring a bell, signaling the next station in sequence that the circuit was clear. Station B would then report its weather, and so on down the line until all stations had the most current reports along the route. Before takeoff, the pilot would receive a list of all weather along his route. Changing conditions were communicated to the aircraft in flight at designated times.

But weather reporting wasn't the only benefit radio and teletype produced. The ability to keep track of airborne aircraft was a major plus. When a flight plan was filed and an aircraft departed Station A, that information was teletyped to all stations on the flight plan route. Then, when the pilot passed over Station B, he communicated his position by radio. If he had no transmitter, he'd gun his engine a couple of times or blink his navigation lights to signal his position to ground personnel—and so on, to his destination.

With weather information available and radio contact with the ground possible, those flying the airways in the late '20s and early '30s were not completely alone in space or darkness. Aviation was still a child but had emerged from infancy.

RADIO RANGES AND THE FIRST INVISIBLE AIRWAYS

Despite sporadic experiments with radio navigation in the '20s, it took the low-frequency four-course radio range to move aviation from strictly contact to instrument flight. It was the radio range that permitted pilots to fly in or above an overcast, and navigate by aural signals coming through their headsets.

Without getting into the technicalities, the range consisted of four towers, erected to form a square. Two of the towers transmitted the Morse Code letter "A" (dot-dash). The other two transmitted the letter "N" (dash-dot) (FIG. 1-2).

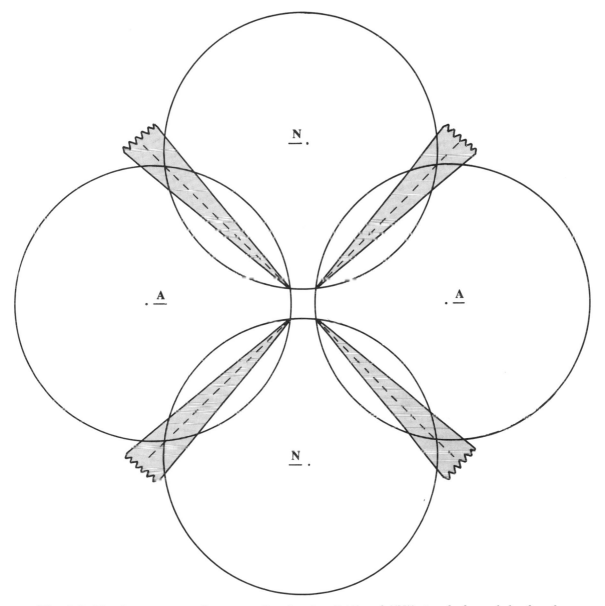

Fig. 1-2. *The four-course radio range. Overlapping "A" and "N" signals formed the four beams.*

When the two signals overlapped, the "A" and "N" codes meshed, and the pilot heard a steady hum-like signal. He then knew that he was on one of the four "beams" leading to or from the range station.

Whether he was flying to or from the station was determined by the change in volume or intensity of the signal. If flying inbound, the volume steadily increased until the aircraft was over the station. At that point, all sounds ceased—the aircraft was in the "cone of silence". The cone fanned outward from the ground up, and at low altitudes, say 800 or 1000 feet, the silence was very brief. The pilot could be in and out of the cone in only a couple of seconds—or even miss it entirely, if he were not smack dab on the beam, which was also extremely narrow at that point—sometimes little more than the wingspan of the aircraft. On the other hand, at 8000 feet, 10,000 feet, or higher, the silence would last several seconds, thus providing a very imprecise position fix. The installation of radio marker beacons identifying the cone did, however, reduce the imprecision.

If the pilot tuned to the range frequency and heard only a clear "A" or a clear "N", all he would know was that he was in one of the "A" or "N" quadrants. If he was unsure of his position and wanted to get on the beam, he then had to follow a set of prescribed orientation procedures, which could be both time- and fuel-consuming.

Once on the beam, the practice was to fly the right side, or "feathered edge", when inbound or outbound. The primary signal, then, would be the on-course hum, with a faint "A" or "N" in the background, depending on which quadrant was on the pilot's right.

The beam could be received up to about 100 miles, and stations were spaced approximately 200 miles apart. Somewhat akin to VOR tracking today, when outbound from one station and the on-course signal became fainter and fainter, the pilot tuned to the next station ahead, probably picking up an equally faint hum that gradually increased in volume as he approached the station.

As valuable an addition as the ranges were to navigation and instrument flight, they had their deficiencies. Generated by low-frequency transmitters, the beams could be bent or thrown off their published compass heading by mountains, mineral deposits, changing weather conditions, static, railroad tracks, even the rising and setting of the sun. As Komons indicates, and from personal experience as well, their inherent undependability was particularly hazardous in mountainous terrain or when weather factors demanded reliability. Plus, they were anything but precise as aids for instrument approaches and landings.

Nevertheless, the range was a most important aid to navigation, and by 1933, 90 stations had been established, producing 18,000 miles of aural airways. Overcoming the inherent low-frequency range deficiencies, however, was several years down the road.

THE START OF AIR TRAFFIC CONTROL

As of the late 1920s and early '30s, "congestion" at some of the larger airports demanded at least a modicum of traffic control on the ground. At some airports this became the role of a gentleman who waved red and green flags to advise pilots to stop or proceed. According to John Knoell, an early pioneer who helped establish the St. Louis Airway Traffic Control Station, one of the first flag-wavers was a gentleman named Archie W. League. Archie would sit at the end of a runway at St. Louis, under a sun-protecting umbrella, and "control" traffic by these visual signals.

Obviously, such a communications medium was useless at night and of almost no help to aircraft in the pattern or on final approach. Becoming more sophisticated, the flags were soon replaced by a red and green light system, but this too, was useless beyond a certain visual range.

The First Control Tower

The next, and most logical step, was radio. The first radio-equipped control tower was constructed in Cleveland in 1930 (FIG. 1-3). Its range was limited to about 15 miles, and the controller tracked the progress of inbound aircraft on a position map, based on periodic reports from the pilot. To call the controller a "controller," however, is not quite accurate. In those days, he could clear an aircraft to land or takeoff, but the pilot was under no obligation to follow his instructions. He really was little more than an advisor or traffic reporter, and it would take later federal regulations to make him a true controller.

The experiment at Cleveland, however, did demonstrate the value of a form of tower control at and in the vicinity of the busier airports. Consequently, about 20 additional structures were erected between 1930 and 1935 (FIG. 1-4).

"Controlling" the Airways

During this period, when the airlines were growing in size and numbers, and instrument flight was increasing, traffic control along the airways and into the airport vicinities was primarily a matter of coordination among the airlines. Glen Gilbert recounts the beginning of a control system in his book, *Air Traffic Control—The Uncrowded Sky*. Gilbert, then with American Airlines, initiated a program of tracking American's flights into Chicago from about 100 miles out via pilot radio reports.

Following Gilbert's initiative, the other major carriers serving Chicago soon formed an informal group, doing the same for their own carriers and keeping each other alerted if an arrival conflict seemed likely. The airlines involved would then mutually coordinate the approach and arrival of their aircraft, and do the same with the control tower by telephone. Radio contact along the airways in those days was primarily between the pilot and his company radio operator/dispatcher (FIG. 1-5). Not until the pilot was within the vicinity of the airport did the tower enter the picture and take over visual control of the aircraft.

Based on the Chicago experiment, in 1935 the airlines operating into Chicago and Newark (then the primary airport serving New York) agreed to set up a system to control the flights at both locations. Called "Airway Traffic Control Stations," the first Station was established at Newark (FIGS. 1-6 and 1-7), followed in 1936 by Cleveland and Chicago. Once again, misnomers enter the picture. These were not literally "airway" control stations, because each station controlled airline activity within only about a 50-mile radius of its airport. Furthermore, the control

Fig. 1-3. *The first control tower. The device on the top of the greenhouse is the wind tee.* (National Air and Space Museum, Smithsonian Institution)

was through the various airline radio operator/dispatchers and their ultimate coordination with the tower personnel.

The fact that the facilities were manned and operated by airline employees for their airlines was an obvious deterrent to uniform traffic control, because one airline had no authority to regulate the operations of another. And, to muddle the airways further, neither private nor military pilots had any requirement to take orders from a commercial operator.

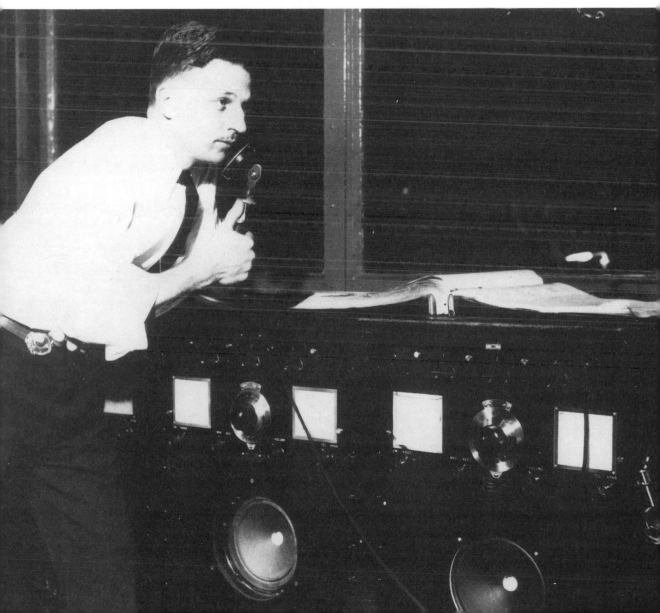

Fig. 1-4. *Archie League eventually put down his flags and went inside to work the radios at the new St. Louis Tower.* (FAA)

Fig. 1-6. *Aircraft plotting position in the Newark, New Jersey, Airway Traffic Control Station. Seated at the map table is Earl F. Ward, the first supervisor of Airway Traffic Control for the federal government.* (National Air and Space Museum, Smithsonian Institution)

Quite understandably, government and airline apprehension over the increasing potential of ground and midair collisions was mounting. Both parties were vociferous in their agreement—federal control of the airways was essential. Finally, on July 6, 1937, after overcoming budgetary problems and a lot of confusing and internal problems, the Bureau of Air Commerce took over the Newark, Cleveland, and Chicago Stations. The airways, current and future, were now under federal control. Regulation compliance at last had the bite of law behind it.

Fig. 1-5. *An early Braniff radio operator.* (National Air and Space Museum, Smithsonian Institution)

Fig. 1-7. *Another view of the Newark "Center" in early 1936, showing the blackboard method of posting flight information. The lantern and flashlight were used because of frequent power failures.* (National Air and Space Museum, Smithsonian Institution)

Back to the Control Towers . . .

The airways came under federal control in 1937, but one facility did not— the tower itself. Each tower was still the responsibility of the municipality in which the airport was located.

Depending on the individual airport and the whims of the city fathers, control tower personnel could have a variety of duties, ranging from communicating with dispatchers and pilots to acting as airport switchboard operators. In some cases, Akron for one, they also sold airline tickets and assisted with passenger baggage as late as 1939. To compound matters, no uniform employment, training, or licensing standards existed. With such informality, standardized airport operations across the system were difficult, if not impossible.

Despite concerns and valid arguments to the contrary, Congress took no action to extend federal control to the towers until, as Komons put it, ". . . forced to do so by the exigencies of war." It wasn't until November of 1941 that the federal government (under its newly established Civil Aviation Administration) assumed control of both airway and tower operations.

Amidst these spotty endeavors, and something that may ring a bell today, was the rising criticism of private flying and its interference with commercial aviation. As Komons summarized it, near-collisions, "miscellaneous flyers" getting in the way of airliners, private pilots landing at congested airports, small planes plying the airways in instrument conditions without flight plans—these and similar concerns were raised in growing volume. With talk of banning private planes without two-way radios at the large terminals "like Newark, Chicago, or Kansas City" increasing, Eugene L. Vidal, then head of the Bureau of Air Commerce, forecast in 1936 that privately owned aircraft would be prevented from landing at congested airports under any condition. His point: Itinerant flyers should not operate in or out of airports used by air carriers. Sound familiar?

During this period (and we're talking about the latter half of the '30s), the airlines were facing economic as well as operational crises. Back in February 1934, the Roosevelt administration had cancelled all airmail contracts and turned the responsibility for carrying the mail back to the Army. The cancellation was an almost-fatal blow to the airlines, because those mail contracts were practically their only source of revenue. The Army, however, was ill-prepared for the responsibility foisted on it, and its accident record over the next few weeks aroused public ire as well as deep concern within government circles.

Recognizing its mistake and misjudgment, the government, in April 1934, opened bidding to the airlines for new routes and mail contracts for what was supposed to be a temporary 90-day period. Some carriers, wanting to retain the routes they had pioneered and had been serving, bid so low—perhaps 17 cents per aircraft mile versus the Post Office Department's limit of 45 cents—that operating at a profit was just about impossible. Had they known that the so-called temporary routes and rates would later be made permanent by Congress, the bidding for both routes and rates might have taken on a different character.

The passing of time brought little relief. By 1937, the airlines were still afflicted with economic problems, and their safety record was a matter of serious concern. In that year alone, there were five fatal accidents in one 28-day period. Coupled with unreliable navigation facilities, air commerce was in deep trouble. The industry was crying for federal regulation. No one, not even those in the government, argued the point, but they could not agree on the solution. Self-interests, politicking, and departmental chauvinism ran rampant through the halls of the nation's capital.

Finally, after months of governmental bickering, President Roosevelt signed the Civil Aeronautics Act into law in June 1938. The law created the Civil

Aeronautics Authority and gave the Authority the power to issue air carrier routes and regulate airline fares. In 1940, Roosevelt split the Authority into two agencies—the Civil Aeronautics Board (CAB) and the Civil Aeronautics Administration (CAA). The CAB, an independent agency, was responsible for economic and safety rulemaking and accident investigation. The CAA, lodged in the Department of Commerce, was charged with air traffic control, airman and aircraft certification, safety enforcement, and airway development.

This organization existed until 1958, when the Federal Aviation Act was passed, creating the Federal Aviation Agency (FAA), and, in the process, transferred the CAA's functions to this new independent body. It also took safety rulemaking from the CAB and entrusted it to the FAA. Of even greater significance, it gave the FAA the sole responsibility for developing and maintaining a common civil-military system of air navigation and air traffic control—a responsibility the CAA had previously shared with others.

In 1967, the Department of Transportation (DOT) was established, absorbing the FAA and other transportation agencies. The FAA was then renamed the "Federal Aviation Administration." This is the FAA we know today, although it has assumed several other responsibilities not originally envisioned in the Federal Aviation Act—responsibilities such as prescribing aircraft noise standards, establishing minimum airport safety standards, improving the ATC radar- and computer-based system. In 1981, the FAA revealed its National Airspace System Plan, which is a blueprint for a state-of-the-art air traffic control and navigation system to accommodate the projected growth in air travel up to the turn of the century.

LANDING BLIND IN THE '30s

But now to go back in time again. As noted earlier, the radio range had a number of inherent weaknesses, many of which were not corrected until the '40s. One that defied correction, however, was its imprecision for instrument landings.

In a certain sense, if a beam was aligned with a runway, which was sometimes not the case, it was very broadly akin to a localizer, in that it did provide guidance to the airport. At an airport very close to the station, however, the cone of silence was so small and the beam so narrow that only a perfect on-course approach—heading, altitude, timing, and rate of descent—would get you to the runway. Conversely, when the airport was some distance away, say 10 or 12 miles, the width of the beam was such that the on-course signal might lead you to the airport, but being lined up with the runway was more a matter of good fortune. It too required stopwatch timing, maintaining the published feet-per-minute descent and airspeed, and flying exactly on the outbound course radial.

Something better was essential for both military and commercial operations. Two systems thus emerged: Ground Control Approach, and the Instrument Landing System.

Ground Control Approach (GCA)

GCA came into being with the development of radar (the acronym for radio detection and ranging). Developed in the United States and used primarily by the military or at very large airline airports, the GCA system consisted of two six-inch diameter cathode ray tubes (CRTs), which with their support equipment, were installed in mobile tractor-trailers (FIG. 1-8). One CRT scanned the immediate airport vicinity for aircraft, and its operator, via radio communications, directed each aircraft in sequence into position for the initial landing approach. The second CRT, manned by the talkdown controller, determined the aircraft's position

Fig. 1-8. *An early Ground Control Approach mobile trailer.* (National Air and Space Museum, Smithsonian Institution)

in relation to the proper heading and approach angle. He then literally talked the pilot down to the runway by verbally communicating course direction and descent instructions.

Housed inside the darkened trailer, the controllers had no visual contact with the outside world (FIG. 1-9). Their "windows" were the CRTs in front of them. Suffice it to say that it was an interesting experience to be a pilot locked in the soup with your immediate future in the hands of a small tube and the verbal instructions from a voice you just had to trust. Despite the fact that many civil pilots didn't like the system because they didn't feel in control of their own destiny, those who manned these units did a fantastic job, and many a pilot owed his well-being to their expertise.

One advantage of the GCA was its mobility. Being motorized, the entire facility could be shifted from one runway to another so that landings were always, or generally, into the wind. The risks of touching down in a strong crosswind were thus minimized. The units could also be moved from one field to another, if military circumstances dictated.

With later technical advances, the system was transferred to the tower. Mobility was lost, but precision enhanced. In fact, it became known as Precision Approach Radar (PAR), and has been used extensively, particularly by the military, into the '80s. Because of its maintenance and operational costs, however, no civilian airports in the U.S. have PAR today.

The Instrument Landing System (ILS)

ILS is often perceived as a fairly recent development in aviation technology. Not so. One ILS form or another has been off the drawing board since the late 1920s. Experimenting with a system developed by a U.S. Army Captain Hegenberger, Jimmy Doolittle made the first completely blind flight and landing in 1929, and the Army used that system for several years thereafter. In fact, the Bureau of Air Commerce announced in 1934 that it would adopt it as its standard and that installation of the ground equipment would begin immediately at 36 commercial airports. The airlines, however, claimed the system to be "unflyable" in their aircraft for technical as well as safety reasons. That ended that.

One version that did survive was started in 1928 by a group of engineers in the Bureau of Standards and became operational in 1931. After the all-too-typical government delays of that era—both bureaucratic and economic—the system was finally refined and made adaptable for commercial use in 1938. What emerged was called "Air Track."

In many respects, the elements of Air Track were the same as today's ILS: a localizer, a glide path, and two marker beacons—an outer marker and a boundary marker. The cockpit instrumentation closely resembled the localizer/glide path needles in use today.

Fig. 1-9. *The controllers at work inside the GCA trailer.* (National Air and Space Museum, Smithsonian Institution)

One difference was that the glide path was a curved beam rather than the straight-line approach we have now. The curve was formed by an infinitude of transmitted signals, rising to about 1500 feet above the airport, that resembled giant teardrops. The pilot picked up the glide slope signal and then flew the underside of the teardrop that best suited the airspeed and descent rate of his particular aircraft. This he did the usual way by keeping the glide path needle generally centered.

Although about a half a dozen other systems existed at the time, Air Track has a special place in history. As related in the June 1938 issue of *Fortune* magazine, a Pennsylvania-Central Airlines (PCA) Boeing 247-D took off on January 26, 1938, from Washington, D.C. for Pittsburgh. Approaching Pittsburgh in a swirling snowstorm, the pilot, strictly on instruments, tuned to the Pittsburgh ILS frequency, centered the localizer, and "played" with the glide slope as he flew down the curved beam. About 50 feet above the ground, he received the shrill beep of the boundary marker. Although the ground was in sight, the pilot forced himself not to look out. The copilot sat ready to take over in case anything went wrong. Seconds later, with the pilot still glued to the instrument panel, the wheels touched the ground.

It was a blind landing, but not that unusual. Thousands had been made before in actual as well as simulated conditions. What made it historic was that is was the first blind landing of a U.S. airliner on a scheduled flight with passengers on board. It also marked the start of the first formal blind-landing training program by a U.S. airline. (The term in those days was "blind"—not "instrument"— flight or landing.)

Conflict still persisted, however, over what ILS system the Bureau of Air Commerce would ultimately adopt. The military had its own, and the airlines wanted something else. Two or more different systems, of course, wouldn't do. Commonality was essential for the safety of all types of operations and operators.

Despite all of the airline, military, and Bureau debates, despite the pressures and divergent points of view in the decision-making process, the 1938 *Fortune* article concludes with this prognostication:

> With all of the negative factors at work, we can neither say in what final form blind landing will come nor fix a date for its arrival. But you can be sure that it *will* arrive. Or as sure, at any rate, as you can be that air safety is a good thing, and that the airline operators want to make money, and that men will continue to fly.

The promise would come true, but completely blind landings wouldn't be realized until well into the postwar years.

Meanwhile, agreement on an ILS system was reached. A unit created to meet the rigid safety specifications of the CAA had been installed at the Indianapolis Municipal Airport in 1939 and tested extensively in all sorts of instrument weather. Its reliability established, the system was approved and accepted by the military in early 1940. A February 3, 1940, *Science News Letter* reported:

> A committee of the National Academy of Sciences, headed by Dr. Vannevar Bush, President of Carnegie Institution of Washington, recommended to President Roosevelt that the Indianapolis CAA system be extended to other airports in the nation, military and commercial, as the best blind-landing system now developed.

In 1945, the Army introduced its own ILS version by using Very High Frequency (VHF) transmitters which eliminated the effects of static on the operation of the glide path. Also, VHF beams were straighter and less inclined to fade, swing, or form false courses than the conventional low-frequency radio beams. The Army called this unit the ''Army Air Forces Instrument Approach System,'' or, more tersely, SCS-51 (Signal Corps Set 51). The initial Technical Order, published January 15, 1945, introducing the system, contained explanations and approach procedures that would be very familiar today. Only references to the initial orientation by using the radio range make it seem a little archaic.

VHF was nothing new, but the old radio ranges were still using the low-frequency transmitters that were responsible for the range unreliability. It wasn't until 1945 that the CAA acted to modernize that vital navigation equipment.

In early 1946, a fogbound American Airlines plane crashed into a California mountain, killing 27 people, the worst commercial air disaster on record, up to that time. *Time* magazine, in its March 18, 1946 issue, observed:

> This accident would perhaps never have happened had all the war-born safety devices been in general use . . .
> But as far as U.S commercial airlines are concerned, there has been no basic change in air traffic control, airway marking, or instrument landing equipment in 15 years—a period that has seen an enormous increase in scheduled flights and the advent of 300-mile-an-hour transports.

The wheels of government do indeed spin slowly.

In 1949, the International Civil Aviation Organization (ICAO) adopted ILS as the standard international approach and landing aid. It was not until the 1960s, however, that equipment had been sufficiently developed to make full automatic blind landings (called ''Category III'') operationally feasible.

Is ILS the final answer? No. Somewhat like the old radio range, it too has its frailties, including its susceptibility to interference from structures in the airport vicinity and the terrain itself, and the fact that it's locked into a single approach path to the runway. As Arnold Field puts it in his book, *International Air Traffic Control*:

> . . . there have been virtually no advances in performance since the introduction of the first Category III compatible equipment in the late 1960s.

The next step is the Microwave Landing System (MLS). That, however, is another story for another time.

INTERNATIONAL STANDARDIZATION THROUGH ICAO

An excerpt from ICAO's brochure *Facts About ICAO*, November 1987, reads:

> In an afternoon's flight, an airliner can cross the territories of several nations, nations in which different languages are spoken, in which

different legal codes are used. In all of these operations, safety must be paramount, there must be no unfamiliarity or misunderstanding. In other words, there must be international standardization, agreement between nations in all technical and economic and legal fields so that the air can be the high road to carry man and his goods anywhere and everywhere without fetter and without halt.

In a few words, that excerpt sums up ICAO's reason for being.

With end of World War II in sight and the potential of international civil aviation obvious, representatives from 52 countries met in Chicago in 1944. Their purpose: to lay the groundwork for worldwide standardization of civil aviation policies and practices. From that meeting, a treaty was signed in December 1944, creating ICAO—the International Civil Aviation Organization. Today, 159 states comprise its membership. Its headquarters are in Montreal, Canada, and it has regional offices in Bangkok, Cairo, Dakar, Lima, Mexico City, Nairobi, and Paris.

ICAO's Purpose and Functions

As implied in the opening quote, standardization, with safety the paramount issue, was and is ICAO's principal charge. This means that international commonality of operating rules, navigating procedures, language, and phraseology must prevail. National self-interests or favored ways of doing things cannot be allowed to interfere with the common good. The fact that ICAO has been so successful in achieving standardization speaks volumes for what nations can do when they're willing to work together, negotiate, and then come to agreements that have universal application.

The agreements reached, however, are not just international in scope. Each member state must abide by them within its own boundaries and see that they are enforced. In our country, that is the responsibility of the FAA. There may be minor local variations, but any that do exist are indeed minor and do not violate the ICAO intent.

In addition to standardization and safety, ICAO's interests reach across the whole gamut of civil aviation. It has been the front runner in working to remove unnecessary customs and immigration formalities, improving international airport passenger facilities, automation of air traffic services, aircraft noise control, unlawful interference with civil aviation, and aviation and the human environment. It is also involved in international legal matters concerning ground damage to aircraft, crimes committed on aircraft, and it has been active in providing technical and economic assistance for aviation development in Third World nations.

Accomplishing all of this takes coordination and cooperation. In 1947, ICAO became a specialized agency of the United Nations and thus works closely with other UN organizations, including the World Meteorological Organization, International Telecommunications Union, the Universal Postal Union, and the

World Health Organization. The same working relationship exists between ICAO and non-UN agencies such as the International Air Transport Association (IATA), the International Federation of Airline Pilots Association (IFAPA), and the International Council of Aircraft Owners and Pilots Associations.

The ICAO Organization Structure

Very sketchily, the ICAO organization structure includes:

Assembly: Composed of all member states, this is the sovereign body. It meets every three years to review the work done and set policy for the coming years.

Council: Selected by the Assembly for a three-year term and is made up of representatives from 33 states. The states chosen are based on three criteria: (1) the importance of the states in air transport; (2) the states that make the largest contribution to providing air navigation facilities; and (3) states which will assure that all areas of the world are represented. The Council is the governing body of ICAO and adopts recommended practices and standards.

Secretariat: Headed by the Secretary General, this has five divisions: Air Navigation, Air Transport, Technical Assistance, Administration and Services, and Legal. Members of these divisions are highly qualified in their fields and are recruited from all over the globe to ensure, as *Facts About ICAO* states, ". . . a truly international approach."

One Example of Standardization

To a measurable degree, universal standardization of civil aviation demands standardization and simplicity of language. It would hardly do to have a Saudi pilot who spoke no English milling around over New York while attempting to communicate with an American controller who spoke no Arabic—or the reverse situation of an American trying to land at Riyadh. Language commonality and standard terminology and phraseology are essential in international operations.

Addressing the problem, ICAO members agreed that English was the most universal language, or at least the language most frequently used in international trade and commerce. It was thus logically adopted as the international aviation language.

Then came the task of simplifying words and expressions so that they could be mastered by those for whom English was not the mother tongue.

The phonetic alphabet is one example. For some time, the U.S. had its own aviation and military alphabet, which was fine for Americans but apparently caused non-English speakers certain pronunciation problems. Without going through it from A to Z, the U.S. phonetic alphabet used to be *Able, Baker, Charlie, Dog,*

Easy, Fox, George, How, Item, and so on. The ICAO revision gave us *Alpha, Bravo, Charlie, Delta, Echo, Foxtrot, Golf, Hotel, India,* and so on to *Zulu* versus the old *Zebra* (or sometimes *Zed,* the French pronunciation of ''Z'').

Phraseologies and terms were also standardized, such as ''Roger,'' ''Affirmative,'' ''Acknowledge,'' ''Say again,'' ''How do you read?,'' ''Stand by,'' ''Hold short,'' ''Taxi into position and hold''—and the examples could go on.

The same standard phraseology between controller and pilot exists in all phases of flight operations from initial aircraft movement to landing and parking on the ramp. VFR or IFR, many terms and expressions are those of ICAO and thus of international usage.

Quoting again a portion of the *Facts About ICAO* brochure:

> ICAO provides the machinery for the achievement of international cooperation in the air; successful results depend on the willingness of the nations of the world to make concessions, to work together to reach agreement. The success which international civil aviation has achieved in the past four decades is abundant proof that nations can work together effectively to achieve the common good.

There can be little argument about that.

CONCLUSION

And so, in one respect, this brings us full circle—ICAN to ICAO. The first effort to establish rules of the air was the initiative of ICAN, back in 1919. ICAO closes the loop by internationalizing the rules through the agreement of the participating member states. What ICAO has accomplished on a global level took us, in the United States, almost 20 years to achieve. Through it all, however, we were the leaders in technical and commercial development, partly, and perhaps primarily, because of the size of our country and our early recognition of the importance of aviation as a tool of commerce.

Whatever the case, whatever the cause, we are enjoying today the technical and electronic fruits of the pioneers who preceded us. The skies are more crowded, but they're safer than ever, despite headline publicity to the contrary. Safety has many fathers, however, including a well-maintained aircraft, pilot knowledge and skill, and a constant awareness that ''it could happen to me.''

In addition, safety is the product of understanding our national airspace and the air traffic control system that makes it work. That's the theme of the chapters that follow, so let's get on with it—with the hope that those chapters will contribute to your understanding and thus your confidence in using the system as it is intended to be used.

2

Introducing
The ATC System

LET'S FACE IT: IT'S A SIMPLE FACT THAT MANY NONINSTRUMENT-RATED PILOTS either don't use the full range of the air traffic control (ATC) facilities available to them, or they do so with an unnecessary degree of apprehension. The reasons may be varied, such as lack of knowledge, inexperience, fear of making mistakes, or any combination thereof. Whatever the case, there seems to be a need to clear the air and try to replace reluctance with confidence—or at least understanding. I realize that no one chapter or series of chapters in any one book can fully accomplish that, but we can at least make a start.

This, then, is an introduction to the airspace system and the air traffic control facilities that make it work. For illustrative purposes, a simulated VFR cross-country flight is probably the best vehicle because it is the most inclusive. You're going from A to C: What FAA facilities would you *normally* use? What control agencies *must* you contact? What agencies *should* you contact for traffic advisories and enroute information?

The intent of this simulation is to introduce those of us who are not entirely familiar with them to the various ATC facilities that are involved in a cross-country flight. A more in-depth look at each will follow in the succeeding chapters. These facilities are classified by the FAA as terminal, Flight Service Stations, and enroute.

A SIMULATED FLIGHT

To set the scene:

- The flight will be nonstop from the Kansas City Downtown Airport to the Memphis, Tennessee, International Airport. We'll fly the Victor 159 Airway, which runs generally southeast/northwest, via Springfield, Missouri, and Walnut Ridge, Arkansas.

- We're going to file a flight plan with the Columbia, Missouri, Automated Flight Service Station (AFSS) which serves Kansas City, and close it on arrival with the Jackson, Tennessee, AFSS, serving Memphis.

- Kansas City Downtown Airport lies under–not in–the Kansas City Terminal Control Area (TCA). The floor of the TCA is 3000 feet over the airport and 5000 feet a few miles to the south.

- Kansas City Departure Control is located in the Kansas City International Airport tower, 15 miles to the northwest of the Downtown Airport.

- We're going to request enroute VFR traffic advisories from the Kansas City Air Route Traffic Control Center (ARTCC or "Center"), Memphis Center, and Memphis Approach Control.

- Memphis International is in an Airport Radar Service Area (ARSA). Two-way radio communication with Memphis Approach Control is mandatory before entering the ARSA.

Filing the Flight Plan

The first facility we'll contact is the Columbia AFSS—to get a weather briefing and to open our flight plan. To get the best briefing possible, the FAA recommends a certain sequence of information that you should give to the specialist as soon as you have him or her on the line. When we get to the Flight Service Station chapter, we'll summarize that sequence as well as the information the specialist will normally provide, and in what order.

Satisfied that the weather will be no problem, we give the briefer the balance of the information he or she needs to file our flight plan. All done through a computer, the flight plan is stored in the AFSS until we call in and ask that it be opened.

Pre-Takeoff

ATIS. We've completed the preflight check, and started the engine. What's next?

With radios on and the transponder in the standby (SBY) position (so that it can be warming up), the first "what's next" is to dial-in the published frequency for the Automatic Terminal Information Service (ATIS). ATIS is a recorded report, updated hourly, that provides, in sequence, the following local airport information:

- Airport name

- Information code, using the phonetic alphabet

- The UTC time (Coordinated Universal Time—the 24-hour clock time, followed by the "Zulu weather")

- Sky conditions

- Visibility and obstruction to vision
  (Omitted if ceiling $\geq 5000'$ and visibility ≥ 5 miles)

- Temperature and dew point

- Wind direction (magnetic) and velocity

- Altimeter setting

- Visual/instrument approach(es) in use (and landing runway(s), if different)

- Departure runway(s) in use (if different from landing runway)

- Information code repeated (phonetic alphabet)

Additional information may be included, such as reports of severe weather, NOTAMs, warnings of construction work near the runway, and similar conditions of which the pilot should be aware. The fact that you have monitored the current ATIS should be communicated to Ground Control before taxiing out and in the initial contact with the tower or Approach Control when landing.

Ground Control. The ground controller operates from the tower and is responsible for directing all aircraft and ground equipment movements on the taxiways or when crossing an active runway. If you're just shuttling your plane around the ramp, you can do that all day without calling GC. Before you touch wheels to a taxi strip, however, you must contact Ground Control for clearance to proceed.

The call is usually very brief. In this case, we simply give the aircraft type and N-number, where we are on the airport, and that we have Alpha, Bravo, or whatever the current ATIS information happens to be. GC will then authorize us to taxi to the active runway.

Even though cleared to taxi out, it's important to stay tuned to the GC frequency. We're still under the controller's jurisdiction and will be until we're at the hold line and ready to contact the tower. In a word, Ground Control is to be monitored from the ramp, through run up, to the hold line. After landing do not switch to GC until the tower controller tells you to (ask for permission if he forgets). Them's the rules.

Flight Service Station. We've taxied to the run up area, completed the pre-takeoff checks, and are ready to go. First, though, it's time to open the flight plan. This involves a change to one of the published FSS frequencies and, this, too, is both simple and brief (but don't forget to ask Ground Control for permission to switch frequencies). One thing to keep in mind, though: the call is addressed to "Columbia Radio," not "Columbia Flight Service." "Radio" is the standard term in all radio communications with any FSS. There is only one exception, and that is when you want to contact Flight Watch for an inflight weather update. Then the call is addressed to "(Blank) Flight Watch."

Something else is important: In all FSS radio calls include the frequency you're calling on and your location. In the automated FSSs, an inflight specialist can have up to 48 frequencies to monitor, with some frequencies being duplicated. Unless you tell him or her which one you're on and where you are, he may find it impossible to respond. (We'll have more on this in the Flight Service Station chapter.)

With the flight plan opened, we taxi to the hold line.

Control Tower. At the hold line—and not before—we change frequencies and contact the tower for takeoff clearance, including in the call the intended direction of flight. Don't make his call when you're back in the run up area, maybe a hundred yards away. You're not ready to go that far from the runway. Get up to the yellow hold line so that when the tower clears you, you're in a position to move and move without delay (FIG. 2-1).

Either while taxiing out to the runway or during the actual takeoff run, change the transponder from the SBY position to ON or ALT. The latter puts the unit in the altitude-reporting mode, assuming of course, that you have that equipment on board (a "Mode C" transponder). From here on, like it or not, when you're within radar range of any controlling agency, your aircraft will be on the radar screen. And there's no choice. FAA regulations say that if the aircraft is transponder-equipped, the set must be turned to ON. If it has Mode C, the set must be switched to ALT.

Airborne

Departure Control. The next service we want, once off the runway, involves traffic advisories out of the area. This help will come from Kansas City Departure

---

Fig. 2-1. *Takeoff and landing clearances are issued by the local controller in the cab of the control tower.* (FAA)

Control. Consequently, when airborne and established in a climb, we ask the tower to approve a frequency change. The controller may tell us to "stay with me for a while," if the volume of local traffic in the immediate vicinity is heavy. Otherwise, he'll come back with "Frequency change approved."

When we hear that, we switch to the Departure frequency, establish contact, and then tell the controller where we are, our present altitude, heading, and destination, and request traffic advisories. Some other things will come into play at this point, such as being asked to change the transponder to a "discrete" code, but let's leave those "other things" for the moment. If his workload permits, the controller will alert us to other traffic and perhaps ask us to change headings to avoid a potential conflict. Or, if there are no "targets" out there to interrupt our course of flight, we may hear nothing. Whatever the case, our responsibility is simple: Keep our heads out of the cockpit, listen, acknowledge advisories or instructions, and do what the controller says. The controllers will give advisories, but their first responsibility is to IFR operations. The monkey for protection is on the VFR pilot's back, so head up and unlocked is the best protective measure available.

In a short while, Departure advises that we're leaving his radar area and to contact Kansas City Center on such-and-such frequency. This is a "handoff," meaning that Departure has advised Center of our existence and intentions, has asked the Center controller if he or she can accept a VFR handoff, and the controller has said yes, in effect "buying" the handoff. Our only task now, after changing frequencies, is to establish contact with Center and verify our altitude, even if we have a Mode C transponder. That's all there is to it.

On the other hand, if Departure says, "Radar service terminated. Squawk one two zero zero," that means he is not handing us off. We then must initiate the contact with Center if we want enroute VFR advisories. In that contact, the acronym "IPAIDS" comes into play, meaning Identification (aircraft type and N-number), Position, Altitude, Intentions or Destination, and transponder Squawk code. Conclude with, "Request VFR advisories."

Center. Once in contact with Center, our progress will be monitored by a facility which, in the case of Kansas City, is physically located in Olathe, Kansas, about 25 miles southwest of the Downtown Airport. This is one of 20 Centers in the contiguous United States, each responsible for the control of IFR traffic over its assigned area, and when conditions permit, providing traffic advisories to VFR aircraft.

That last being the case with our flight, as we move down the airway toward Springfield, along with some possible advisories of traffic, the controller tells us to "Contact Kansas City Center on frequency (blank)." This means that we're leaving his sector of responsibility and he's turning us over to another controller, perhaps sitting a few feet away, who will be monitoring our progress on his frequency. All we do now is acknowledge receipt of the instruction, repeat back the new frequency (to be sure we've copied it correctly), enter it in the radio, and contact the new controller with, "Kansas City Center, Cherokee Eight Five One Five November is with you. Level at seven thousand five hundred."

Nearing Springfield, Center will tell us to contact Springfield Approach Control on such-and-such frequency. We're not going to land there, so why Approach? We'll be passing through the airspace for which Approach is responsible, and will thus be under their surveillance. Once out of that airspace, Springfield will hand us off to Center again—assuming Center's workload in that sector will be able to handle us.

Depending on the length of the flight, the process of transfer could happen several times until, in the example we're using, we get about 50 miles southeast of Springfield. At that point, Kansas City will come on the air and tell us to contact Memphis Center on a certain frequency. We're now in Memphis's territory, and future advisories will come from them.

Regardless of the Center, we might hear at any time something like this: "Cherokee Eight Five One Five November, traffic at one o'clock, three miles, also southeast bound, altitude unknown." The controller has spotted another aircraft on his screen at our one o'clock position and is alerting us to its presence. We first acknowledge that we have received the call and, if we see the aircraft, tell the controller. "Roger, Center, Cherokee One Five November has traffic." If we haven't spotted it, the response goes, "Roger, Center, Cherokee One Five November, negative contact. Looking." And then we do look!

ATIS. About 40 or so miles out of Memphis, we tune to the Memphis ATIS for the latest weather information and the runway(s) in use. Knowing the active runway this far out gives us time to visualize and plan the probable traffic pattern we'll fly.

Approach Control. About 30 miles out, Center turns us over to Memphis Approach Control for vectors (headings) and advisories into the ARSA surrounding the airport. Remember that we *must* establish "two-way radio communication" with Approach before entering any ARSA, whether we've been in contact with Center of not (more on this in Chapter 6). If you're ever unfamiliar with the location of an airport, don't be afraid to tell Approach. The controller will give you the vectors that will lead you straight to it.

Control Tower. Finally, when within a few miles of the airport, Approach tells us to contact Memphis (International) Tower on the published frequency. This is the last lap, and the tower sequences us into the traffic pattern and gives the clearance to land.

Back on the Ground

Ground Control. On the ground and clear of the runway, the tower tells us to call Ground Control for taxi clearance to whatever location or fixed base operator we've selected. In real-life situations, if you're not sure where to go or how to get there, ask Ground for *progressive* taxi instructions.

Flight Service. When parked at the ramp, the final radio call is to Jackson "Radio" (Flight Service) to close out the flight plan. We can do this by phone in the operator's facility, but it's a good idea to make the call as soon as we've shut down the engine. It's an easy call to forget—and if you do, remember that people will start looking for you 30 minutes after your estimated arrival. A needless search does not make for happy authorities.

By Way of Summary . . .

In sequence, the FAA service and controlling facilities involved in this example were:

> Columbia Flight Service (telephone)—Downtown ATIS—Downtown Ground Control—Columbia Flight Service—Downtown Tower—Kansas City Departure Control—Kansas City Center—Springfield Approach—Memphis Center—Memphis ATIS—Memphis Approach Control—Memphis Tower—Memphis Ground Control—Jackson Flight Service.

That's 14 facilities, with an absolute minimum of one telephone call and 13 radio frequency changes—which may give the impression that you were a little busy. Were they all mandatory? No. Going VFR, you are *required* to contact Downtown Ground Control, the Downtown tower, Memphis Approach (because Memphis is in an ARSA), Memphis Tower, and Memphis Ground Control. Listening to ATIS is not required, but has become standard operating practice, because it's the smart, efficient thing to do.

CONCLUSION

The objective of this scenario was to introduce the basic elements of the airspace system and the various FAA agencies that would or could enter the picture on a typical VFR cross-country. It was a sketchy overview—details have been reserved for the next chapters when we look at the three key types of ATC facilities and what goes on behind the scenes as we file flight plans, get handoffs, and all the rest.

What I've outlined, however, is part of the National Airspace System (NAS), which includes operations in controlled as well as uncontrolled environments. So with this as a start, the next logical step is to take a closer look at that system and the regulations pertaining to it.

3

A Closer
Look at the
Airspace System

A S I SAID IN THE INTRODUCTION, REVIEWING OR DESCRIBING THE AIRSPACE system at the start of the '90s has certain risks. What is valid today may be invalid tomorrow. Major changes are in the wind or are already blowing across the pilot's horizon.

The recent rash of midair collisions and reported near-misses has stirred the Department of Transportation and its Federal Aviation Administration into a welter of activity uncommon in the bureaucracy. Things are moving rapidly. Regulations are getting tougher; uncontrolled airspace is shrinking; airspace violators are being tracked and punished more severely; and general aviation is finding freedom of the air a diminishing privilege. In the process, it is the general aviation VFR pilot who is bearing the brunt of the increasing restrictions. Some of the prophecies of the 1930s are coming true.

To a certain degree, however, perhaps the VFR pilot population brought at least a portion of the restrictiveness on itself. While the volume of incidents is relatively small, there have been too many cases of illegal penetration of controlled airspaces and violations of VFR flight regulations. Whether products of carelessness, inattention, or ignorance matters little. The fact remains that the federal authorities are taking action to reduce the hazards of the "crowded skies."

That said, we still have considerable freedom to go almost anywhere, if we have at least a private license and the aircraft has the required avionics. We say we have the freedom, but freedoms or rights are not always honored. Denial or delay of clearances into controlled areas are not rarities these days. The cause is not all regulatory, although it is certainly a contributor. The more the restrictions, the greater become the demands placed on the controllers and their hardware. Until the ATC facilities are fully staffed and the equipment matches today's state of the art, additional regulations may further impinge on the freedoms that remain.

Whatever the future, the basic elements of the airspace system will probably survive. If that's a reasonable prophecy, let's begin with a general review of the system as it is currently structured, followed by a discussion of Special Use Airspace in Chapter 4. In succeeding chapters, we'll look at tower-controlled airports more closely, including the control areas that surround an increasing number of the busier terminals.

SOURCES FOR IDENTIFYING AIRSPACE

Before venturing forth, it behooves us to determine what airspace we will or might be penetrating—controlled, uncontrolled, prohibited, restricted, Military Operation Areas (MOAs), or whatever. Three basic determining sources exist, and can be used singly or in combination, depending on the nature of the flight. These are the Sectional Aeronautical Chart (or just plain Sectional), the Enroute Low Altitude Chart (ELAC), and the *Airport/Facility Directory (A/FD)*.

The Sectional is well-known to every pilot, even the raw beginners. It contains a multitude of information and depicts in color many of the types of airspace. It's thus an indispensable reference for VFR flight planning. Published by the National Ocean Service (NOS), 37 geographically-designated charts (not "maps") cover the 48 conterminous states and are updated twice a year.

Primarily designed for instrument operations, the ELAC is also an excellent reference for VFR cross-country operations, *if* it is used in conjunction with the Sectional. Unlike on the Sectional, ground details, such as rivers, highways, obstructions, terrain altitudes, towns, and the like are omitted. Instead, the ELAC focuses on radio navigation facilities and includes a wealth of data not found on the Sectional. Combined, the two charts provide about all the information you could want on a cross-country journey. Updated about every two months by NOS, 48 charts cover the 48 states.

The *Airport/Facility Directory*, as the name implies, contains data about airport facilities and services, including runways, types of fuel available, communication facilities, frequencies, radio aids to navigation, and other information not readily available elsewhere. Again a NOS publication, the *A/FD* is updated six times a year.

Just a reminder about any of these sources: Be sure to refer to the current issue! Because of changes, what was fact on the last chart or *A/FD* may not be valid today. Flight Service Stations are being consolidated and automated; new Airport Radar Service Areas (ARSAs) are being added, replacing the nearly extinct

Terminal Radar Service Areas (TRSAs); additional Terminal Control Areas (TCAs) have been proposed; and we could go on. Just don't rely on an out-of-date chart. It could be embarrassing and costly.

"CONTROLLED" AND "UNCONTROLLED" AIRSPACE DEFINED

Logic would have it that the airspace is either controlled or it isn't. That's not quite true, however. You can be in some controlled areas but not controlled by any air traffic control (ATC) facility—which, on the surface, doesn't make a lot of sense. Nor does the definition of controlled airspace in the Federal Aviation Regulation (FAR) 1.1 add much in the way of clarity:

> "Controlled airspace" means airspace designated as a continental control area, control area, control zone, terminal control area, or transition area, within which some or all aircraft may be subject to air traffic control.

This definition means that under certain conditions, *some* aircraft *may* be subject to air traffic control. It depends where you are and whether you're VFR or IFR. For example, when landing at an airport with an operating control tower, there's no question. VFR or IFR, you're under the control of the tower when you are within at least five miles of the airport. On the other hand, if you're flying VFR along a Victor airway on a VFR flight plan, whether obtaining traffic advisories from a Center or not, you are *not* under ATC control. All you have to do is abide by the VFR altitude, visibility, and cloud separation regulations. So, even in an area designated as "controlled," as a VFR pilot you may not be subject to a controlling agency.

Conversely, the *Airman's Information Manual*, Paragraph 80, defines uncontrolled airspace as:

> . . . that portion of the airspace that has not been designated as Continental Control Area, Control Area, Control Zone, Terminal Control Area, or Transition Area.

In other words, it's all the airspace that isn't classified as controlled. That tells you a lot, doesn't it?

Figure 3-1 illustrates the airspace configuration. Being merely a cutaway profile, however, it requires at least a modicum of explanation to understand it.

Perhaps you have found a clearly written description of uncontrolled and controlled airspace, but if one exists, it has so far eluded me. Despite the definitions and the chart (FIG. 3-1), neither of which adds much to comprehension, there are a fair number of pilots who are confused, or at least uncertain, about the structure of the airspace and the rules and regulations when operating within it.

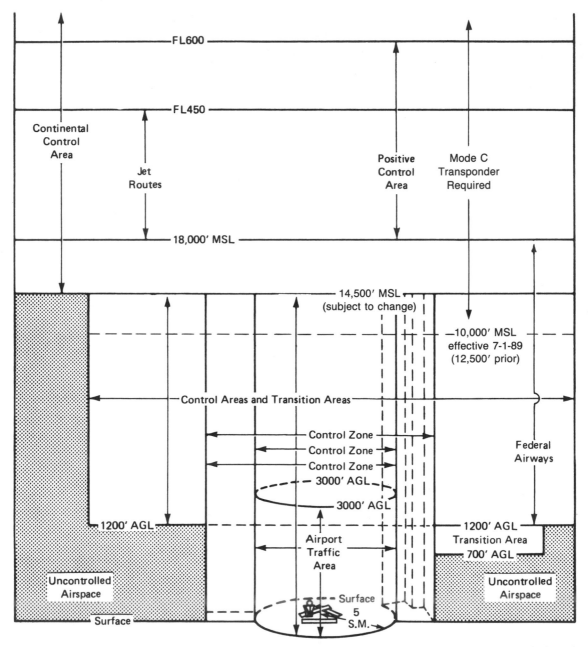

Fig. 3-1. *This figure illustrates the vertical and horizontal dimensions of controlled airspace, including the Mode C requirement at and above 10,000 feet MSL, effective July 1, 1989. Prior to that date, the requirement applies above 12,500 feet MSL.*

UNCONTROLLED AIRSPACE

Figure 3-1 indicates three levels of uncontrolled airspace: surface to 700 feet AGL, surface to 1200 feet AGL, and surface to 14,500 feet MSL.

That's well and good, but it, along with the *AIM* definition, still leaves a fair number of questions unanswered. Finding the answers is where the Sectional Chart comes into play.

If you check any Sectional, you'll see a lot of airports surrounded by blue and magenta designs—some circular, others irregular in structure. The Sectional legend flap then implies—but doesn't state as such—that *within* the areas bounded by the magenta, the ceiling of uncontrolled airspace ceiling is 700 feet AGL. It further implies—but doesn't state—that from the blue coloring *outward*, the ceiling of the uncontrolled airspace is 1200 feet AGL.

In either case, you'll note a distinct demarcation or separation line where the blue and magenta meet. Moving toward the airport, the magenta fades slightly or becomes fuzzy. The blue does the same in the outward direction.

The fading or fuzziness indicates that everywhere inside the magenta, the 700-foot ceiling prevails, except at those airports where a clearly defined Control Zone (CZ) exists. (We'll discuss CZs later in this chapter.) By the same token, the outward fading of the blue identifies the geography where the 1200-foot ceiling prevails. Accordingly (other than for any intervening Prohibited or Restricted areas), in the open country between any airport with blue to any other airport with blue, the ceiling/floor is 1200 feet AGL. So it's simply a matter of remembering that throughout the country, up to 14,500 feet MSL, blue-to-blue identifies the 1200-foot uncontrolled airspace ceiling. Below 1200 feet, the VFR visibility/cloud separation minimums for uncontrolled airspace must be observed. Above it, the regulations for controlled airspace prevail.

Fine, but what about the uncontrolled airspace that goes up to 14,500 feet MSL, per FIG. 3-1? Answer: As a general rule, the 1200-foot ceiling/floor exists over most of the United States. It's a different story, however, in the mountainous regions of the West.

For example, look at the excerpt from the Denver Sectional (FIG. 3-2). This is just a segment of an airway, but you'll notice that the outside lines of the airway (in blue on the original chart) are sharp, while the blue shading fades inward toward the airway centerline. The controlled airspace thus starts at 1200 feet AGL within the eight nautical mile width of the airway. Outside the airway, however, beyond the sharp blue line of demarcation, it's a different story. In the areas *between* any two demarcation lines, the airspace is uncontrolled up to the 14,500-foot level. Again, the outward or inward shading of the blue establishes the existence of the 1200-foot AGL ceiling/floor.

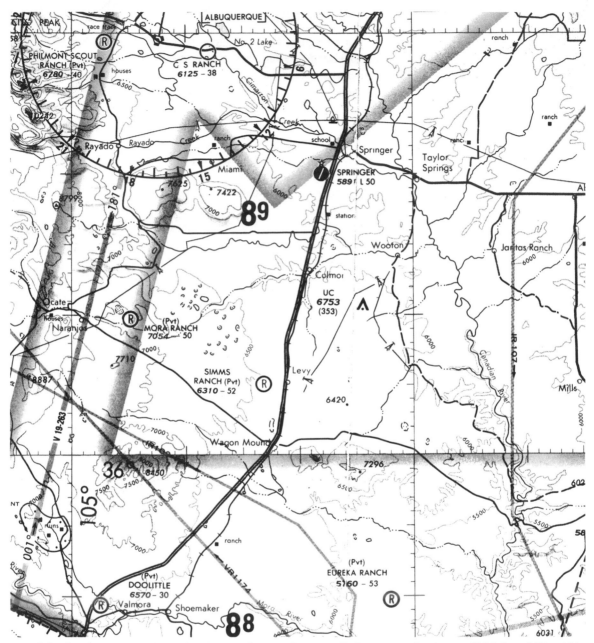

Fig. 3-2. *On this excerpt from the Denver Sectional, controlled airspace begins at 1200 feet AGL within the airway. Outside of the airway, controlled airspace doesn't start until 14,500 feet MSL, as indicated by the sharp edge of the shading (blue on the original chart).*

CONTROLLED AIRSPACE

Disregarding airports and their immediate surroundings for the moment, FIG. 3-1 depicts other controlled airspace, such as the Continental Control Area and the Positive Control Area. Even according to FAA personnel, the Continental Control Area is really a hangover from the days of commercial piston aircraft when operations were generally in the 14,500 to 25,000-foot altitude ranges. About all the Area does today is establish the fact that some aircraft may be subject to ATC control between 14,500 and 18,000 feet MSL—the base of the Positive Control Area. On a VFR flight plan in this altitude range, you are not subject to control. IFR is another matter. (The FAA is proposing to lower the floor of the Continental Control Area. So, wherever you see "14,500" in this book, be aware that a new number may apply by the time you read these words.)

The Positive Control Area, however, offers no choice. Regardless of the weather, you must file an IFR flight plan and adhere to all IFR regulations and procedures. Control from 18,000 to 60,000 feet is, indeed, Positive. To confuse matters a bit, the FAA has recently classified the Positive Control Area into two categories: the Continental Positive Control Area (over the lower 48 states) and the Alaska Positive Control Area, but these are just technical distinctions.

As to the Federal Airways: Except in Hawaii, where there are no vertical limits, the normal 8 nautical mile width of airspace along the airways, from 1200 feet AGL up to 18,000 feet MSL, is identified as "controlled." I say "normal" because the 8-mile width prevails up to about 50 miles from the VOR transmitting station. Beyond that, the airway gradually fans out to a 20-mile width (10 miles either side of the centerline) 130 nm miles from the transmitter.

Remember, however, that if you are flying an airway on a VFR flight plan, or no flight plan at all, you'll be in a controlled airspace but not under ATC's control. You may have established contact with an Air Route Traffic Control Center for traffic advisories or enroute flight following, and, if so, you'll probably have several communication exchanges with Center or Approach Control personnel as you proceed along the airway. You're still VFR, however, in VFR conditions. Accordingly, your only responsibilities are to adhere to the VFR flight altitudes and visibility/cloud separation regulations, to advise Center if you are going to change altitudes or deviate from your announced route of flight, and to keep your eyes open.

Until you near a Terminal Control Area (TCA), an Airport Radar Service Area (ARSA), or an airport with an operating control tower, you can fly the airways all day and never call or be in contact with any controlling agency. That's not necessarily a good idea, but it's still the VFR pilot's privilege.

VFR REGULATIONS:
Altitudes, Visibility, and Cloud Separation

With the basic structure of the airspace out of the way (except for airports), a brief review of the altitude, visibility, and cloud separation regulations affecting VFR pilots is in order. These may be well known, but no discussion of operating within the airspace system would be complete without at least a short summary.

Flying VFR places that old and oft-repeated responsibility on the pilot: the responsibility to "see and avoid"—whether the airspace is controlled or uncontrolled. That's as applicable in the open country as in the vicinity of a tower-operated airport. In a controlled environment, as around an airport, you may be given advisories that you ". . . have traffic at two o'clock," but the ultimate responsibility for conflict avoidance is still yours.

Despite that obvious fact, the skies would be chaotic and infinitely more dangerous if we were allowed to roam about completely at will, relying solely on the hope that we and others will "see and avoid." Consequently, and to minimize the potential of conflict, regulations have been established governing altitudes to be flown as well as visibility and cloud separation minimums that must be observed.

Altitudes

First, the altitudes, again from the *AIM*, as illustrated in FIG. 3-3. The chart is self-explanatory, but an easy way to remember whether the VFR altitude should

CONTROLLED AND UNCONTROLLED AIRSPACE VFR ALTITUDES AND FLIGHT LEVELS			
If your magnetic course (ground track) is	More than 3000' above the surface but below 18,000' MSL fly	Above 18,000' MSL to FL 290 (except within Positive Control Area, FAR 71.193) fly	Above FL 290 (except within Positive Control Area, FAR 71.193) fly 4000' intervals
0° to 179°	Odd thousands, MSL, plus 500' (3500, 5500, 7500, etc.).	Odd Flight Levels plus 500' (FL 195, FL 215, FL 235, etc.).	Beginning at FL 300 (FL 300, 340, 380, etc.)
180° to 359°	Even thousands, MSL, plus 500' (4500, 6500, 8500, etc.).	Even Flight Levels plus 500' (FL 185, FL 205, FL 225, etc.).	Beginning at FL 320 (FL 320, 360, 400, etc.)
UNCONTROLLED AIRSPACE - IFR ALTITUDES AND FLIGHT LEVELS			
If your magnetic course (ground track) is	Below 18,000' MSL fly	At or above 18,000' MSL but below FL 290, fly	At or above FL 290, fly 4000' intervals
0° to 179°	Odd thousands, MSL, (3000, 5000, 7000, etc.).	Odd Flight Levels, FL 190, 210, 230, etc.).	Beginning at FL 290, (FL 290, 330, 370, etc.)
180° to 359°	Even thousands, MSL, (2000, 4000, 6000, etc.).	Even Flight Levels (FL 180, 200, 220, etc.).	Beginning at FL 310, (FL 310, 350, 390, etc.)

Fig. 3-3. *The odd and even VFR and IFR flight altitudes. Note that IFR altitudes apply only within uncontrolled airspace.*

be in odd or even thousands of feet is to use the acronym WEEO—westbound even, eastbound odd—plus 500. And remember that those altitudes don't apply when flying at 3000 feet AGL or below.

If everyone would adhere to the prescribed altitudes, we'd have a lot fewer near-misses. Evasive action is too frequently necessary when you're at the right altitude but some sightseer barrels toward you head-on at the same altitude. This often happens above 3000 feet AGL within 30 or 40 miles of an airport where, for some reason, altitude-adherence seems less important.

And then there are cases when both aircraft are going by the book, but one is headed southeast, the other northeast. A disaster is in the making, unless at least one pilot has alert and roving eyes. If you have your head in the cockpit much over 10 seconds instead of scanning the surrounding atmosphere, you ought to be getting a little nervous. The rate of closure, even between light aircraft, will not tolerate inattention to the outside world.

Visibility and Cloud Separation

Now let's look at the visibility/cloud separation minimums. Figure 3-4 tells the story, and there's not much to add. Okay, you're at the proper altitude, but

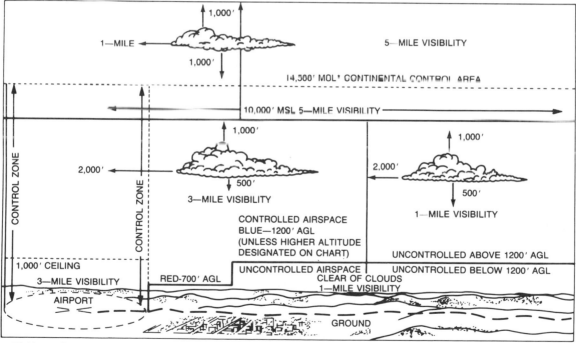

*Subject to Change

Fig. 3-4. *Basic VFR Weather Minimums.*

the visibility is decreasing or there's a bunch of puffy clouds up ahead. Again, to see and avoid, the FARs are very specific about visibility minimums and separation from clouds or overcasts.

Have trouble remembering the numbers? Follow the sequence of: feet below, feet above, feet laterally. Then double the figures as you go: 500, 1000, 2000. Just don't forget that 2000 feet from one cloud also means 2000 feet from the next, or actually a 4000-foot separation between those puffy whites.

Despite the regulations, there are those for whom the desire to skim along a few feet above or below a cloud layer is irresistible. It's a great way to get the sensation of speed. Others have trouble overcoming the temptation to burst into a nice white cloud just for the fun of it or to see if they really can fly on instruments.

Are you a gambler—or a Russian roulette devotee? That's what it's all about. Some other character may also be testing his new-found instrument skills in the same cloud. Or a perfectly legitimate IFR aircraft may be climbing or letting down through the cloud layer. Suddenly there he is and there you are. He's legal, you're not, but that won't make much difference to the surviving families (except for the few million bucks the other guy's relatives will get from your estate).

There's an old saying: "There are old pilots and there are bold pilots, but there are no old bold pilots." It's a time-worn adage, but age has not dimmed its validity. Violating the rules may give some people a sense of bravado and make for good hangar talk. In those cases, though, bravado is called stupidity.

UNCONTROLLED AIRPORTS

Now let's focus on the airports, beginning with the many that are uncontrolled and then to those that fall under the "controlled" category. A disclaimer of sorts, however, relative to radio frequencies and whom to call under what conditions, is necessary at this point. So many combinations of facilities and frequencies at uncontrolled airports are possible that what we say or describe in the following pages may not cover every single situation you might encounter. Only one constant prevails at uncontrolled airports: Either the field has no tower at all, or the tower is part-time and closed. Considering the other variations that could exist, the reason for this disclaimer should become more evident as we move into the subject.

"Uncontrolled" does not mean total freedom to operate as you please in and around the many "uncontrolled" airports across the country. The FAA visibility and cloud separation minimums still apply, as do radio communication responsibilities and the traffic patterns to fly. What distinguishes the "controlled" from the "uncontrolled" is the existence or non-existence of an *operating* control tower. If the field has no tower at all, it is uncontrolled. If there is a tower but it is part-time, the field is uncontrolled when the tower is closed. All told, over

95 percent, or roughly 12,000 out of 12,500 airports in the United States available for unrestricted public use, not including heliports, are uncontrolled, in the sense that no tower exists on the property.

Of those, there are two types: one designated as MULTICOM and the other UNICOM. Both are easily identified on the Sectional by the fact that they are magenta-colored, while tower-controlled airports (even ones with part-time towers) are always depicted in blue.

MULTICOM

MULTICOM is identified by the *absence* of frequency information. If you look at FIG. 3-5, you'll see that at T-Bar Airport at Tahoka, Texas, only the field elevation (3126 feet) and the length of the runway (33, or 3300 feet) are indicated. (The letter L does not mean runway length but rather that the runway is lighted for night operations.) By inference, then, the airport has no tower, no Flight Service Station, no UNICOM. It is uncontrolled in every sense.

So what does this mean to the VFR pilot? Simply that:

- You can operate in and around the airport at will, observing only the basic rules of traffic pattern flying and right of way.

- If you maintain an altitude of 1200 feet AGL or less, the visibility must be at least one statute mile and you must be able to remain clear of any clouds.

- Above 1200 feet AGL, the visibility must be at least three miles and the standard cloud separation 500 feet below, 1000 feet above, and 2000 feet horizontally.

- Radio position reports and intentions are communicated on the 122.9 frequency—the Common Traffic Advisory Frequency (CTAF) for all MULTICOM airports—and all calls are addressed to ''(Airport Name) Traffic.''

Fig. 3-5. *T-Bar Airport at Tahoka, Texas is an uncontrolled airport where the MULTICOM CTAF (122.9) is the only means of radio communications.*

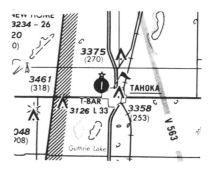

UNICOM

The second type of uncontrolled airport also has no tower but UNICOM service is available. UNICOM is a non-government radio facility usually manned by the local fixed-base operator (FBO), and its presence on the field can be determined from the Sectional (FIG. 3-6) or the *A/FD* (FIG. 3-7). As with a MULTICOM airport, the field elevation and the longest runway length are recorded, but the slanted figures (*122.8* in FIG. 3-6) tell you that UNICOM is available. At airports such as this, which have no tower and no Flight Service Station, the UNICOM frequencies are almost universally *122.7, 122.8,* or *123.0.*

The advantage of UNICOM, when contacted for a "field advisory," is that the FBO will give you the current wind direction and velocity, the favored runway in use, and the existence of any reported traffic in the pattern or area. In no way, however, is UNICOM a controlling agency. It is merely a field advisory service offered by the local FBO. It can also be used to request a taxi, ask the FBO operator to make a phone call for you, relay messages to people waiting for you, alert the operator of needed mechanical repairs, and so on. These services are available

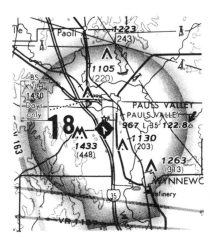

Fig. 3-6. *How a Sectional identifies a UNICOM airport.*

PAULS VALLEY MUNI (F61) 2 S UTC-6(-5DT) 34°42'40"N 97°13'23"W	DALLAS-FT. WORTH
968 B S4 FUEL 100LL, MOGAS	L-13C
RWY 12-30: H3500X150 (CONC) S-42, D-55, DT-110	IAP

RWY 12: Road.   RWY 30: Trees.
RWY 17-35: H3500X150 (CONC)   S-42, D-55, DT-110   LIRL
  RWY 17: P-line.   RWY 35: Trees.
AIRPORT REMARKS: Attended 1400-2330Z‡. After hours call 238-6762.
COMMUNICATIONS: CTAF/UNICOM 122.8.
  MC ALESTER FSS (MLC) Toll free call, dial 1–800–WX–BRIEF. NOTAM FILE MLC.
Ⓡ FORT WORTH CENTER APP/DEP CON 128.1
RADIO AIDS TO NAVIGATION: NOTAM FILE ADM.
  ARDMORE (H) VORTACW 116.7   ADM   Chan 114   34°12'41"N 97°10'05"W   346°30.1 NM to fld. 930/09E.
  NDB (MHW) 384   PVJ   34°42'55"N 97°13'44"W   at fld. VFR only. NOTAM FILE MLC.

Fig. 3-7. *Determining a UNICOM airport in the Airport/Facility Directory.*

wherever UNICOM exists, whether the airport is controlled or uncontrolled. To obtain either those services or a field advisory, the initial radio contact is addressed to "(Airport name) UNICOM" and all subsequent position reporting calls are made to "(Airport name) Traffic" over the airport's published UNICOM frequency.

Uncontrolled Airports with Closed Towers

Here we have a tower on the airport, but it's only a part-time operation, as, for example, from 0700 to 1900 local time. When open, the airport is controlled and the rules for operating within at least a 5-mile radius of it apply. (We'll get into that later.) When the tower is closed, however, it's just like a MULTICOM or UNICOM field. The only difference, radio-wise, is that field advisories would be obtained by first contacting UNICOM on its frequency (assuming the FBO is open) and then addressing position reports to "(Airport name) Traffic" over the *tower* frequency—even though the tower is closed.

But a question: How do you know whether the tower is full- or part-time? The Sectional will tell you, as will the *A/FD*. Find a blue-colored airport on any Sectional. If you see a star or asterisk immediately following the tower frequency, the tower is part-time. For example, take Fort Smith, Arkansas (FIG. 3-8). The star to the right of the frequency—CT **118.3** —is the clue. Now turn to the inside flap of the Sectional and the data under "CONTROL TOWER FREQUENCIES ON MEMPHIS SECTIONAL CHART" (FIG. 3-9). Along with other information, you'll note that the Fort Smith tower is in operation between 0600 and 2300 local time. During those hours, the airport is controlled. At all other times, it's uncontrolled.

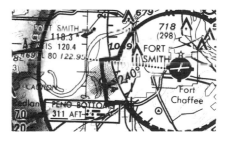

Fig. 3-8. *A star to the right of the tower frequency indicates a part-time operation.*

Another variation: There is a part-time tower and a Flight Service Station on the airport (although this is becoming a matter of history as more and more FSSs are being consolidated into regional locations). With the tower closed, the FSS provides the airport with advisories but on the *tower* frequency, not 123.6 or any of the published FSS frequencies. It does *not* control traffic, however. At no time is a Flight Service Station a controlling agency. Other than being capable of providing accurate and complete weather information, and on-field

CONTROL TOWER FREQUENCIES ON MEMPHIS SECTIONAL CHART

Airports which have control towers are indicated on this chart by the letters CT followed by the primary VHF local control frequency. Selected transmitting frequencies for each control tower are tabulated in the adjoining spaces, the low or medium transmitting frequency is listed first followed by a VHF local control frequency, and the primary VHF and UHF military frequencies, when these frequencies are available. An asterisk (*) follows the part-time tower frequency remoted to the colocated full-time FSS for use as Airport Advisory Service (AAS) during hours tower is closed. Hours shown are local time. Radio call provided if different from tower name.

Automatic Terminal Information Service (ATIS) frequencies, shown on the face of the chart are normal arriving frequencies, all ATIS frequencies available are tabulated below.

ASR and/or PAR indicates Radar Instrument Approach available.

CONTROL TOWER	RADIO CALL	OPERATES	ATIS	FREQ	ASR/PAR
ADAMS		CONTINUOUS	125.6	118.7 257.8	ASR
BARKSDALE AFB		CONTINUOUS	375.8	126.2 295.7	ASR
BLYTHEVILLE AFB		CONTINUOUS		126.2 255.9	ASR/PAR
BRAVO OLF (NAVY)		0800-1700 MON-FRI		279.2	
COLUMBUS AFB		0700-1800 MON-THU 0700-2000 FRI 0900-1600 SAT 1000-1600 SUN CLSD HOL & OT EXC EMERG	115.2 273.5	126.2 289.6	ASR
DRAKE		0600-2200	133.1	118.5* 369.0	
FORT SMITH		0600-2300	120.4	118.3 381.6	ASR
GREENVILLE		0700-1900		119.0 256.9	
GREGG CO		0600-2200	119.65	119.2 257.8	ASR

Fig. 3-9. *Another source to determine a tower's period of operation: the reverse side of the Sectional's "Legend."*

FSS functions basically like UNICOM as far as flight operations—not personal telephone calls, or the like—are concerned.

Finally, assume the airport has UNICOM, a Remote Communications Outlet (RCO) providing direct radio contact with a distant Flight Service Station, and the FBO is open. Now, whom do you call for advisories? Quite apparently, it's the FBO. On the UNICOM frequency, the FBO will give you current weather and any reported traffic, while the FSS RCO is available for opening and closing flight plans, even while you're on the ground.

But what if the FBO is closed and you want advisories? In this case, first call the FSS on the RCO frequency. They will give you winds, altimeter setting, the favored runway, and any reported traffic. With that data, go to the UNICOM CTAF for position reports and to announce your intentions. You could stay with Flight Service, but the odds are that other arriving or departing traffic would be using the CTAF rather than the RCO. You'll thus have a better idea of the traffic in and around the airport.

If any of this "whom do you call when, and what frequency do you use" leaves you somewhat perplexed, FIG. 3-10 may clarify things.

CONTROLLED AIRPORTS

Now we come to one of the more complicated (perhaps "confusing" is more descriptive) aspects of the airspace system. What with Airport Traffic Areas (ATAs), Control Zones (CZs), Transition Areas (TAs), TCAs, ARSAs, and a few more, it's little wonder that the typical VFR pilot does indeed become confused. Let's see if we can bring some clarity to the subject. Remember, however, that right now we're concerned only with tower-controlled airports and the immediate geography surrounding them. The matter of TCAs, ARSAs, and TRSAs comes later.

One simple fact, repeated only for emphasis, is universal: If the airport has an operating tower, the airport is controlled, and every pilot is under the jurisdiction of air traffic control (ATC). If there is no tower, or it is closed, the airport is uncontrolled, and the normal VFR operating regulations apply.

Airport Traffic Areas (ATAs)

To start with the most basic, every tower-operated airport has what is called an *Airport Traffic Area* (ATA). This, as FIG. 3-1 indicated, is the airspace within a 5 statute mile radius from the center of the airport and rising to, but not including, 3000 feet above airport elevation. You won't find the ATA depicted on any chart or in any airport information publication, but it's there nonetheless.

So what does the existence of the ATA mean to the pilot? Simply that:

- Two-way radio contact with the tower must be established before entering the ATA and maintained while in it.

- You are expected to comply with the control tower instructions, unless doing so would cause you to violate a VFR regulation or create a potentially hazardous situation.

- Controller instructions are to be tersely acknowledged in a few words that tell the controller you have received his message and understand what is expected of you. Merely "Rogering" an instruction does not communicate understanding.

- Permission to transit the ATA at altitudes below 3000 feet must be obtained from the tower controller *before* entering the ATA, preferably 10 to 15 miles from the airport. Above 3000 feet AGL, you are out of the ATA, and no radio contact is required.

- You do not report on downwind, base, or final, as at an uncontrolled field, unless the tower requests you to do so. The controller knows where you are, and these calls only needlessly consume air time and the controller's attention.

It's obvious that if a tower exists, the airport has enough activity to warrant such a traffic controlling agency. Consequently, the initial contact before entering the ATA should be established at least 10 miles from the field. In so doing, merely identify your aircraft (type and N-number), your position, altitude, the fact that

Fig. 3-10. *Use this chart to determine what frequencies to use for field advisories (winds, favored runway, and, in some cases, weather observations) and for self-announce position reporting. Always check the A/FD for exceptions to this chart.*

Tower Status	On-Site FSS Status	On-Site RCO	FBO Status	Field Advisories Type/Radio Frequency	Radio Frequency for Self-Announce Position Reports (CTAF)	ATC Radio Frequency
Tower Open						Tower
Tower Closed	FSS Open			ASS/Tower[5]	Tower	
Tower Closed	FSS Closed	RCO	FBO Open	UFA/UNICOM[1]	Tower	
Tower Closed	FSS Closed	RCO	FBO Closed	FAA/RCO	Tower	
Tower Closed	FSS Closed	RCO	No FBO	FFA/RCO	Tower	
Tower Closed	FSS Closed	No RCO	FBO Open	UFA/UNICOM	Tower	
Tower Closed	FSS Closed	No RCO	FBO Closed	Not Available	Tower	
Tower Closed	FSS Closed	No RCO	No FBO	Not Available	Tower	
Tower Closed	No FSS	RCO	FBO Open	UFA/UNICOM[1]	Tower	
Tower Closed	No FSS	RCO	FBO Closed	FFA/RCO	Tower	
Tower Closed	No FSS	RCO	No FBO	FFA/RCO	Tower	
Tower Closed	No FSS	No RCO	FBO Open	UFA/UNICOM	Tower	
Tower Closed	No FSS	No RCO	FBO Closed	Not Available	Tower	
Tower Closed	No FSS	No RCO	No FBO	Not Available	Tower	
No Tower	FSS Open			ASS/123.6[3]	123.6[2]	
No Tower	FSS Closed	RCO	FBO Open	UFA/UNICOM[1]	123.6[2]	

No Tower	FSS Closed	FCO	FBO Closed	FFA/RCO	123.6[2]
No Tower	FSS Closed	RCO	No FBO	FFA/RCO	123.6[2]
No Tower	FSS Closed	No RCO	FBO Open	UFA/UNICOM	123.6[2]
No Tower	FSS Closed	No RCO	FBO Closed	Not Available	123.6[2]
No Tower	FSS Closed	No RCO	No FBO	Not Available	123.6[2]
No Tower	No FSS	RCO	FBO Open	UFA/UNICOM[1]	UNICOM
No Tower	No FSS	FCO	FBO Closed	FFA/RCO	UNICOM
No Tower	No FSS	No RCO	No FBO	FFA/RCO	122.9[4]
No Tower	No FSS	No RCO	FBO Open	UFA/UNICOM	UNICOM
No Tower	No FSS	No RCO	FBO Closed	Not Available	UNICOM
No Tower	No FSS	No RCO	No FBO	Not Available	122.9[4]

1 Last hour's official weather observation available from FSS over RCO if weather observer is on duty.

2 Of as listed in A/FD.

3 Where available. Some AFSSs may not offer this service.

4 MULTICOM.

5 FSS will reply on tower frequency.

AFSS - Automated Flight Service Station

ATC - Air Traffic Control

FBO - Fixed - Base Operator with UNICOM

FSS - Flight Service Station (All AFSSs are open 24 hours.)

RCO - Remote Communications Outlet

AAS - FSS Airport Advisory Service (winds, weather, favored runway, altimeter setting, if observer is on duty at airport)

FFA - FSS field advisories (last hour's winds, weather, and altimeter setting, reported traffic within 10 miles of airport)

UFA - UNICOM field advisories (winds, favored runway, known traffic altimeter setting [at some locations])

51

you have monitored the current ATIS (Automatic Terminal Information Service)—if this service exists on the airport—and your intentions. As an example:

> Billard Tower, Cherokee 8515 November over Perry Dam at three
> thousand five hundred with Charlie (the current ATIS report), landing
> Billard.

If you're below 3000 feet and want to cross through the ATA, the call goes:

> Billard Tower, Cherokee 8515 November over Perry Dam at two
> thousand five hundred. Request approval to transit your area westbound.

From then on, it's just a matter of acknowledging and following the controller's instructions.

By the same token, ground movements around the airport that would put you on any taxiway or runway require approval of Ground Control, as does tower permission to take off and to turn to the heading you have requested after departure. In sum, whether landing, taxiing, departing, or shooting touch-and-gos at a controlled airport, radio contact with the tower personnel, including Ground Control, is mandatory.

That's all well and good, but what happens if the tower is part-time and closed when you want to take off or land? What do you do then? In that case, the ATA does not exist and, unless there's an operating FSS on the field, the radio calls are just like those at any uncontrolled airport—MULTICOM or UNICOM.

Control Zones (CZs) and Transition Areas (TAs)

The second area of "control" is the *Control Zone*, or CZ, and here is where a fair degree of uncertainty is common. What's the difference between an ATA and a CZ? Why a CZ if an ATA already exists? When is a CZ in effect and when isn't it? And so the typical questions go. To clarify things, the following may help:

What is a Control Zone? It is a designated area surrounding certain tower airports (usually coinciding with the Airport Traffic Area radius) as well as many that have no tower at all. In addition, there may be a keyhole-like extension for the purpose of facilitating IFR landings and departures. Unlike the ATA, which rises to, but not including, the 3000-foot AGL altitude, the CZ goes from the ground to the base of the Continental Control Area—currently 14,500 feet MSL. Within the CZ, but beyond the ATA, VFR traffic is "controlled" by ATC only during below-basic VFR conditions.

How are CZs identified? The Sectional identifies CZs by a broken circle surrounding the airport. Depending on the airport, the broken lines may also indicate an extension of the CZ, thus forming the keyhole or cookie-cutter design.

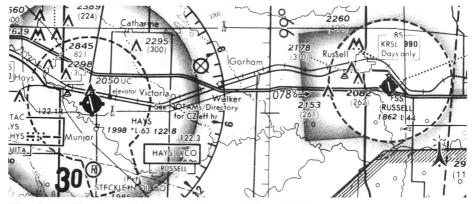

Fig. 3-11. *The Control Zones at Hays and Russell, Kansas.*

Figure 3-11 illustrates both configurations. the circular structure at Russell, Kansas, and the keyhole at nearby Hays.

What is the purpose of a Control Zone? A CZ exists solely to limit VFR traffic during instrument meteorological conditions (IMC) in order to expedite the movement of IFR traffic into and out of the airport.

Is a CZ always in effect? The CZ does not exist in VFR weather when the ceiling is at least 1000 feet and the visibility three miles. In those conditions, mentally wipe all CZs and Transition Areas off the chart. They're simply not there. Also, regardless of the weather conditions, there is no CZ when the tower, if one exists, is closed and there is no qualified weather observer on the airport.

What is required for an airport to have a CZ? To have a CZ, at least one (or a combination) of the following must be located on the airport:

- An operating control tower with a qualified weather observer on duty
- A Flight Service Station
- A federally-designated qualified weather observer
- A National Weather Service Office

The basic requirement is an on-the-field resource qualified to report accurate and current airport weather data, *plus* communications capability within the CZ down to the runway surface of the primary airport (the airport upon which the CZ is designated).

What does the magenta indicate when a CZ exists? You'll recall that within the boundaries depicted by the magenta, the floor of the controlled airspace is normally 700 feet AGL. When an airport has a Control Zone, however, that floor exists only between the limits of the CZ (the five-mile radius) and the magenta band. Within the CZ, the airspace is controlled from the surface up to 14,500 feet. Consequently, to operate VFR below the 700-foot floor, you must have at least one mile visibility and be able to remain clear of clouds. Entrance into or departure from the CZ, however, is prohibited during instrument meteorological conditions unless a Special VFR (SVFR) clearance, which we'll discuss in a minute, is authorized by ATC.

Does the blue/magenta band have any other significance? Yes. It defines what is called the Transition Area (TA). This is the airspace reserved for IFR aircraft that are transitioning from an enroute-to-landing or a departing-to-enroute status in IMC. If you look at any Sectional, you'll see a lot of blue/magenta TAs surrounding MULTICOM or UNICOM airports that have no Control Zone, as well as airports with towers and clearly identified CZs. The purpose, once again, is to expedite as well as protect departing and arriving IFR traffic in IMC.

But if there is no CZ, as such, how is IFR traffic controlled? To a large extent, that depends on the individual location. At MULTICOM or UNICOM airports located near a tower-controlled CZ, Approach Control (through its radar facilities) would assume the responsibility. In another situation, the non-CZ field might be miles from any tower airport but perhaps near a Center-remoted outlet. Then, Center would provide the necessary radar coverage and instructions, probably down to the final approach.

Many times, however, radar service may be available only to a point. Gage, Oklahoma, is one example. Gage is located at the very fringe of the Kansas City Center's area of responsibility and the nearest remoted radar site is at Garden City, Kansas, about 115 nautical miles to the northwest. That far from the target means that radar coverage is ineffective much below 7000 feet. ATC can provide vectors and altitude changes down to approximately that altitude, but from there on, Center would apply non-radar rules and practices to ensure the separation of participating IFR aircraft.

Fine, but how does all this affect the VFR pilot? Let's set up four situations, remembering that VFR minimums in a control zone are 1000-foot ceiling and 3 miles visibility.

Situation One: The airport is below basic VFR minimums, and you want to take off. You can't do it, except with a Special VFR clearance.

Situation Two: You want to land at an airport which has a CZ, but the weather at that airport is below basic VFR minimums. You are nearing one of the transition areas identified by the blue/magenta shadings, still perhaps 20 or 30 miles from the airport. Is a call to one of the ATC facilities or the nearest Flight Service Station required, this far from the CZ? No, but it's wise to make your intentions known as far in advance as practicable. Although it may be VFR where you are, you are about to enter airspace that is controlled in IMC conditions. You cannot penetrate the control zone, whether a tower is on the field or not without first obtaining an SVFR clearance.

Situation Three: You're flying cross-country at 5500 feet AGL. Approaching the Transition Area of a CZ airport, you run into a thick haze, reducing your forward visibility. If you continue, visibility may go below the basic 3-mile minimum. IMC conditions exist at the airport you are nearing (but no ceiling is reported), and you don't want to land there anyway. What can you do? Perhaps a one-eighty out of the area would be the smartest maneuver. You can penetrate the TA without ATC approval if visibility stays at least 3 miles. But since the airport is already reporting IMC, a Special VFR clearance is required to enter the Control Zone, and if there is a fair amount of IFR traffic, the chances of getting that clearance are remote.

Situation Four: You're completely VFR in bright sunshine at 5500 feet AGL, but the airport in the CZ you want to transit is socked in with ground fog. Is contact with ATC necessary? No. A clearance is not *required* to transit a CZ if you are flying in basic VFR conditions above the ceiling layer and are not penetrating the airport traffic area.

For reemphasis only, CZs exist solely to facilitate IFR arrivals and departures in conditions below basic VFR. They are there to limit or exclude any VFR activity within those boundaries that could impede or unduly delay IFR traffic.

What is this "Special VFR" (SVFR)? It's simply this: If the visibility is at least one mile and you are able to remain clear of clouds, you can request an SVFR clearance from the tower or the controlling ATC facility. As a rule, however, only one fixed-wing (FW/SVFR) aircraft at a time is permitted in the CZ, so approval will depend on the existing traffic and whether that approval would delay IFR operations. Also, the FW/SVFR clearance applies only to operations within the CZ. Outside the CZ, you must be able to adhere to the basic VFR minimum ceiling and visibility regulations, both below and above the 700/1200-foot floors.

Regardless of IFR traffic, no SVFR would be approved unless the minimum safe altitudes in FAR 91.79 can be adhered to. Basically, these say that:

- No pilot may operate an aircraft over any congested area of city, town, or settlement, or over any open air assembly of persons below 1000 feet above the highest obstacle within a horizontal radius of 2000 feet of the aircraft.

- The minimum altitude for fixed-wing aircraft over other than congested areas is 500 feet AGL, except open water or sparsely populated terrain.

Thus, if the ceilings are such that this FAR would be violated, the request for an SVFR would be denied. And, by the same token, no matter what the weath-

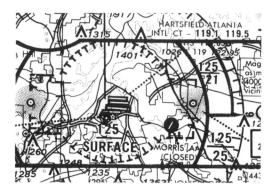

Fig. 3-12. *The ''T's'' around the Atlanta airport indicate ''No SVFR.''*

er, these minimums must not be violated by fixed-wing aircraft. (They're a little more lenient for helicopters.)

What about a night SVFR? This is prohibited between sunset and sunrise—unless the pilot is instrument rated and the aircraft is equipped for IFR flight.

Can SVFRs be obtained at all CZ airports? No. Some of the busier airports will not grant SVFRs. Those CZs are indicated on the Sectional by a circle of T's instead of dashes (FIG. 3-12).

How is an SVFR obtained if there is no tower on the field? In those cases, the SVFR is requested through the nearest Flight Service Station, operating tower, or Air Route Traffic Control Center.

Why contact a FSS? It's Not a Controlling Agency. True, but the FSS will relay the SVFR request to the appropriate ATC facility, such as Approach Control or Center. That facility will approve or disapprove the request, based on existing traffic, and inform the FSS accordingly, which, in turn, will advise the pilot.

Can you clarify what ATC agency is contacted for the various SVFRs? That will vary, depending on where you are and the facilities on or off the airport. If you initially call the ''wrong'' agency, you will be asked to contact another that is in more direct control. Here are some guidelines on how to obtain an SVFR clearance:

Departing

- Uncontrolled airport: Call the nearest FSS

- Controlled airport: Call Ground Control

Arriving and/or Transiting

- Uncontrolled airport and beyond radar range of an Approach Control (or Center) facility: Call FSS

- Uncontrolled airport and within radar range of Approach Control (or Center): Call Approach (or Center)

- Controlled airport with tower, no Approach Control: Call tower

- Controlled airport with tower and Approach Control: Call Approach

- Controlled satellite airport with tower, but Approach Control at primary airport: Call tower

Some of this, no doubt, gets confusing, partly because so many different possibilities exist. And, perhaps I've belabored the subject of both Control Zones and SVFRs. They're all part of the airspace system, though, and thus warrant understanding by the VFR pilot. You never know when knowledge of CZs and the regulations pertaining to them could be important to your well-being.

TEMPORARY FLIGHT RESTRICTIONS

Curiosity and/or morbidity are rather common human traits. A major fire is raging; an explosion has devastated a wide area; a tornado has wiped out a portion of a town; a major sporting event is underway. Whatever the incident, many of us are tempted to get airborne and see what's going on from above. Before doing so, we would be wise to do a little checking.

If there is an incident that warrants temporary flight restrictions, the restrictions are established by the area manager of the Air Route Traffic Control Center that has jurisdiction over the area in which the incident has taken, or is taking, place. Then, through FAA procedures, a NOTAM is issued stipulating what restrictions are in effect. Largely these are designed to bar sightseers from the area and to prevent interference with emergency, rescue, or disaster relief measures.

Normally, the restricted airspace extends to 2000 feet AGL within a 2 nautical mile radius of the event. These dimensions can vary, however, with the seriousness of the occurrence and the rescue/relief operations involved. The NOTAM fully explains the restrictions, how long they will be in effect, what aircraft are permitted within the area, and the military or federal agency responsible for coordinating emergency activities.

FAR 91.91 states the restriction regulations and *AIM*, Paragraph 133 provides further explanation. Recognizing the occasional tendency to be ambulance-chasers or just plain gawkers, a review of the regulations, as well as checking for NOTAMs that might have been issued, could keep us out of trouble.

CONCLUSION

That's a good part of the airspace story—controlled and uncontrolled. Flying VFR in most of the so-called controlled airspace, whether on a VFR flight plan or not, places relatively few restrictions or requirements on us. That freedom, however, demands that we adhere to the prescribed VFR flight altitudes and that we scrupulously observe the visibility and cloud separation minimums. It further demands that we comply with the established traffic pattern and communication procedures when operating in and around uncontrolled airports. Perhaps above all is the VFR pilot's responsibility to have alert and roving eyes in a head that is out of the cockpit and on a constant swivel.

As far as airports in general are concerned, we can summarize the principles this way:

If an airport has an operating tower, the airport is controlled. It thus has an ATA during all operating times. It also (almost always) has a CZ which imposes additional requirements for VFR pilots during instrument meteorological conditions. Furthermore, radio contact with, and approval from, the tower is required before entering the ATA for landing, when transiting the ATA below 3000 feet AGL, for takeoff and departure direction, and for ground movement of the aircraft on any taxiway or runway. Those are the basics. Operating in a TCA or ARSA, where Approach or Departure Control become involved (which we'll discuss in later chapters), requires additional procedures and equipment above and beyond the basics.

The airspace story, however, is not yet complete. Except for a brief reference, we have not said anything about the Special Use Airspace—those pieces of geography that are classified as Prohibited, Restricted, the vast chunks of air called Military Operations Areas (MOAs), or the Military Training Routes (MTRs). As these can offer some unwanted excitement to the unwary VFR pilot, they warrant a chapter unto themselves—the chapter that follows.

4

Special Use
Airspace

A GLANCE AT ALMOST ANY SECTIONAL WILL REVEAL A VARIETY OF LINES AND designs that depict airspace set aside for "special use." In all cases, these are blocks of space that have been established for purpose of national security, welfare, or environmental protection; or, military training, research, development, testing, and evaluation ("training/RDT&E").

Although the airspace reserved for security, welfare, and the environment could require flight detours or altitude changes, their size and sparsity make them relatively minor obstacles to VFR and IFR operations. Not so, however, with the areas set aside for military training/RDT&E. These provide space for all sorts of flight training maneuvers, bombing runs, missile launching, aerial gunnory, or artillery practice. It's thus patently apparent that unauthorized or careless penetration of active Special Use Airspace (SUA) could be somewhat hazardous to the unwary pilot. That being the case, let's start with a summary of the policy behind this airspace, followed by the various types of Special Use Airspace and the VFR pilot's responsibilities relative to them.

MILITARY OPERATIONS REQUIREMENTS

The FAA has a controller's handbook titled *Special Military Operations* (7610.4G) which summarizes the basic FAA policy relative to military operations requirements. In essence, the policy recognizes that the military has a continuing need to conduct certain training as well as research, development, testing, and evaluation activities, and that these activities should be conducted in airspace large enough to contain the planned activity and as free from nonparticipating aircraft as is practical. Accordingly, four types of Special Use Airspace exist primarily but not exclusively for military purposes: *Restricted Areas* (R), *Military Operations Areas* (MOAs), *Alert Areas* (A), and *Warning Areas* (W). In addition, but not considered Special Use Airspace, are the *Air Defense Identification Zones* (ADIZs) and cross-country low-level VFR and IFR *Military Training Routes* (MTRs).

The one other type of SUA, classified as *Prohibited Areas* (P), is established for national security, national welfare, or environmental protection. As we said, however, these are relatively few in number and small enough in area to be of only infrequent concern to the pilot. Prohibited Areas, along with MTRs, ADIZs, and the varieties of military SUA, are depicted on Sectional and other aeronautical charts.

As a further matter of policy, the government agency, organization, or military command responsible for establishing SUA must specify the proposed area's:

- vertical limits;

- horizontal limits;

- the hours of use, plus notations indicating whether the use is "Continuous," "Intermittent," "By NOTAM" (Notice To Airmen), or otherwise.

The policy also states that:

- the SUA will be limited to the minimum area(s) necessary to support operational requirements.

- the area be designed to conduct the maximum number of different types of military activity in the same airspace area.

- the military shall provide procedures for joint-use scheduling in the area ("joint-use" meaning use by both participating and nonparticipating aircraft).

Does the military just grab a chunk of airspace that it decides it needs? Hardly. Take the case of an MOA. The only aspect of the process occasionally subject to whimsy is the MOA's name. From the time the Air Force determines the need for the airspace until the FAA headquarters in Washington issues the final approval, eight or nine steps have intervened. These include reviews by, and coordination with, the military's regional office, the Air Route Traffic Control Center responsible for the area in which the SUA will be established, the FAA's regional office, interested entities on whom the airspace might have impact (such as airport managers, pilot organizations, and pilots themselves), and if military activities are proposed below 3000 feet AGL, the Environmental Protection Agency. Above 3000 feet, a "categorical exclusion" exists, and the EPA does not become involved. What with consultations, negotiations, and the need to follow the military/government chain of command, it can easily take up to two years from start to finish to establish military SUA.

Not only that, but once the SUA comes into being, each using agency (as defined below) must submit annual reports on the previous 12 months' activity. In the case of Restricted Areas, this includes the usage by daily hours, days of the week, and the number of weeks during the year that the space was released to the controlling agency for public use. In effect, the report justifies the existence of the space as it stands or reflects the need for revisions.

Some definitions may help in understanding the basic policy:

- *Using agency:* This refers to the agency or military unit that is the primary user and scheduler of the particular airspace.

- *Controlling agency:* The FAA facility, almost always the Air Route Traffic Control Center (ARTCC), in which the airspace is located. Depending on a variety of factors, Center may or may not exert direct control of military traffic operating within that airspace.

- *Participating aircraft:* Aircraft, usually but not necessarily military, that are involved in the training/research, development, testing, and evaluation activities ("training/RDT&E," again).

- *Nonparticipating aircraft:* Those aircraft for which a Center has separation responsibility (meaning IFR aircraft) but which have not been authorized by the using agency to operate through or in the SUA.

Before discussing SUA in a little more detail, how many parcels of SUA are we talking about?

- *Prohibited:* Excluding those set aside for wildlife protection, at this writing, seven areas are classified as Prohibited: The White House and government buildings, mostly along the Mall, in Washington; Mount Vernon, Virginia: Kennebunkport, Maine (President Bush's summer residence); Camp David near Thurmont, Maryland; Plains, Georgia (President Carter's hometown); a Department of Energy nuclear facility in Amarillo, Texas; and President Reagan's ranch near Santa Barbara, California.

- *Restricted:* Approximately 180 R-Area complexes exist across the country, with many composed of subsegments, such as A, B, C, etc. The subsegments, however, are not counted as part of the 180 total.

- *Military Operation Areas:* Again, approximately 180, with each named MOA counted as a single complex, regardless of its number of subsegments.

Finally, you who fly exclusively in Connecticut or Rhode Island are lucky. Those are the only two states of the 50 that have no Special Use Airspace within their borders.

THE TYPES AND PURPOSES OF SPECIAL USE AIRSPACE

Now for a closer look at the types of SUA, why they exist, and the restrictions, if any, they place on the VFR pilot.

Prohibited Areas (P)

Again, these exist for reasons of national interest, environmental protection, or national security. As an example, take Plains, Georgia. This is charted on the Jacksonville Sectional (FIG. 4-1) by a blue racetrack design and "P-77." Next, if you check the SUA table on the Sectional (FIG. 4-2), you'll see that flight below 1500 feet MSL over Plains is prohibited, the ban is continuous, and any proposed flight below that altitude must be requested through and approved by the FAA in Washington. Above 1500 feet MSL, there are no restrictions.

The same principle applies elsewhere. From the surface to whatever altitude is specified, the area is Prohibited—and that means *prohibited*. No ifs, ands, or buts—unless prior approval to penetrate the area has been obtained.

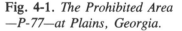

Fig. 4-1. *The Prohibited Area
—P-77—at Plains, Georgia.*

SPECIAL USE AIRSPACE ON JACKSONVILLE SECTIONAL CHART

Unless otherwise noted altitudes are MSL and in feet; time is local.
Contact nearest FSS for information.
†Other time by NOTAM contact FSS

The word "TO" an altitude means "To and including."
FL – Flight Level
NO A/G – No air to ground communications

U.S. P-PROHIBITED, R-RESTRICTED, A-ALERT, W-WARNING, MOA-MILITARY OPERATIONS AREA

NUMBER	LOCATION	ALTITUDE	TIME OF USE	CONTROLLING AGENCY
P-77	PLAINS, GA	TO 1500	CONTINUOUS	ADMIN, FAA WASHINGTON, D.C.
R-2903 B	STEVENS LAKE, FL	TO FL 230 WITHIN 5 NM RADIUS CENTERED AT 29°53'04"N, 81°59'09"W TO 7000 & 5000 WITHIN SE EXTN TO 7000 WITHIN NE EXTN	CONTINUOUS	JAX TRACON
R-2904	STARKE, FL	TO BUT NOT INCL 1800	0800-1700 DAILY APR-AUG 0800-1700 SAT-SUN SEP-MAR†	JAX TRACON
R-2906	RODMAN, FL	TO 14,000	CONTINUOUS	JAX TRACON
R-2907 A	LAKE GEORGE, FL	TO FL 230	CONTINUOUS	ZJX CNTR

Fig. 4-2. *The Special Use Airspace table on the Sectional details the flight restrictions.*

Restricted Areas (R)

More common, and larger in territory, are the areas classified as "Restricted." These are the blocks of space that, when active, pose serious and often invisible hazards to nonparticipating aircraft and those not specifically authorized to enter the area. What sort of hazards? Well, how about artillery fire, missiles, aerial gunnery, or bombing, as examples? Enough to discourage violation of the area by any VFR pilot when it's active.

The areas are easy to spot on the Sectional because of the diagonal blue lines that establish the horizontal perimeters. Figure 4-3 illustrates two areas located near Brookfield, Kansas, identified as R-3601A and R-3601B. The table on the Wichita Sectional (FIG. 4-4) provides further information about the altitudes within

Fig. 4-3. *The slanted border (blue on the chart) indicates the existence of Restricted Areas 3601A/B. In this case a Military Operations Area borders the Restricted Areas on the south and west.*

SPECIAL USE AIRSPACE ON WICHITA SECTIONAL CHART

Unless otherwise noted altitudes are
MSL and in feet; time is local.
Contact nearest FSS for information.
†Other time by NOTAM contact FSS

The word "TO" an altitude means "To and
including."
FL – Flight Level
NO A/G – No air to ground communications

U.S. P-PROHIBITED, R-RESTRICTED, A-ALERT, W-WARNING, MOA-MILITARY OPERATIONS AREA

NUMBER	LOCATION	ALTITUDE	TIME OF USE	CONTROLLING AGENCY
R-3601 A	BROOKVILLE, KS	TO FL 180	0830 TO 1630 CST MON, TUES, WED, FRI, SAT, 0830 TO 2100 CST THURS, O/T BY NOTAM 24 HRS IN ADV.	ZKC CNTR
R-3601 B	BROOKVILLE, KS	TO 6500	0830 TO 1630 CST MON, TUES, WED, FRI, SAT, 0830 TO 2100 CST THURS, O/T BY NOTAM 24 HRS IN ADV.	ZKC CNTR
R-3602 A	MANHATTAN, KS	TO 29,000	CONTINUOUS	ZKC CNTR
R-3602 B	MANHATTAN, KS	TO 29,000	CONTINUOUS	ZKC CNTR
A-562 A	ENID, OK	TO 10,000	SR TO 3 HR AFTER SS MON-FRI	NO A/G
A-562 B	ENID, OK	TO 10,000	SR-SS MON-FRI	NO A/G
A-683	McCONNELL AFB WICHITA, KS	TO 4500	0800-1900 MON THRU FRI	NO A/G

Fig. 4-4. *Another example of how the Special Use Airspace data is determined from the Sectional.*

which military activity can be conducted, the time(s) of use, and the controlling agency—in this case, ZKC, or the Kansas City ARTCC.

A question: You're flying VFR at 7500 feet and would like to cross through R-3601B going west to east (disregard the existence of the adjacent MOA for the moment). Can you do it without permission or clearance? Yes. The Area's altitude of use is from the surface to and including 6500 feet MSL. Above that altitude, R-3601B doesn't exist, thus no approval to transit the airspace is required and there is no threat from ground or airborne military activities.

Transiting R-3601A is a different story, however. The altitude here goes from the ground up to FL180, and during the hours of use, ZKC (Kansas City Center) would route even IFR aircraft around or above the area. Obviously, VFR flight should not even be contemplated.

During the published hours of use, the using agency is responsible for controlling all military activity within the R-Area and determining that its perimeters are not violated. When scheduled to be inactive, the using agency releases the airspace back to the controlling agency (Center), and, in effect, the airspace is no longer restricted.

By the same token, it's entirely possible that no activity will be scheduled during some of the published hours of use. In those instances, the using agency again releases the space to the controlling agency for nonmilitary operations in that period of inactivity.

From a VFR point of view, then, the pilot's responsibility is rather apparent:

- When plotting a VFR flight and the route crosses a Restricted Area, determine from a *current* Sectional the altitudes of activity and the days/hours of use. If the flight would penetrate the area when it is active, there's only one admonition: Stay out! An active R-Area is a land for no man who shouldn't be there. Furthermore, if you should wander into such an area intentionally or carelessly, anticipate a chat with the FAA and a resulting violation filed against you.

- If the flight is planned during a period when the area is published as inactive, don't plod ahead in blind confidence. Note the likely statement "O/T by NOTAM"—meaning possible use at times other than stated. When this occurs, the using agency notifies the controlling ARTCC (24 hours in advance, in the cases of R-3601A and B). Center then advises all Flight Service Stations within 100 miles of the area, and the FSS(s) issues a Notice to Airmen (NOTAM) reflecting the nonpublished activation of the area. So, even though you're planning to head out on a Sunday morning or any other time when an R-Area is apparently not in use, don't do so until you have contacted the appropriate FSS. Then specifically ask if there is a NOTAM indicating that the R-Area will be active at the time you will pass through it. If there is such a NOTAM, you again have only one choice: Reroute and stay out! An R-Area is not to be fooled with.

- Even though a chart may indicate that a military-related R-Area is effective, say, 8:00 AM until noon, Monday through Friday, it doesn't mean that the R-Area is always *active* during that period. If the military is not using the airspace and has released it to the controlling agency, you can get permission from the controlling agency (usually Center) to pass through the R-Area. All it takes is a telephone or radio call, and it can save you time and money. Be sure you call within two hours of your estimated transit through the Area, to make sure that the military does not intend to reactivate it on short notice.

Military Operations Areas (MOAs)

Military Operations Areas pose the largest potential obstacle to direct VFR flight between two points because of their relative size and number. Not always, of course, but frequently enough to cause diversions or detours when an MOA is active.

What is an MOA? Well, it's the vertical and horizontal chunk of airspace established to segregate certain military flight training exercises, such as combat maneuvers, acrobatics, and air intercept training, from nonparticipating IFR traffic. While activity in a Restricted Area is described as potentially "hazardous" to nonparticipating aircraft, the same adjective is not employed in describing an MOA. Perhaps that's a matter of semantics, however. An F-16 barreling straight up or straight down could be considered somewhat hazardous to an aircraft that had penetrated an active MOA.

To draw a clearer distinction between a Restricted Area and an MOA: Restricted Areas are established primarily for artillery, missiles, lasers, ground-to-ground and air-to-air gunnery, bombing practice, and similar training/RDT&E exercises. Because of the nature of the activities, the ground and airspace above a Restricted Area are, in effect, "deeded" to the military by the government and made a matter of record in the Federal Register.

An MOA, on the other hand, is designed for the flight training exercises cited above. Furthermore, the airspace may be requested by the military (Air Force, Navy, or Air National Guard), but it is the FAA in the final analysis that agrees to establish an MOA. In other words, one might say that an MOA comes into being only at the pleasure of the FAA.

Identifying MOAs. Undoubtedly familiar to every pilot are the diagonally striped magenta bands on the Sectional that block off those large chunks of terrain and the airspace above them. Designed as they are with consideration for both military and nonmilitary operations, the length and width of an active MOA could add miles and certainly minutes to a VFR flight. (As an aside, "hot" is the usual pilot jargon when referring to an active MOA or Restricted Area.)

As just one example of size, take the Ada East and West MOAs in central Kansas (FIG. 4-5). Combined, they're not unusually large, but they do stretch 70nm east/west and 18 to 41nm north/south. That could be a fair piece of geography to circumnavigate if the MOAs were hot.

Should you or should you not avoid an MOA? First, check the Sectional table (FIG. 4-6). Printed in magenta is the MOA name, altitudes of use, time(s) of use, and the controlling agency. Note particularly the Ada altitudes of use—7000 feet. This means that the MOA can be active from 7000 to flight level 180 (approximately 18,000 feet), as per the asterisked footnote, and the time of use is from sunrise (SR) to sunset (SS) Monday through Friday, and Saturday and Sunday by NOTAM. As a matter of general information, MOAs may extend vertically above FL180 through the designation of the airspace as an "ATC Assigned Airspace" (ATCAA).

The "Time of Use" raises a point. These are the *published* periods during which the MOA is most likely, but not necessarily, active. Said another way, these are the times that the using agency has identified as the *probable* periods of activity based on operations schedules, availability of aircraft, pilots, and similar considerations. The Area's using agency, let's say an Air Force unit, has, in each case, a scheduling office that is responsible for establishing a real-time activity schedule for the MOA and forwarding it, as well as any subsequent changes, to the controlling ARTCC. That office is also responsible for developing procedures with other Air Force user units to ensure that those units notify the

Fig. 4-5. *This excerpt from the Wichita Sectional indicates the expanse of the Ada MOAs.*

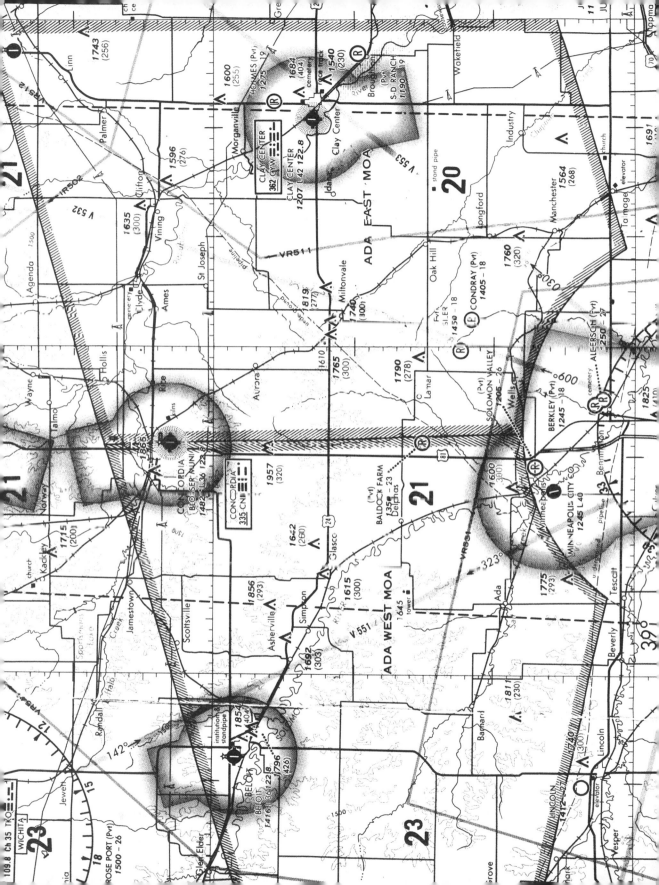

MOA NAME	ALTITUDE OF USE*	TIME OF USE†	CONTROLLING AGENCY
ADA EAST	7,000	SR-SS MON-FRI SAT-SUN BY NOTAM	ZKC CNTR
ADA WEST	7,000	SR-SS MON-FRI SAT-SUN BY NOTAM	ZKC CNTR
BISON	1,000 AGL	0830-1130 & 1330-1600 MON-FRI & ONE WEEKEND PER MONTH	ZKC CNTR
KIT CARSON A	100 AGL TO 9,000	INTERMITTENT BY NOTAM	ZDV CNTR
KIT CARSON B	9,000	INTERMITTENT BY NOTAM	ZDV CNTR
LINCOLN	8,000	NORMALLY 0900-1600 TUE-SUN BY NOTAM	ZMP CNTR
PINON CANYON	100 AGL TO 10,000	INTERMITTENT BY NOTAM	ZDV CNTR
SMOKY	500 AGL TO 5,000	0900-2200 TUE-SAT	ZKC CNTR
TRACY 1	10,000 TO 17,000	0800-1700 MON-FRI	ZKC CNTR
TRACY 2	5,000 TO 17,000	0800-1700 MON-FRI	ZKC CNTR
VANCE 1A	10,000	1 HR BEFORE SR- 1 HR AFTER SS MON-FRI	ZKC CNTR
VANCE 1B	7,000	1 HR BEFORE SR- 1 HR AFTER SS MON-FRI	ZKC CNTR

*Altitudes indicates floor of MOA. All MOA's extend to but do not include FL 180 unless otherwise indicated in tabulation or on chart.

Fig. 4-6. *The MOA data on the Sectional details the altitudes, time(s) of use, and the controlling agency (in this case, ZKC, meaning the Kansas City Center).*

scheduler as soon as possible of any periods (one hour or longer) of MOA nonuse after the initial schedule has been established. The purpose, of course, is to permit the scheduling office to return complete control of the airspace to Center for nonmilitary use. As with Restricted Areas, however, "O/T By NOTAM" also applies to the MOAs.

Consequently, keep in mind that the "Time of Use" only establishes the hours during which the using agency is free to schedule activity. It must, however, through its scheduling office, advise the ARTCC on a daily basis of the planned schedule, as well as changes in that schedule that might occur. Otherwise, the MOA cannot be used for its designated purposes.

MOAs and the VFR Pilot. Can you, as a VFR pilot, enter an MOA at any time, whether it is active or not? Yes. It is not a Prohibited or Restricted Area. Should you? If the Area is hot at your intended altitude, the answer is No! It's like cloud-busting—you're playing Russian roulette.

For one thing, an active MOA may be full of fighters zipping around you at near-Mach 1 speeds. Also, military training involves acrobatics and abrupt maneuvers. To permit such training, participating aircraft in an MOA are exempt from FAR 91.71 which states:

> No person may operate an aircraft in acrobatic flight . . . within a
> control zone or a Federal airway . . . [or] below an altitude of 1500
> feet above the surface . . .

Freed of these regulations, you could have aircraft going straight up, straight down, inverted in flight, or whatever, while you're plodding along in their training airspace. To compound the risk, despite the fact that military pilots are probably far better trained in the see-and-avoid concept than the typical civilian, they are often very busy while maneuvering in an MOA and can't devote sufficient time or attention to clearing nonparticipating aircraft.

A point of clarification: Participating aircraft are exempt from FAR 91.71 only when they are operating *between* the published MOA floor and ceiling. In the Ada example, from 7000 feet MSL to FL180, the FAR doesn't apply. Below 7000 feet, however, participating aircraft must abide by all FARs. The rules for them are the same as for any pilot—VFR, IFR, airline, or general aviation.

So, once again, how do you know whether you should or shouldn't penetrate an MOA? Let's go back to the Ada East and West example. If you planned a daylight trip during the week and wanted to cruise at any altitude above 7000 feet MSL through the area, you'd be wise to forget it. Either figure a lower altitude or detour the whole MOA. Not that you are *prohibited* from cruising at 7500 or 8500 feet, but you're likely to encounter activity anywhere between 7000 and 18,000 feet. Unless, within a few hours of your departure, you can determine from Flight Service that no operations have been scheduled, despite the published time of use, it's just not worth the risk.

On the other hand, suppose you want to venture forth on a weekend. Presumably the MOA will be quiet, per the Sectional, and a flight through it at any altitude would pose no problem. But don't be too sure. A call to your Flight Service Station is in order. During the briefing, if the information is not volunteered, specifically ask if any NOTAMs have been issued about activity in the Ada MOAs.

Assuming there are none, it appears that you might be in good shape. But let's say that your last phone call to the FSS was four or five hours ago. Now you're airborne, and what was fact then may not be fact now. The using agency could have scheduled an activity in the interim. If so, you ought to know about it. So what do you do? As you're flying along and approaching the MOA, get on the radio and call the controlling Air Route Traffic Control Center—in the Ada case, Kansas City Center. If you have not been in contact with Center for traffic advisories up to now, the call is simple:

You: Kansas City Center, Cherokee Eight Five One Five November.

Ctr: *Cherokee Eight Five One Five November, Kansas City Center, go ahead.*

You: Center, Cherokee Eight Five One Five November is about twenty miles north of Ada East, level at seven thousand five hundred. Can you advise if the Area is hot?

Ctr: *Cherokee One Five November, negative. There is no reported activity at this time and no NOTAMs issued.*

You: Roger, Center. Thank you. Cherokee One Five November.

If the area is hot, Center will confirm that fact and probably advise of the type of activity that is going on.

Instead of contacting Center, why not call the nearest FSS? The reason: Although both Center and the FSS will have the same schedule of activity, only Center has the most accurate reading of what participating aircraft are actually in the Area and where they are. It is thus the best source for determining the current, real-time MOA activity.

Let's say the MOA is hot. Who provides any control of the participating aircraft? An ATC facility, such as Center, may assume the responsibility when requested by the military. Otherwise, when certain conditions are met and a letter of agreement exists, control of an MOA, or any other ATC assigned airspace (ATCAA), can be transferred to a Military Radar Unit (MRU). It is now the MRU's responsibility to keep its aircraft within the altitudes and boundaries of the airspace, to provide traffic advisories to participating aircraft, to separate participating aircraft, and to advise Center immediately when participating aircraft cannot remain within the allocated airspace. So, in this case, there is control, but it is of the military, by the military.

Suppose, going VFR, you have been warned that an MOA is hot, but you choose to enter it anyway. What can you expect from Center?

First, Center *may* advise the military radar facility that you have penetrated the MOA, and Center *might* give you advisories of potential conflicting military traffic. Then again, it might not. One common concern of controllers about committing to giving advisories is the possibility of not being able to maintain continuous radar contact with the military aircraft during their maneuvers and altitude changes, and yet potentially being held accountable if a midair incident occurred. It's a logical concern. Traffic advisories are meaningful only when the traffic can be seen on the radar scope and its altitude confirmed.

So don't rely totally on help from Center in an active MOA. Center will provide separation between nonparticipating IFR aircraft cleared into an MOA or ATCAA, but it's a different matter when VFR aircraft are involved. You've been warned that the MOA is hot. You're within your rights to enter the area, but you have to assume the risk and the responsibility to "see and avoid." Is the risk really worth the miles and minutes you're saving? You be the judge.

MARSA

Here's an acronym—MARSA—with which many pilots may not be familiar. It stands for "Military Assumes Responsibility for Separation of Aircraft." This means that when an agreement between the military and the FAA controlling agency has been reached (via letter or otherwise), the military using agency has the right to invoke MARSA. Depending on the conditions or purposes for doing so, separation and control of participating aircraft become the responsibility of the Military Radar Units, Airborne Radar Units (ARUs), or it may be nothing more than visual separation and the pilots' responsibility to see, avoid, and stay within the confines of the assigned airspace.

One example cited by Lt. Col. John Williams, Air Force Representative to the FAA's Central Region, was the Williams MOA, just east of Phoenix, Arizona. Designed for extensive pilot training, the MOA was divided into several horizontal and vertical internal segments, with one aircraft assigned to a specific segment. Albuquerque Center, through radar coverage, was responsible for keeping each aircraft within its assigned segment, thus ensuring proper separation. The problem was that the Center controllers, trying to do their jobs, were on the air so much with the participating aircraft that the flight instructors found it difficult to communicate with their students. Consequently, an agreement was engineered with Center that MARSA would automatically be in effect during student training exercises.

Another example is aerial refueling operations. MARSA begins when a tanker and receiver are in the Air Refueling Airspace and the tanker advises ATC that it is accepting MARSA. From then on, until MARSA is terminated, the tanker/receiver are responsible for their own separation.

The FAA's *Special Military Operations* handbook, Paragraph 1-33, states that "The application of MARSA is a military service prerogative and will not be invoked indiscriminately by individual units or pilots . . . ATC facilities do not invoke or deny MARSA. Their sole responsibility concerning the use of MARSA is to provide separation between military aircraft engaged in MARSA operations *and other nonparticipating IFR aircraft.*" (Italics ours.)

This is perhaps a matter of little concern to the VFR pilot, but if you should be considering entering an MOA or flying along a Military Training Route (we'll discuss those in a moment), recognize that MARSA may have been invoked, and that the military is assuming responsibility for the separation of *its* aircraft and its aircraft alone. ATC is now out of the picture entirely, other than separating its nonparticipating IFR aircraft from those of the military.

That's pretty much the MOA story. Of all Special Use Airspace, MOAs typically offer the largest obstacle to a direct flight between two points. The VFR pilot, however, can penetrate them safely if:

- he flies above or below the altitudes of scheduled activity, *or*

- he determines from the FSS the extent of activity, if any, within the assigned altitudes by asking for MOA NOTAMs, and then establishes contact with the controlling Center for current activity updates.

Otherwise, be wise. Stay out of MOAs if you don't know what's going on within those magenta boundaries.

Alert Areas

Now we come to a slightly different breed of SUA, for the reason that, except for Prohibited Areas and Air Defense Identification Zones, Alert Areas are the only type of Special Use Airspace that exist for other than just military operations. Alert Areas may contain a high volume of pilot training or unusual types of aerial activity, neither of which is classified as hazardous to aircraft. While most do indicate areas of military pilot training, those near Miami, Wichita, and along the Texas and Louisana gulf coast, for example, denote heavy civilian flying activity. In essence, they exist to "alert" pilots to areas of high-density air traffic.

As with the other Areas discussed, the Alerts are depicted on the Sectional by the familiar blue bands that define the perimeters (FIG. 4-7), and are further detailed on the Sectional table (FIG. 4-8), outlining location, altitudes of use, and time(s) of use. Note, however, under "Controlling Agency," the "No A/G" (no air/ground communications). This means that there is no controlling agency dedicated specifically to the Alert Area and no special frequency assigned for operations within the Area.

That might require a little more explanation. Take the case of the Alert Area A-683 at Wichita (FIG. 4-9). If you are coming from the east and want to land at Wichita's Mid-Continent Airport, you'll be going right through A-683. Since FIG. 4-8 says "No A/G" for this Area, does this mean that there will be a complete communications void while you are in the Area? No. You're approaching Wichita's ARSA (Airport Radar Service Area), and you must establish "two-way radio communications" with Wichita Approach Control before entering the ARSA's outer circle. So even though you'll still be in the Alert Area for awhile, once you enter the ARSA you will receive vectors and/or advisories from Approach. So there will be radio communications, but they will relate to operations within the ARSA prior to landing, and not to traffic conditions in the Alert Area.

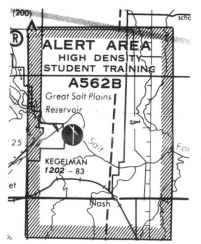

Fig. 4-7. *Alert Area A-562B northwest of Enid, Oklahoma, is the "little sister" of A-562A at Vance Air Force Base (not shown).*

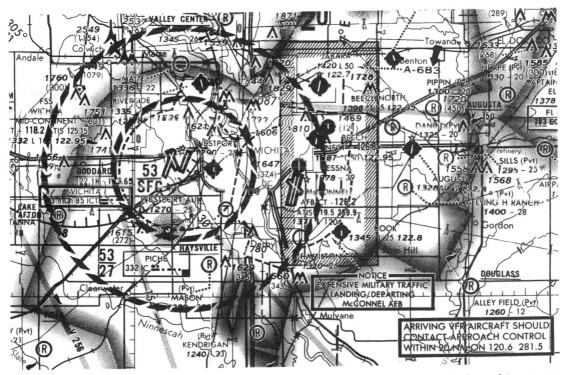

SPECIAL USE AIRSPACE ON WICHITA SECTIONAL CHART

Unless otherwise noted altitudes are
MSL and in feet; time is local.
Contact nearest FSS for information.
†Other time by NOTAM contact FSS

The word "TO" an altitude means "To and
including."
FL – Flight Level
NO A/G – No air to ground communications

U.S. P-PROHIBITED, R-RESTRICTED, A-ALERT, W-WARNING, MOA-MILITARY OPERATIONS AREA

NUMBER	LOCATION	ALTITUDE	TIME OF USE	CONTROLLING AGENCY
R-3601 A	BROOKVILLE, KS	TO FL 180	0830 TO 1630 CST MON, TUES, WED, FRI, SAT, 0830 TO 2100 CST THURS, O/T BY NOTAM 24 HRS IN ADV.	ZKC CNTR
R-3601 B	BROOKVILLE, KS	TO 6500	0830 TO 1630 CST MON, TUES, WED, FRI, SAT, 0830 TO 2100 CST THURS, O/T BY NOTAM 24 HRS IN ADV.	ZKC CNTR
R-3602 A	MANHATTAN, KS	TO 29,000	CONTINUOUS	ZKC CNTR
R-3602 B	MANHATTAN, KS	TO 29,000	CONTINUOUS	ZKC CNTR
A-562 A	ENID, OK	TO 10,000	SR TO 3 HR AFTER SS MON-FRI	NO A/G
A-562 B	ENID, OK	TO 10,000	SR-SS MON-FRI	NO A/G
A-683	McCONNELL AFB WICHITA, KS	TO 4500	0800-1900 MON THRU FRI	NO A/G

Fig. 4-8. *How the Sectional denotes A-562B's altitudes and times of use.*

Fig. 4-9. *There are no A/G communications in the Wichita A-683 Alert Area, as indicated in* FIG. 4-8, *other than the normal contacts with Approach Control, so extreme caution is essential.*

Unlike the other military-use airspace, the type of activity in the Alert Area is stated on the Sectional, such as ''High Density Student Training'' in A-562B, or perhaps ''High Volume of Helicopter and Seaplane Traffic,'' or whatever the reason for existence of the Area might be.

Okay, but what's the difference between this and the other Areas we've been discussing? For one, participating aircraft in an Alert Area are governed by all FARs, including the ban on acrobatics in a Control Zone, a Federal Airway, and below 1500 feet AGL. Second, no permission is required to enter an Alert Area. And third, participating as well as nonparticipating aircraft are equally responsible for collision avoidance.

In reality, then, the only major differences between an Alert Area and other airspace is the high density of traffic in a relatively confined area—and the fact that there is no agency (other than routine FAA or military air traffic control) issuing traffic advisories, alerts, or providing any sort of separation between aircraft within the area, whether IFR or VFR. ''Alert'' is thus a good adjective to describe the Area.

Warning Areas (W)

Another of the chunks of Special Use Airspace is the Warning Area (FIGS. 4-10 and 4-11). These, however, should be of little concern to the typical VFR pilot because they are located offshore. Actually, there is almost no difference between Warning and Restricted Areas in terms of the types of activity and the hazards to nonparticipating aircraft.

Fig. 4-10. *Just one of the many Warning Areas off the Atlantic Coast, beginning only a few miles from Melbourne, Fla. Between 3 and 12 miles from the U.S. coast, aircraft still must obey the operating rules of FAR Part 91.*

W-158 D	MAYPORT, FL	1200 TO 12,000 AGL	CONTINUOUS	ZJX CNTR
W-158 E	MAYPORT, FL	TO 1200	0500-2300 MON-FRI	JAX TRACON
W-158 F	MAYPORT, FL	1200 TO 1700	0500-2300 MON-FRI	JAX TRACON
W-159 A	JACKSONVILLE, FL	UNLIMITED	INTERMITTENT	ZJX CNTR
W-159 B	JACKSONVILLE, FL	TO FL 240	INTERMITTENT	ZJX CNTR
W-470 A, B,C,D,E	PANAMA CITY, FL	UNLIMITED	INTERMITTENT	ZJX CNTR
W-497 A	PATRICK AFB, FL	UNLIMITED	BY NOTAM	ZMA CNTR
W-497 B	PATRICK AFB, FL	UNLIMITED	BY NOTAM	ZMA CNTR

Fig. 4-11. *Further Sectional identification of W-497B and the fact that the Area, when activated by NOTAM, has an unlimited ceiling.*

Nowadays, there are two types of Warning Areas.

Nonregulatory Warning Areas. These Areas are designated over international waters in international airspace beyond 12 nautical miles from the U.S. coast, and thus cannot legally be regulated by the FAA. For any nonparticipating pilot, however, the admonitions about penetrating a Restricted Area apply equally when a Warning Area is active. Simply put, stay out!

Regulatory Warning Areas. These areas extend from 3 to 12 nautical miles from the U.S. coast (over areas now considered U.S. territorial waters) and contain the same kinds of hazardous activity as nonregulatory Warning Areas, and Restricted Areas. They serve to warn nonparticipating pilots of the potential dangers. Within regulatory Warning Areas, pilots must abide by the operating rules of FAR Part 91.

Air Defense Identification Zones (ADIZs)

Finally, we have those offshore areas called "Air Defense Identification Zones", or "ADIZs." Unlike the airspace reserved for training, research, development, testing, and evaluation, these fit more under the national security category. Specifically, FAR 99.3(a) offers this definition:

> The Air Defense Identification Zone (ADIZ) is an area of airspace over land or water in which the ready identification, location, and control of civil aircraft is required in the interest of national security.

Amendments to FAR Part 99 that became effective in 1988 focused on certain ADIZ realignments as well as nomenclature changes. The amendments, originally initiated by the Joint Chiefs of Staff back in 1986 and followed by subsequent requests to the FAA, included:

- Realigning the ADIZs abutting Mexico so that they do not infringe on Mexican airspace.

- Deleting ambiguous terms, such as "Coastal," "Gulf," "Pacific," and "Distant Early Warning Identification Zones (DEWIZs)" and adopting the common term of "Air Defense Identification Zone."

- Realigning the Alaskan ADIZ and simplifying flight plan and position reporting requirements of pilots operating in and out of the Aleutian Islands and who routinely must exit and reenter the ADIZ.

- Realigning the Guam ADIZ.

Flight Regulations. Considering the purpose of an ADIZ, specific regulations pertain to operations into and within one of these security areas. Some of the more pertinent are:

- As FAR 99.7 puts it, anyone operating in an ADIZ or Defense Area must comply with Part 99 and the special security instructions issued by the FAA Administrator in the interest of national security.

- Aircraft must have a functioning two-way radio and, if equipped with a transponder, the transponder must be in the ON position (or ALT if Mode C equipped). The only exception to the radio requirement pertains to procedures for aircraft without two-way radios and operated on a DVFR (Defense VFR) flight plan. (At this writing, the FAA has proposed to make Mode C transponders mandatory for aircraft penetrating an ADIZ.)

- An IFR or DVFR flight plan must be filed.

- IFR and DVFR position reports are required.

- Flight plan deviations by IFR aircraft in uncontrolled airspace, and by DVFR aircraft, are prohibited unless the appropriate aeronautical facility has been notified prior to the deviation.

- Radio failures must be reported to the proper facility as soon as possible.

These are a few of the regulations which make it rather clear that unauthorized penetration of an ADIZ could be serious matter.

The whole ADIZ concept, however, shouldn't concern most of us. With only a few exceptions, the areas are well off the coasts, and, other than for those who have aircraft equipped for extensive overwater flight, the ADIZs would typically stretch the range of the average general aviation plane. Despite that, no discussion of the Special Use Airspace would be complete without at least a brief mention of ADIZs and some of the rules pertaining to them.

Controlled Firing Areas

This is one we haven't mentioned for a couple of reasons. First, although the activities within the area could be hazardous, those activities are suspended immediately when radar, spotter aircraft, or ground lookout positions detect an approaching aircraft. Secondly, because of this feature, and the fact that they do not cause nonparticipating aircraft to alter their flight route, the Areas are not identified on any aeronautical chart. They pose no problem to either VFR or IFR flight, but just be aware that such things exist.

If some of what I've said about the SUA is a little confusing, perhaps FIG. 4-12, will provide a more succinct summary.

MILITARY TRAINING ROUTES (MTRs)

No review of the airspace system would be complete without a brief discussion of those thin gray lines on the Sectional or the brown lines on the Enroute Low Altitude Charts that identify the Military Training Routes (MTRs) (FIG. 4-13). (They're shown in pink on VFR Wall Planning Charts.)

What They Are

Similar to Special Use Airspace, MTRs exist because of the recognized need for high-speed, low-altitude military pilot training in the interests of national security. A Department of Defense-FAA joint venture, MTRs come in two forms: IFR, charted as "IR", and VFR, charted as "VR."

How They Are Identified

All routes flown exclusively below 1500 feet AGL are assigned a four-digit number, as "IR-1221" or "VR-1756." Routes with one or more segments flown above 1500 feet have three numbers, e.g., "IR 804." Thus a route with, say, three segments below 1500 feet and only one above, has a three-digit identification.

As FIG. 4-14 indicates, the numbers are allocated in blocks and identify the FAA region in which the route's entry point is located. Note that three-digit numbers are not used in the Southern region.

Route Structures

One other aspect of the structure: Note the small arrow adjacent to the route number in FIG. 4-13. Although probably obvious, the arrow indicates the direction of flight along the route. In other words, a given numbered route is always one-way. But there may be traffic in the opposite direction along the same route line on the Sectional but with a different MTR number. An example is illustrated in FIG. 4-15, taken from the Wichita Sectional, where aircraft on VR1174 go east,

Fig. 4-12. *A summary of the types, purposes, and general characteristics of Special Use Airspace.*

SPECIAL USE AIRSPACE MATRIX

Type of Airspace	Purpose/Activity	Dimensions	Designated Hours of Operation	Nonparticipating Aircraft Permitted During Designated Hours?	Chart/ Publication
PROHIBITED AREA	to prohibit flight over a surface area in the interests of national security or national welfare.	VERT: Min. Required FLOOR: Surface HORZ: As Required	Continuous	No	Sectional/WAC ELAC IFR Planning *Federal Reg.*
RESTRICTED AREA	To confine or segregate activities considered hazardous to nonparticipating aircraft. Guns and Bombs	VERT: As Required FLOOR: As charted HORZ: As Required	Charted times	No[1]	Sectional/WAC ELAC IFR Planning *Federal Reg.*
WARNING AREA (Non regulatory)	To contain activity that may be hazardous to nonparticipating aircraft. Guns and Bombs	Defined dimensions over international water outside 12-nautical mile limit	Charted times	Yes[2]	Sectional/WAC ELAS IFR Planning *Federal Reg.*
WARNING AREA (Regulatory)	To contain activity that may be hazardous to nonparticipating aircraft. Guns and Bombs	Defined dimensions between 3 and 12 nautical miles offshore	Charted times	Yes[2]	

MILITARY OPERATIONS AREA	To contain, nonhazardous training activity in airspace as free as possible of nonparticipating aircraft. Acrobatics, maneuvers	VERT: As Required to FL180 FLOOR: Normally 1200' HORZ: As Required	Charted times	Yes[2]	Sectional/WAC ELAC IFR Planning
ALERT AREA	To alert nonparticipating pilots of high volume nonhazardous activity. Fixed-wing, oil rigs helicopter training, etc.	VERT: To FL180 FLOOR: Surface HORZ: Avoid airways airports	Charted times	Yes[3]	Sectional/WAC ELAC
CONTROLLED FIRING AREA	Hazardous to nonparticipating aircraft. Rockets, blasting, field artillery	VERT: 1000' above highest altitude activity FLOOR: Surface HORZ: 5 statute miles visibility - 360	By NOTAM	Yes	Not charted

1 unless airspace has been released to ATC and pilot obtains ATC permission

2 but not recommended when active

3 use caution

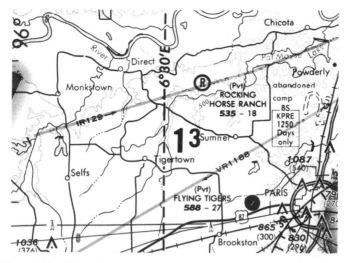

Fig. 4-13. *IR and VR Military Training Routes, as shown on a Sectional. Note the small arrows indicating the direction of the military traffic.*

and those on VR1574 fly the reciprocal route westbound. The one constant is that if there is a reciprocal route, it is always given a different MTR number. This is unlike the Victor airways, where the airway number is the same regardless of the direction in which it is flown.

When an MTR is indeed one-way throughout, it does have a couple of advantages for the nonparticipating pilot: If you're crossing or paralleling the

	ROUTE NUMBERS	
FAA REGION	**One Or More Segments Above 1500 Feet**	**All Segment At Or Below 1500 Feet**
Southern	1 thru 99*	1001 thru 1099
Southwest	100 thru 199	1100 thru 1199
Western-Pacific	200 thru 200	1200 thru 1299
	980 thru 999	1980 thru 1999
Northwest Mountain	300 thru 499	1300 thru 1499
Central	500 thru 599	1500 thru 1599
Great Lakes	600 thru 699	1600 thru 1699
Eastern	700 thru 799	1700 thru 1799
New England	800 thru 899	1800 thru 1899
Alaska	900 thru 979	1900 thru 1979
*Leading zeros are dropped		

Fig. 4-14. *The numbering system for Military Training Routes.*

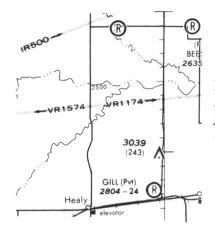

Fig. 4-15. *An illustration of how an MTR is numbered when traffic flows in both directions along the route.*

route, you at least know the flow of the military traffic and in which direction to keep your eyes peeled. Also, in planning a cross-country, should your route coincide with a one-way MTR, you'd be wise to plot your course well to the right or left of the MTR centerline, especially if you're travelling in the same direction as the potential traffic. A jet coming up behind you at 250+ knots might find you a little hard to spot if you're in its direct line of flight—and, unless you've got a rearview mirror and a swivel neck, you'd probably never see him at all. Which is just another reason for getting a thorough FSS briefing and maintaining contact with the ARTCC for enroute traffic advisories. Those are the folks who can help keep you out of trouble.

Whether IR or VR, the routes below 1500 feet are structured to skirt uncontrolled but charted airports by at least 3 nautical miles or 1500 feet altitude. Similarly, the routes are designed to avoid populated areas and controlled airport areas, and to cause as little disturbance as possible to people and property on the ground.

Although the Sectional and the ELAC depict an MTR with a thin colored line, let not the thinness deceive you. The actual width of an MTR can be considerably greater than the charts would intimate. If there is any standard at all, it is probably 5/5 (meaning 5 miles either side of the centerline).

Don't take that as a rule, however. The variations are considerable. For example, IR-514, originating at Lincoln, Nebraska, varies from 4/4 to 16/25; IR-608, Pensacola, Florida, is 10/10 throughout; VR-1128, Tinker Air Force Base, Oklahoma, is 2/2; while VR-1180, Cannon Air Force Base, New Mexico, fluctuates from 5/5 to 7.5/7.5; and so on.

The point for the nonmilitary VFR pilot is that just because you are a little to the right or left of an MTR centerline doesn't mean the potential for conflict no longer exists. Those B-52s, or what-have-you, could be anywhere within the route's established limits. Once again, vigilance is the key.

Military Pilot Rules on an MTR

Whether VFR or IFR, the military pilot is responsible for remaining within the confines of the published MTR width and altitude. Speedwise, flights are to be conducted at the minimum speed compatible with the mission requirements. However, while on the MTR and if below 10,000 feet MSL, military aircraft are not bound by FAR 91.70, which limits aircraft speed to 250 knots indicated (288 mph) below that altitude. When exiting or before entering an MTR, that FAR does apply, unless the aircraft manual recommends a higher speed for safe maneuverability.

Weatherwise, VFR operations on a VR route are conducted only when conditions are *above* standard VFR minimums (1000 and 3). More specifically, flight visibility must be 5 miles or better, and flights are not conducted when the ceiling is less than 3000 feet AGL.

If operating IFR, on an IR route, will the military pilot get the standard services and aircraft separation from ATC? Perhaps, but mission requirements, the altitudes flown, or the inability of Center's radar to pick up the target could make those services impossible. In such cases, through a letter of agreement between the scheduling unit and the appropriate ATC facility, the route or routes may be designated for MARSA. Then, the military assumes sole responsibility for separation of its aircraft.

Route Scheduling

Each MTR has a designated military unit responsible for scheduling all military flights intending to use that route. When it is practical to do so, the scheduling unit, each day and prior to 2400 hours, confirms with the appropriate FSS (called the "tie-in" FSS), the next day's planned route utilization. When that much advance notice is not possible, and barring any other agreement, the scheduling must be accomplished and communicated to the FSS at least two hours before use.

The schedule confirmed with the tie-in FSS is the hourly schedule for each IR and VR route, and includes the route number, aircraft type, the number of aircraft on the mission, the proposed times when the aircraft will enter and exit the MTR, and the altitude(s) to be flown. If a given route is closed or a scheduled aircraft cancels out, the scheduling unit is required to relay any changes to the tie-in FSS as soon as possible.

With this information on hand, the Flight Service Station tonight would be able to give you a reasonably accurate briefing on tomorrow's activity. Changes can occur, however, so the closer the briefing to your actual departure time, the more accurate the MTR's status will be.

MTRs and the VFR Pilot

A few precautions will minimize the risks MTRs present to the VFR pilot:

- In planning a cross-country trip, note what MTRs will cross or parallel your route of flight.

- When you call the Flight Service Station for a briefing, specifically ask for the scheduled military activity at the approximate time you would be on or crossing an MTR.

- Get an updated activity report from the nearest FSS when within 100 miles of the MTR.

- Establish and maintain contact in flight with the appropriate Air Route Traffic Control Center for routine traffic advisories as well as the actual, real-time military activity on the MTRs in your line of flight.

- Keep your transponder on. (If you have one, that's an FAA requirement anyway.) Many military aircraft have airborne radar and could spot you as a target and take evasive action before an emergency arose.

- Stay above 1500 feet AGL. That sounds like an obvious admonition, but do remember that there could be a fair volume of high-speed, low-level operations anywhere from 100 feet on up.

- Finally, keep your head out of the cockpit and your eyes open. Military aircraft aren't easy to see. They've been camouflaged to blend in with the sky or the terrain.

In Summary

MTRs are rarely discussed or considered as potential hazards to the VFR pilot—but they can be. And what perhaps adds to the potential is their apparent innocence. Unlike the distinct definition of an MOA or a Restricted Area, there are just those gray lines on the Sectional—nothing to cause us to sit up and take notice. But take notice we should. That empty sky out there could soon be darkened by a stream of B-52s or some other sample of airborne military machinery. As the *Airman's Information Manual* puts it:

> Nonparticipating aircraft are not prohibited from flying within an MTR; however, extreme vigilance should be exercised when conducting flight through or near these routes. Pilots should contact FSSs within 100nm of a particular MTR to obtain current information or route usage in their vicinity. Information (available) includes times of scheduled activity, altitudes in use on each route segment, and actual route width.

Route width varies for each MTR and can extend several miles on either side of the charted MTR centerline . . . When requesting MTR information, pilots should give the FSS their position, route of flight, and destination in order to reduce frequency congestion and permit the FSS specialist to identify the MTR routes which could be a factor.

The paragraph seems to sum up MTRs.

CONCLUSION

Discussions with many pilots, experienced as well as student, tend to point to two principal areas in which initial and refresher training are deficient: radio communications and Special Use Airspace. The obvious intent of this chapter was to fill in some of the possible gaps in your knowledge of the latter.

SUAs do consume a fair amount of airspace, but it is airspace set aside with the mutual consent of several agencies of the government—and for the best possible purpose: our national defense and security. That purpose can be achieved, however, only through the training, research, development, testing, and evaluation of our defense resources—both human and material. The MOAs, Restricted Areas, and so on, may, indeed, present barriers to direct-line flight or require altitude deviations, and we might complain silently or loudly about those infringements on our freedom, but they are small prices to pay for the reasons this airspace exists.

5

The Transponder

A S WE MOVE INTO DISCUSSIONS OF TERMINAL CONTROL AREAS (TCAs), AIRPORT Radar Traffic Areas (ARSAs), and the like, the role of the transponder becomes critical. Without it, or without an understanding of its use and the terminology associated with it, operating in many types of controlled airspace will be next to impossible. Accordingly, we'll first outline the radar beacon system, then the transponder and what it does, followed by a few comments about the coming of Mode S and, finally, transponder terminology.

To avoid confusion, it's important to note that the system and the radarscope images discussed here pertain only to terminal approach control facilities. This is called an Automated Radar Terminal System (ARTS) and is a different system than that used in the en route centers. ARTS II and ARTS III identify advanced models of the basic system.

THE AIR TRAFFIC CONTROL
RADAR BEACON SYSTEM (ATCRBS)

ATCRBS permits more positive control of airborne traffic and consists of two basic sky-scanning features. The first is called *primary* radar, the other, *secondary* radar. Primary radar sweeps its area of coverage and transmits back to the radarscope images of obstacles it encounters, such as buildings, radio towers, mountains, heavy precipitation, or aircraft. The size of the return depends on the reflective surface encountered by the radar sweep. A small fabric-covered aircraft would produce an almost negligible reflection on the radarscope compared to that of an all-metal Boeing 747. Whatever its construction, an aircraft appears on the controller's scope as merely a small blip, showing the aircraft's range (distance) and direction (azimuth) from the radar site. These limited returns produce a very imprecise means of identification, other than to indicate to the controller that there's an airplane out there on a certain bearing from, and so many miles from, the radar site. With such scant data, a controller would be hard-pressed to track, control, separate, or identify traffic in the aircraft's vicinity with any degree of accuracy.

To overcome those limitations, a secondary system exists which incorporates a ground-based transmitter/receiver, called an *interrogator*, along with an operating aircraft transponder. The two radar systems—primary and secondary—then function in unison and constitute the Air Traffic Control Radar Beacon System.

What happens is that, as the two systems make their 360-degree sweep, the secondary beacon antenna transmits a signal that "interrogates" each transponder-equipped aircraft (or *target*, in controller parlance), and "asks" the transponder to "reply." As the transponder does, the synchronized primary and secondary signals produce a distinctly shaped image on the radarscope. The image, however, only indicates that the transponder is on and, unless the pilot has been otherwise directed, it has been set to the standard VFR transmitting code of 1-2-0-0. As the terminology goes, it is "squawking one two zero zero," or "squawking twelve hundred," or "squawking VFR."

But this, too, is limited data, particularly in a heavy-traffic area. For more specific identification, each transponder has a small button which, when the pilot activates it, more definitively identifies his particular aircraft. Thus, when a controller tells you to "Ident" and you push the IDENT button, the radarscope image changes again, permitting the controller to positively identify your aircraft among all of the targets on his screen.

Very superficially, that's the basic principle of the radar beacon system. The transponder, however, is the airborne unit that maximizes the system's value in the traffic control process.

TRANSPONDER "MODES" AND FEATURES

Undoubtedly, most general aviation pilots have at least a speaking acquaintance with this piece of equipment installed in the instrument panel. That acquaintanceship is particularly likely if they have been flying in or around any type of high-density terminal airspace. For others, not entirely conversant with the transponder or the regulations pertaining to its use, a few words may be in order.

Transponder Modes

Transponders are usually referred to in terms of types or *modes*, of which seven are either in use or available.

Modes 1 and 2:	Assigned to the military
Mode 3/A:	Used by both military and civilian aircraft
Mode B:	Reserved for use in foreign countries
Mode C:	Mode 3/A transponder equipped with altitude-reporting capabilities
Mode D:	Not presently in use
Mode S:	A new Mode that will come into more common use later in the 1990s

For those of us in general aviation, only Modes 3/A and C are of current interest.

The Features

Mode 3/A is the standard transponder which does a reliable job of establishing radarscope identification of a given aircraft. The one pictured in FIG. 5-1 happens to be a Narco AT-50A, but all makes are basically the same.

The unit is activated by the switch at the extreme left of the set. The switch positions, as the picture shows, range from OFF to SBY (standby), ON, or NORMAL on some sets), ALT (altitude), and TST (test).

Once the engine is started, the switch should be turned to SBY. This allows the set to warm up, which normally takes two to three minutes. Meanwhile, it is not transmitting any signal. At the same time, check to be sure that the transponder has been set to 1200, unless ATC has given you a different code. When cleared for takeoff, or during the takeoff run, turn the switch to ON, if you don't have altitude-reporting capabilites (Mode C). The set is now in the Mode 3/A posture, and after you're airborne, this symbol would appear on the radarscope (FIG. 5-2).

The symbol, however, will reflect only your relative geographical position in the airspace and the fact that you're transmitting the 1200 code.

Fig. 5-1. *This is a typical Mode 3/A transponder that also has altitude-reporting capabilities, making it a Mode C.*

If the set has altitude-reporting capabilities (Mode C), the switch should be turned to ALT. Then, this symbol will appear on the controller's scope, once the aircraft is airborne:

—045

Now the controller can determine your azimuth, range, and current altitude, in this case, 4500 feet.

A firm FAA ruling: The transponder *must* be in the ON position, or in the ALT position if it has altitude-reporting capabilities. And it must be left on from takeoff until landing, unless a controller instructs otherwise.

Moving to the right of the switch positions in FIG. 5-1, the next prominent features are the 1-2-0-0 numbers. Directly below each number is a knob or dial. These change the numbers to whatever code ATC requests. The 1200 code is the standard VFR code and, under normal operating conditions, should never be changed unless ATC so advises. A change is likely to be requested, however, if you are in a controlled area, such as a TCA, an ARSA, or, in most cases, when you're receiving enroute traffic advisories from an Air Route Traffic Control Center on a cross-country excursion. In any of these situations, you may still be flying VFR, but ATC will assign you a specific, or *discrete*, code so that your aircraft can be identified from all others in the airspace. That discrete code will be yours alone as long as you are in that ATC facility's airspace and being controlled or given advisories.

Relative to the codes, reference is often made to a "4096 transponder." What this means is that each of the four knobs can dial in eight digits, from 0 to 7. Combined, the four knobs thus produce a total of 4096 different codes: $8 \times 8 \times 8 \times 8$. Anticipating what discrete code ATC might assign you is impossible. With only a few exceptions, which we'll review in a moment, the code is selected by a computer according to the National Beacon Allocation Plan. It thus could be anything within the block of codes assigned to a given facility.

If ATC asks you to *squawk* (meaning to dial in) a certain code, first, write down the numbers so you won't forget them (it's easy to confuse "0465" with "0456" or any other potential combination). Next, repeat the code back to the controller to confirm that you have copied it correctly. Then immediately enter the code in the transponder. When you do, an image similar to this will appear on the radarscope:

The diagonal line is called the *leader line*; 045 is the altitude—4500 feet (assuming Mode C capability); 13 represents the aircraft's ground speed—130 knots; and W indicates that the west sector controller is handling the aircraft.

Further to the right, on the transponder, is that small semi-transparent button I mentioned earlier. The button serves two purposes:

- Every time the transponder is interrogated by the radar beacon, a light within the button blinks momentarily. The blinking indicates that the set is working and transmitting a signal, representing your aircraft, back to the radarscope. In effect, it is "replying" to the interrogator.

- When a controller asks you to "Ident", he's telling you to push the button once—and only once. As you do, the image on the scope "blossoms", further identifying your aircraft among others in the area:

It's important, however, to activate the Ident feature only when instructed to do so. Don't touch the button unless you hear something like: "Cherokee Eight Five One Five November, ident." Then push the button once.

TRANSPONDER CODES

As I've said, 1200 is the standard VFR code and should always be entered in the transponder during normal flight operations, unless ATC directs otherwise. There are some other codes, however, with which every pilot should be familiar.

For instance, if you have a bona fide emergency—a fire, engine failure, loss of control, whatever—and if time permits, immediately enter the code 7700. When you do, as the controllers describe it, "Lights light up and bells ring." All radarscopes within range will signal an emergency, and controllers at a nearby radar-equipped tower, Center, or Approach Control will be trying to contact you by radio. That won't do much good if you're not on (or monitoring) one of their frequencies or the 121.5 emergency frequency, but at least ATC will be able to follow the track of your aircraft and be in a better position to spot your approximate geographical position, should you go down. That 7700 code, however, is strictly an *emergency* code, and, except for what we say next, should never be entered, even momentarily.

The "next" is the 7700/7600 combination code for radio failure. As soon as it becomes apparent that your radios are dead or dying, dial in 7700 for 1 minute and then 7600 for 15 minutes. Then, if you're still airborne, keep repeating

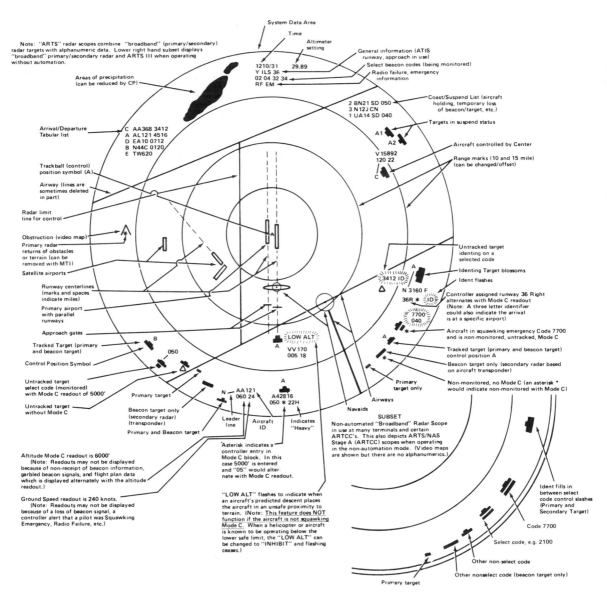

Note: "ARTS" radar scopes combine "broadband" (primary/secondary) radar targets with alphanumeric data. Lower right hand subset displays "broadband" primary/secondary radar and ARTS III when operating without automation.

System Data Area

Time

Altimeter setting

General information (ATIS runway, approach in use)

Select beacon codes (being monitored)

Radio failure, emergency information

1210/31   29.89
Y ILS 36
02 04 32 34
RF EM

Areas of precipitation (can be reduced by CP)

2 BN21 SD 050
3 N12J CN
1 UA14 SD 040

Coast/Suspend List (aircraft holding, temporary loss of beacon/target, etc.)

Targets in suspend status

A1
A2

Arrival/Departure Tabular list

C AA368 3412
A AL121 4516
D EA10 0712
B N44C 0120
E TW620

V 15892
120 22
C

Aircraft controlled by Center

Range marks (10 and 15 mile) (can be changed/offset)

Trackball (control) position symbol (A)

Airway (lines are sometimes deleted in part)

Radar limit line for control

Obstruction (video map)

Primary radar returns of obstacles or terrain (can be removed with MTI)

Satellite airports

Untracked target identing on a selected code

A
3412 ID

N 3160 F
36R * ID

Identing Target blossoms

Ident flashes

Controller assigned runway 36 Right alternates with Mode C readout (Note: A three letter identifier could also indicate the arrival is at a specific airport)

Runway centerlines (marks and spaces indicate miles)

Primary airport with parallel runways

7700
040

Aircraft in squawking emergency Code 7700 and is non-monitored, untracked, Mode C

Approach gates

LOW ALT

A
VV 170
005 18

A
*

Tracked target (primary and beacon target) control position A

Beacon target only (secondary radar based on aircraft transponder)

Tracked Target (primary and beacon target)

Control Position Symbol

B

050

Primary target only

Non-monitored, no Mode C (an asterisk * would indicate non-monitored with Mode C)

Untracked target select code (monitored) with Mode C readout of 5000'

Primary target

Untracked target without Mode C

N — AA 121
060 24

A42816
050 * 22H

A

Airways

Navaids

Beacon target only (secondary radar) (transponder)

Primary and Beacon target

Leader line

Aircraft ID

Indicates "Heavy"

SUBSET
Non-automated "Broadband" Radar Scope in use at many terminals and certain ARTCC's. This also depicts ARTS/NAS Stage A (ARTCC) scopes when operating in the non-automation mode. (Video maps are shown but there are no alphanumerics.)

Altitude Mode C readout is 6000'
(Note: Readouts may not be displayed because of non-receipt of beacon information, garbled beacon signals, and flight plan data which is displayed alternately with the altitude readout.)

Ground Speed readout is 240 knots.
(Note: Readouts may not be displayed because of a loss of beacon signal, a controller alert that a pilot was Squawking Emergency, Radio Failure, etc.)

Asterisk indicates a controller entry in Mode C block. In this case 5000' is entered and "05" would alternate with Mode C readout.

"LOW ALT" flashes to indicate when an aircraft's predicted descent places the aircraft in an unsafe proximity to terrain. (Note: This feature does NOT function if the aircraft is not squawking Mode C. When a helicopter or aircraft is known to be operating below the lower safe limit, the "LOW ALT" can be changed to "INHIBIT" and flashing ceases.)

Ident fills in between select code control slashes (Primary and Secondary Target)

Code 7700

Select code, e.g. 2100

Other non-select code

Other nonselect code (beacon target only)

Primary target

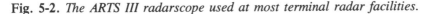

ARTS III Radar Scope with Alphanumeric Data. Note: A number of radar terminals do not have ARTS equipment. Those facilities and certain ARTCC's outside the contiguous US would have radar displays similar to the lower right hand subset. ARTS facilities and NAS Stage A ARTCC's, when operating in the non-automation mode would also have similar displays and certain services based on automation may not be available.

Fig. 5-2. *The ARTS III radarscope used at most terminal radar facilities.*

the 1-minute/15-minute cycle. As with the 7700 code, the combination alerts ATC that you've got a problem but that it's a radio-related problem and not of a serious emergency nature.

Figure 5-3 recaps these and other standard codes. The starred ∗ codes should never be used by civilian pilots.

A FEW WORDS ABOUT MODE C

Some additional comments about Mode C are essential, especially in light of the FAA regulations effective in 1989 and 1990. Until recently, Mode C for strictly VFR operations was more of a voluntary addition to the Mode 3/A transponder than a necessity. True, it was mandatory for flight above 12,500 feet MSL and in the TCAs, but otherwise it was not a requirement. Times have changed, however.

TRANSPONDER CODE	TYPE OF FLIGHT	WHEN USED
0000*	Military	North American Air Defense
1200	VFR	All altitudes, unless instructed otherwise by ATC
4000*	Military VFR/IFR	In Warning and Restricted areas
7500	VFR/IFR	Hijacking
7700	VFR/IFR	In an emergency--"Mayday"
7700 (1 min.) 7600 (15 min.)	VFR/IFR VFR/IFR	Loss of radio communications
7777*	Military	Intercept operations
Any code	VFR/IFR	When using center or Approach Control and ATC assigns a specific, or "Discrete" code

Note: The starred (*) codes are for military operations only, and are never to be used by civilian pilots.

Fig. 5-3. *These are the standard military and civilian transponder codes, of which 1200 is the most commonly used in general aviation VFR operations.*

The rash of midair collisions in high-density traffic areas during the latter part of the 1980s triggered that change. Coupled with more and more reported near-misses, the public, the media, and Congressional pressure forced the FAA to take prompt action. The FAA responded by tightening pilot and equipment requirements in controlled airspace—particularly terminal areas. Mostly, but not exclusively, the tightening related to the transponder and its ability to report aircraft altitudes in those terminal areas. Enter, then, Mode C.

What Makes a Transponder "Mode C"?

A regular Mode 3/A transponder becomes Mode C by one of two adaptations.

The first is to remove the present altimeter and replace it with an *encoding* altimeter. Externally, this looks just like any ordinary altimeter. Internally, however, there are some modifications. Electronically connected to the transponder, the altimeter aneroid bellows expand and contract with altitude changes, and the changes are converted to coded responses by the transponder. When interrogated by the sweeping radar beacon, the transponder replies by transmitting those responses, which are then decoded on the ground. The process concludes when the target's altitude appears on the radarscope, as illustrated earlier.

The second conversion option is to leave the old altimeter right where it is and install a *blind encoder*. This unit does just what the altimeter does, differing only in that it is a small black box, usually physically mounted on the firewall or elsewhere under the instrument panel and out of the pilot's sight.

Which is preferable? Operationally, both are equally effective. The blind encoder, however, has one advantage: If it malfunctions, it can be removed for repairs and the airplane is still flyable—except, of course, where Mode C is required.

On the other hand, if the encoding altimeter goes on the fritz, it has to be removed, you'll have no altimeter, and the aircraft is grounded pending repairs. Plus, you've probably removed a perfectly good altimeter. If you're lucky, you might be able to sell it; otherwise, you're stuck with a reliable but useless instrument.

From a cost point of view, assuming the aircraft already has a transponder, adding Mode C is a relatively inexpensive proposition. Prices vary, of course, as do installation charges, but here are a couple of examples (1988 prices). A Transcal blind encoder costs about $500, with installation in the $175 range. A Narco AR-850 is around $325, and a similar installation charge. Following the blind encoder route, then, would set the purchaser back $500 to $700, depending on type and local labor charges. By comparison, a new encoding altimeter goes for about $900, plus $175 installation.

Starting with a new transponder adds a few more bucks. A King KT-76, for example, lists for $1175—which is reasonably representative of the models on the market. According to one avionics vendor, however, that price is usually discounted by about 30 percent. If that's so, the cost would drop to the $825 vicinity. Add installation, and you're in the $1000 area. Ballparking the maximum total, figure a $1500 bill for a new transponder plus blind encoder. Even if you go the whole route, that's still not a very costly investment.

THE COMING OF MODE S

Nothing seems to remain constant in the world of flight, electronics, and avionics—nor should it. The National Airspace System Plan (NASP), that I'll summarize later has 92 separate projects designed to move aviation into the next century. Just one of those projects is the *MODE S transponder*, the "S" standing for *selective address*.

For all intents and purposes, this transponder closely resembles a Mode C. The main difference lies internally, wherein the aircraft type and N-number are permanently programmed on a microchip. When interrogated, Mode S automatically transmits that data, which then appears on the controller's scope, along with the aircraft's altitude and ground speed. This feature eliminates the need for the controller to enter the aircraft type and N-number manually in the computer, and, for the pilot, the dial-twisting required to squawk different ATC-requested codes. That's about all the basic Mode S will do.

If you need greater sophistication, you can add an onboard computer, printer, and screen. As an example, you want to get your IFR flight clearance. By punching the right buttons on your keyboard, the clearance will automatically be addressed to your aircraft and appear on your screen. If you want a hard copy, punching another combination of buttons will produce the copy on your printer.

The same procedure applies for weather data, emergency routings, Special Use Airspace information, or conflict warnings via the Traffic Alert and Collision Avoidance System (TCAS) that Mode S permits. Whether requested by the pilot or initiated by ATC, the information can be selectively addressed to just that one aircraft without a single radio transmission—which, obviously, will reduce clutter over the air. It's all done through data links between ground and air and the Advanced Automation System (AAS) that will prevail in the next decade.

Those benefits, however, come not from the Mode S equipment itself, but from the selective addressing that Mode S makes possible. Without the rather expensive add-ons, the advantages of this new transponder to the average lightplane pilot are relatively limited. I doubt that there will be many Cessnas or Cherokees flying around with computers and printers dressing up their cockpits.

All transponders manufactured after January 1, 1990, and installed after January 1, 1992, must have Mode S capabilities. That doesn't mean, though, that Mode S is mandatory after 1992. The FAA has stated that as long as your Mode C is working or can be repaired, it doesn't have to be tossed out. Only when it finally dies must it be replaced with a Mode S.

There's more to the Mode S story than this brief overview. It is, however, an important element in the FAA's NAS plan to increase safety, provide better collision avoidance capabilities, reduce radarscope clutter, simplify the pilot's radio communication and dial-twisting requirements, and permit the selective addressing of computerized data directly to the printer/screen of the concerned aircraft. Mode S, along with the automated ground equipment, makes possible these forward leaps.

TRANSPONDER TERMINOLOGY

To round out the transponder picture, the terminology associated with transponder use comes into play. The most common terms or expressions (some of which I've already touched on), whether the equipment is Mode 3/A or C, are these:

Squawk: Back in the World War II days, the Allies had a radar beacon system known as IFF (Identification Friend or Foe). Our aircraft were equipped with transmitters which, when queried by the radar sweeps, sent back a sound similar to that of a parrot's squawk, identifying themselves as friends. That "squawk" has carried over and is used by controllers and pilots alike to mean that the transponder has been turned on and that a certain code has been, or should be, dialed in. When a controller tells you to "squawk four three two one", he's telling you to enter those digits in the unit. In essence, all "squawk" means is "transmit." The two words could be used interchangeably, but "squawk" has hung on, reminiscent of those days 50 years ago.

Ident: When you hear "Cherokee One Five November, ident," the controller wants you to push the ident button one time so that he can more positively identify your aircraft on his radarscope. At this point, it's appropriate, but not required, to acknowledge his call with a simple "Roger." Say no more. Just push the button. Saying "Roger, Cherokee One Five November identing," is unnecessary. As the "ID" on his scope blossoms, the controller will know that you followed his instruction.

Squawk (number) and Ident: This instruction means to enter a certain four-digit code in the transponder and then ident. For example, "Cherokee Eight Five One Five November, squawk one two zero zero and ident." If you've already got that standard VFR code in the unit, nothing more needs to be done than the act of identing. If you've been given a different code, say, 4321, then it's proper to read back the code to be sure you understood it. "Roger, Four Three Two One." Now enter it and ident—if the controller told you to. If you don't hear "Ident", don't touch the button.

Stop Squawk: This is an instruction to turn the transponder off entirely.

Squawk Standby: For whatever reason, the controller says this if he wants you to stop transmitting any signal but not turn the set off. So, merely switch from ON or ALT to the SBY position. You won't be transmitting, but the set will still be warm for immediate future use.

Stop Altitude Squawk: If you hear this, turn the switch to the ON (or in some sets, NORMAL) position—not to OFF. ATC wants you to continue transmitting your position on Mode 3/A, but not your Mode C altitude.

Recycle or *Reset:* Occasionally, a squawk will transmit a questionable signal or one that is the same code given to another aircraft. Also, one of the code numbers may not quite slot into place. Whatever the case, ATC is asking you to reset the four digits so that you are transmitting the assigned code.

Squawk Mayday: If you've reported an emergency of some sort, the controller, with whom you've been in contact, may tell you to "squawk Mayday," meaning that you are to dial in the 7700 emergency code. ("Mayday" comes from the French *M'aidez*, pronounced "mayday," meaning "Help me.")

CONCLUSION

More and more aircraft will have to have Mode C transponders to operate in any environment other than uncontrolled airports, away from terminal areas, and below 10,000 feet MSL. The specific requirements that come into effect in 1989 and 1990, will be covered in Chapter 6.

Requirements aside, transponders are one more piece of equipment that enhance safety in the air. Without them, ATC would be hard-pressed to direct and separate terminal or enroute traffic with any degree of accuracy.

Despite the furor raised by many general aviation interests over the FAA's recent Mode C rulings, the cost to equip an aircraft with that altitude-reporting capability is minor when the increased safety factor is considered. It's also a minor price to pay for the privilege of entering and operating in the most strictly controlled airspace—near the busy air carrier airports of some 150 major U.S. cities. Those cities and their terminal airspace, along with the associated transponder requirements are the subjects of the next chapter.

6

Terminal ATC

IN EARLIER CHAPTERS, I TALKED A LITTLE ABOUT SOME OF THE ASPECTS OF THE terminal environment, including Airport Traffic Areas (ATAs), Control Zones (CZs), and made references to Airport Radar Service Areas (ARSAs) and Terminal Control Areas (TCAs). It's time now to be more specific about those airspace "structures" and the FAA facilities—the tower and Approach/Departure Control—involved in the traffic controlling process.

BUT FIRST, A FEW STATISTICS AND COMMENTS

Statistics constantly change, but the latest available figures (May 1988) reveal that there are 16,582 airports in the U.S. Of that total, 10,807 are classified as "private use" and 5,775 as "public use." Among the public use, 416 have FAA-administered control towers, another 24 are joint military/public facilities, and 28 are operated by private contractors. (These 28 are identified on the Sectional by the notation "NFCT" (nonfederal control tower) adjacent to the tower frequency, FIG. 6-1.)

So, rounding off the figures, 5800 airports are for your use and mine, while approximately 500, or seven percent, are classified as "controlled." The remaining 93 percent are uncontrolled fields requiring only self-announce communications. That gives us a lot of room to roam about, unfettered by the rules, procedures, and requirements involved in operating in a controlled-airport environment.

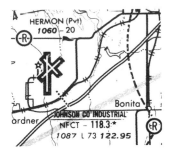

Fig. 6-1. *A nonfederal control tower (NFCT) is operated by a private contractor and staffed, usually, by former FAA and/or military controllers.*

The only problem—if there is a problem—is that these 500 or so aerodromes are located, for the most part, in the more populated areas. Consequently, access to them demands certain pilot qualifications as well as avionics. It further requires pilot knowledge of what these controlled areas are and how to operate within them.

Pilots with a knowledge deficiency will do one of two things: go miles out of the way to avoid an ARSA or a TCA, or—not knowing what they don't know— barge ignorantly into a controlled terminal area, potentially causing all sorts of havoc. The first alternative is needlessly costly in time and fuel; the second is both illegal and dangerous.

In interviews with many *air traffic control specialists* (a synonym for "controller"), one common plea to pilots emerged: Be prepared! Do some homework before sallying forth into a controlled environment. Know the procedures and requirements. Know how and when to use the radio. Know what to say and what you can expect to hear. If you don't understand an instruction, don't be afraid to ask the controller to "say again" or "speak more slowly." Don't just "Roger" an unclear instruction simply because you don't want to reveal your uncertainty to the listening audience.

And there are other elements in this matter of preparation, such as knowing the tower and ground frequencies of the airport you're entering. One controller cited this as a frequent example of unpreparedness—of which even air carrier pilots are occasionally guilty. As he said, "There are three people up there in the front end of a Boeing 727, making pretty good money, and they haven't even taken the time to look up the correct tower frequency."

In another case, a pilot called in for landing instructions and then asked the tower if the airport "was north or south of the river." The controller admitted the temptation to retort that the airport was north of the river, "where it had been for 50 years." He mastered the temptation, but I wonder how many times controllers have bitten their tongues when questions born of ignorance and inadequate preparation have filtered through their headsets. A mere glance at the Sectional before departing, or even enroute, would have told this pilot exactly where the airport was located.

Still another example: Many airports have navigation aids, such as VOR/DME or Non-Directional Beacons (NDBs), right on the field. Controllers say it is not unusual, however, for pilots to contact the tower and ask for vectors or headings to the airport. Of course, if the necessary avionics aren't on board or aren't working properly, the request can be justified. Otherwise, just dialing in the appropriate frequency and centering the needle would lead these pilots directly to their destination. But these same folks probably didn't take a few extra minutes to check the Sectional or the *Airport/Facility Directory* before venturing forth.

Preparation—or rather, the lack of it—arose many times in discussions with controllers, whether based in a tower, Approach Control, or Center, and with specialists at Flight Service Stations. Of course, pilots have to know what they're preparing for, so knowledge becomes the obvious cornerstone. Flying in or out of a controlled environment, requires no rare or elusive skill, but it does demand those two basics of knowledge and preparation.

In looking at the "areas" that surround controlled airports, I'll first briefly review the roles of the two controlling facilities—namely the Tower and Approach/Departure Control. Then I'll summarize the areas that comprise the terminal control environment, including how they're identified, their structure, the pilot and equipment requirements, and finally the operating regulations—particularly the VFR regulations—pertaining to each.

THE TWO TERMINAL CONTROLLING AGENCIES

Two facilities are responsible for the orderly terminal arrivals and departures of both IFR and VFR aircraft. One is the air traffic control tower (ATCT), and the other is Approach/Departure Control.

The tower exercises control *only* over traffic within the 5-mile radius of the Airport Traffic Area (ATA). Where it exists, Approach/Departure is responsible for separating aircraft—particularly IFR—in the area outward from the ATA to about a 35-mile radius around the primary airport. Additionally, Approach/Departure's airspace rises to the upward limits of its radar coverage, which may vary from approximately 10,000 feet to 15,000 feet AGL, depending on the terminal.

Three acronyms commonly identify the Approach/Departure facility. The first, and most common is *TRACON*—terminal radar control. The second is *TRACAB*—terminal radar control in the tower cab. The third is *RAPCON*—radar approach control. What's the difference? It is simply the physical location.

TRACON means that the actual facility, with its radar equipment, computers, phones, and personnel, is housed in the control tower structure but not in the glass-enclosed tower cab itself. All of the larger airports have TRACON because of the space needed for equipment and personnel.

TRACAB is found at a few towers with lower activity, but still requiring on-site radar Approach/Departure Control. In these instances, the equipment and personnel are located in the tower cab, and thus more or less in face-to-face contact with the ATA controllers—something not possible in a TRACON. TRACABs still exist at places like Sioux City, Iowa; Springfield, Missouri; Elmira, New York; and Reading, Pennsylvania.

RAPCON is the Air Force/FAA acronym for radar approach control, and, where it exists, is entirely removed from the tower structure. It interfaces with civilian towers in the traffic controlling process, but it can be at a military airport some miles away.

THE ATA AND CONTROL TOWER

A control tower has four primary responsibilities:

- To separate and sequence aircraft transiting the ATA or in the traffic pattern

- To expedite arrivals and departures

- To control ground movements of aircraft and motorized vehicles

- To provide clearances and local weather and airport information to pilots, the latter primarily, but not exclusively, via the tape-recorded ATIS messages.

The basics of operating within an ATA were covered in Chapter 3. Now for a few additional points:

- The tower has direct and sole control over *only* the traffic that is within the limits of the ATA.

- Outside the ATA, the tower controller *may* issue traffic advisories to other aircraft with which he has been in contact, if his workload permits. That service, however, is secondary to the controller's primary responsibility—namely, to keep track of the types and N-numbers of aircraft that have called in and visually scan the skies within the ATA, for the purpose of sequencing and/or separating landing, departing, and transiting traffic.

- With the above points in mind, the fact that you have established contact with the tower a few miles outside of the ATA should not lull you into a false sense of security. All that inbound radio call does is alert the tower controller to the fact that you are out there, intend to enter the ATA, and, with a transponder, helps to identify your particular aircraft. This information allows the tower controller to plan the flow and sequencing of traffic into the ATA and the traffic pattern. He or she is not staring at a radar screen (even if the tower is so equipped) to separate VFR traffic outside the ATA or to alert pilots to possible conflicts. Whether arriving or departing, it's not uncommon for pilots to be a little more relaxed when in the general area of a tower-controlled airport. Don't let complacency take over.

- We're going to get into this later, but towers at the larger terminals have a radar display of a 35-mile or so radius in the tower cab itself. It is not the clearest image, however, because it is a televised reproduction of the original image received in the TRACON (a room that is dimly lit to give the controllers the clearest possible radarscope picture). What is seen in the tower is thus a second-generation display that is being transmitted from its point of origin by a television microwave link (TML). If it's a satellite airport tower with a radar screen, it is receiving the same second-generation picture, also transmitted by a TML from the TRACON at the primary airport. This radar system is called *BRITE*, the acronym for "Bright Radar Indicator Tower Equipment"—a system described by the FAA itself as "not always reliable." The intent of BRITE, however, is to produce an image that can be easily seen in the bright environment of the tower cab (FIG. 6-2). TRACAB locations also use BRITE.

Coupled with whatever minor deficiencies BRITE might have is the fact that not all tower controllers are radar-qualified. This doesn't mean that they have had no training and are unable to interpret what they see on the scope; it just says that they have not gone through the extensive training as well as current Approach Control experience that is required to classify them as radar-certificated. Without that certification, the controller can *suggest* that a pilot take certain actions outside the ATA, if the radar image so indicates, but he cannot issue directives that would constitute an order or a command. Instead of saying, "Turn left to zero three zero heading", it would be, "Suggest you turn left to zero three zero heading."

Regardless of the existence of an ARSA or TCA, the tower is in complete command of traffic within the ATA. Even though the VFR pilot may still be in a controlled environment and subject to vectors or traffic advisories, he has the neverending responsibility to keep his eyes open and be his own best conflict resolver. That's true anywhere, but especially so near a tower-controlled airport where the volume of traffic is sufficient to warrant the very existence of that tower.

AIRPORT RADAR SERVICE AREAS (ARSAs)

ARSAs are the fastest growing addition to the controlled airspace system and are replacing the Terminal Radar Service Areas (TRSAs) throughout the country. The ARSA concept was developed to provide more positive control of aircraft in the terminal area than under the TRSA system. Pilot participation—meaning establishing two-way radio communication with Approach Control and

receiving traffic advisories—is optional in a TRSA, assuming the flight is VFR. In an ARSA, participation is mandatory.

Qualification Criteria

To qualify as an ARSA, the airport must have:

1) An operating control tower served by radar approach control; and

2) It must meet at least one of the following criteria:

  • 75,000 annual instrument operations at the primary airport; or

  • 100,000 annual instrument operations at the primary and secondary airports in the terminal hub area; or

  • 250,000 annual enplaned passengers at the primary airport.

As of the date of writing, 131 ARSAs have been established, with seven more proposed for activation. For those interested in the specific locations of ARSAs, we suggest that you check the current edition of the *Airman's Information Manual*.

Identifying an ARSA

ARSAs are easy to spot on the Sectional because of the slashed magenta circles surrounding the primary airport. If you glance at FIG. 6-3, you'll note the two concentric circles defining the Little Rock ARSA (actually, "Adam's Field"). The three "spokes" leading from the inner to the outer circle divide the outer circle of this particular ARSA into three sectors, each with a different altitude floor 1500, 1800, and 2100 feet MSL—but all with the common 4300-foot MSL ceiling. Inside the inner circle, the ARSA rises from the surface to that 4300-foot level.

Another ARSA-identifying source is the *Airport-Facility Directory (A/FD)*, FIG. 6-4. The fact that Little Rock has an ARSA is indicated by the "ARSA ctc APP/CON". The *A/FD* also tells you what Approach/Departure frequency to use, depending on where you are in relation to the airport. Clockwise, between 042° and 221°, it's 124.2; from 222° around to 041°, you'd call on 119.5. Using the Sectional, if you turn to the table on the reverse side of the Legend and refer to the "TCA, ARSA, TRSA, and Selected Radar Approach Control Frequencies" (FIG. 6-5), you'll find the same information right there.

Fig. 6-2. *A tower controller scans her BRITE radar screen.* (FAA)

Fig. 6-3. *The Little Rock ARSA, with its slashed magenta inner and outer circles.*

LITTLE ROCK

§   **ADAMS FLD**   (LIT)   2 E   UTC–6(–5DT)   34°43′48″N 92°13′59″W   **MEMPHIS**

     258   B   S4   **FUEL** 100LL, JET A   OX 1, 3   LRA   CFR Index C   **H-4F, L-14E**

     RWY 04-22: H7173X150 (ASPH-GRVD)   S-70, D-90, DT-140   HIRL   **IAP**

       RWY 04: SSALR. Thld dsplcd 303′. Railroad.   **RWY 22:** MALSR. VASI(V4L)—GA 3.0°TCH 52′. Building.

     RWY 18-36: H5124X150 (ASPH)   S-67, D-84, DT-135   MIRL

       RWY 18: VASI(V4L)—GA 4.0°TCH 62′. Thld dsplcd 90′. Road.   **RWY 36:** VASI(V4L)—GA 4.0°TCH 64′.

       Thld dsplcd 90′. Road.

     RWY 14-32: H4039X150 (ASPH)   S-8   MIRL

       RWY 14: Thld dsplcd 355′. Road/Trees.   **RWY 32:** VASI(V4L)—GA 3.0°TCH 53′. Trees.

     AIRPORT REMARKS: Attended continuously. Landing fee. Rwy 14-32 closed to air carriers. Transient acft parking at

       airline terminal ramp ctc arpt police at airline concourse for reentry to locked operations area. From Oct–Apr large

       concentrations of bird in vicinity of arpt most activity between SR–SS up to 1500′ MSL. Flight Notification Service

       (ADCUS) available.

     WEATHER DATA SOURCES: LLWAS.

     COMMUNICATIONS: ATIS 125.6 1200-0600Z‡   **UNICOM** 122.95

       LITTLE ROCK FSS (LIT) on arpt. 122.55 122.35 122.2 Toll free call, dial 1–800–WX–BRIEF, LC 376-0721. NOTAM

       FILE LIT.

     ⒭ **LITTLE ROCK APP/DEP CON** 124.2 (042°-221°) 119.5 (222°-041°)

       TOWER 118.7   **GND CON** 121.9   **CLNC DEL** 118.95   **PRE TAXI CLNC** 118.95

     ARSA ctc **APP/CON**

     RADIO AIDS TO NAVIGATION: NOTAM FILE LIT.

       LITTLE ROCK (H) VORTACW 113.9   LIT   Chan 86   34°40′39″N 92°10′49″W   316° 3.8 NM to fld. 240/05E

       LASKY NDB (H-SAB/LOM) 353   ▪ LI   34°40′08″N 92°18′19″W   042° 4.6 NM to fld.

       ILS 110.3 I-LIT Rwy 04 LOM LASKY NDB

       ILS 110.3 I-AAY Rwy 22

       ASR

Fig. 6-4. *The A/FD identifies the Little Rock (Adams Field) ARSA by the notation "ARSA ctc APP/CON".*

CONTROL TOWER FREQUENCIES ON MEMPHIS SECTIONAL CHART

Airports which have control towers are indicated on this chart by the letters CT followed by the primary VHF local control frequency. Selected transmitting frequencies for each control tower are tabulated in the adjoining spaces, the low or medium transmitting frequency is listed first followed by a VHF local control frequency, and the primary VHF and UHF military frequencies, when these frequencies are available. An asterisk (*) follows the part-time tower frequency remoted to the colocated full-time FSS for use as Airport Advisory Service (AAS) during hours tower is closed. Hours shown are local time. Radio call provided if different from tower name.

Automatic Terminal Information Service (ATIS) frequencies, shown on the face of the chart are normal arriving frequencies, all ATIS frequencies available are tabulated below.

ASR and/or PAR indicates Radar Instrument Approach available.

CONTROL TOWER	RADIO CALL	OPERATES	ATIS	FREQ	ASR/PAR
ADAMS		CONTINUOUS	125.6	118.7 257.8	ASR
BARKSDALE AFB		CONTINUOUS	375.8	126.2 295.7	ASR
BLYTHEVILLE AFB		CONTINUOUS		126.2 255.9	ASR
COLUMBUS AFB		0700-1800 MON-THU 0700-2000 FRI 0900-1600 SAT 1000-1600 SUN CLSD HOL & OT EXC EMERG	115.2 273.5	126.2 289.6	ASR

Fig. 6-5. *The reverse side of the Sectional legend is one more means of determining frequencies at Adams Field.*

The ARSA Structure

The Sectional outlines the circular plan view of the ARSA, but there's more to it than that. FIGURE 6-6, a cross section, illustrates the typical lateral and vertical structure. Surrounding the primary airport is the *inner circle*, rising from the surface to 4000 feet AGL. This may vary slightly, but it is the typical ARSA ceiling. Although not of major importance, note that the radius of the inner circle is 5 *nautical* miles, while the radius of the ATA is 5 statute miles.

Next comes the *outer circle*, with a 10 nautical-mile radius and a 1200-foot AGL floor. The floor, too, may vary slightly in altitude from ARSA to ARSA. The outer circle's ceiling is the same as for the inner circle.

Finally, we have what is called the *outer area*, which is not depicted on any aeronautical chart. Like the ATA, however, it's there nonetheless. The perimeter of this circular area is 20 nautical miles from the airport. The outer area extends from the lower limits of radar coverage upward to the airport's Approach Control vertical limits—approximately 10,000 feet AGL.

Pilot Qualifications and Aircraft Equipment

ARSAs have no minimum pilot requirements. From student on up, any pilot has access to the ARSA.

Equipment-wise, until December 30, 1990, only a two-way radio capable of communicating with the two controlling facilities—Approach and the tower—is required. No transponder, no navigation aids.

Things will change, however, effective December 30, 1990. As FIG. 6-7 illustrates, beginning then, all aircraft operating within an ARSA, and above the ARSA, up to and including 10,000 feet MSL, must be equipped with an operable Mode C transponder.

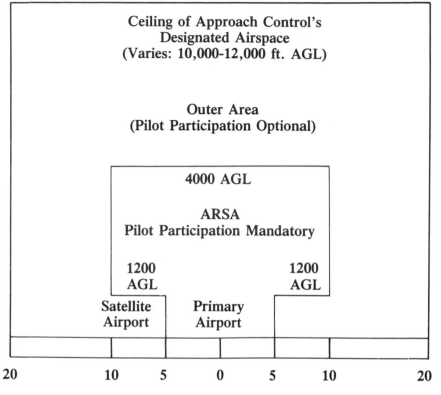

Fig. 6-6. *The structure and dimensions of a typical ARSA. The altitudes and shape may vary slightly from ARSA to ARSA.*

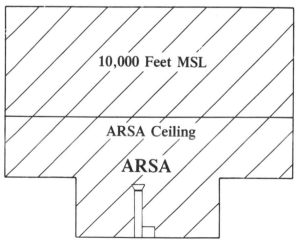

Fig. 6-7. *Effective December 30, 1990, Mode C will be required when operating in or above an ARSA (as indicated by the diagonal stripes).*

Operating Regulations

To approach or depart an ARSA, the following regulations apply.

- When approaching an ARSA with intentions to land at any airport within the inner circle or to transit the ARSA (below the 4000-foot ceiling), ''two-way radio communication'' with Approach Control must be established *before* entering the outer circle (that's the outer *circle*, not the outer *area*). In the outer area, the pilot has the option of establishing contact if he wants traffic advisories. It's up to him. If contact is made, however, Approach has no option. It must provide the advisory service, whatever its workload may be inside the ARSA itself.

- While ''clearance'' into an ARSA is not required, establishment of ''two-way radio communication'' is. To be more specific, if you call Approach and all you hear is ''Stand by,'' you have *not* established ''two-way radio communication'' (by FAA's definition) and may not enter the outer circle. (That ''Stand by'' might have been addressed to another aircraft, unbeknownst to you.) If, however, the controller responds, ''(Your aircraft call sign), stand by,'' you have met the requirement and may proceed into the ARSA. The mere fact that Approach specifically acknowledged *your* call sign is sufficient to allow you to enter the ARSA.

- Once in the ARSA, Approach will issue instructions, vectors, or altitude changes. These should be acknowledged and followed unless doing so would place you in jeopardy or cause you to violate a VFR regulation, such as entering a cloud bank. In such cases, you must advise the controller of the situation so that he can give you alternate instructions.

- Prior to entering the ATA, Approach will turn you over to the tower for final landing instructions and landing clearance.

- In departing the primary ARSA airport, and after monitoring the current ATIS, the first step is to call Clearance Delivery (CD), which is usually located in the tower, next to the Ground Control position. At airports without CD, contact Ground Control. In either case, state your intentions and record the instructions you are given. For example:

You: Memphis Clearance, Cherokee Eight Five One Five November is at Memphis Aero with Hotel. VFR to Birmingham via Victor One Five Niner, requesting five thousand five hundred.

CD: *Cherokee Eight Five One Five November, maintain three thousand. Expect five thousand five hundred ten minutes after departure. Departure frequency 124.15. Squawk zero two three six.*

You: Roger, three thousand, five thousand five hundred in ten, 124.15, zero two three six. Cherokee Eight Five One Five November.

CD: *Cherokee One Five November, readback correct.*

Next is the usual call to Ground Control and then the tower for takeoff clearance.

- If departing a satellite airport within the inner circle, contact with the tower is to be established as soon as possible after takeoff. Established traffic patterns must be obeyed.

- For departures, arrivals, or touch-and-gos at a satellite airport under the outer circle, if you plan to stay under the 1200-foot outer circle floor and will not be entering the ARSA at any time, contact with ATC is unnecessary and shouldn't be established at all.

Services in the ARSA

Once "two-way radio communication is established," Approach or Departure Control will give you vectors and approve altitude changes.

Within the 10-mile radius, Approach will:

- sequence all arriving traffic into the ARSA.

- maintain standard separation between IFR aircraft of 1000 feet vertically and 3 miles horizontally.

- separate IFR and known VFR aircraft through traffic advisories or a 500-foot vertical separation.

- issue advisories and, when necessary, safety alerts to VFR aircraft.

Relative to the last point, ATC does not separate VFR aircraft from other VFR aircraft in an ARSA. The responsibility to see-and-avoid still remains with the pilot. ATC will, however, give advisories to inform pilots of the bearing (usually by the "clock" position), the approximate distance, and the altitude of other traffic that might pose a potential conflict.

A *safety alert* is issued when conflict between two aircraft appears imminent. The pilot to whom the alert is directed would be wise to follow ATC's instructions *immediately*. No arguing, no questioning, no delaying (unless you are aware of a safer alternative). An emergency is in the offing.

Can ATC refuse a pilot entry into the ARSA? Theoretically, no. ATC "clearance" is not required. In reality, though, controllers have occasionally been forced to deny entrance because of traffic saturation within the ARSA and therefore have the prerogative of telling you, "Your aircraft call sign remain outside the

ARSA and Stand by.'' If you are told this, comply without argument. ATC is temporarily just too busy to accommodate any more activity.

Conclusion

ARSAs were designed to replace the TRSAs, in which pilot participation is strictly voluntary. The ARSA removes that option and thus increases the safety factor.

Has it met with popular acclaim? Not entirely. Pilots have been denied entry because of traffic saturation and ATC's resultant inability to sequence, separate, vector, and issue advisories. Early complaints are lessening, however, as both pilots and controllers are mastering the system and polishing local procedures. Perhaps it's not the ideal solution to traffic control in high-density areas, but the ARSA is certainly a better approach to safety than the looseness of the TRSA. In effect, the ARSA is a balanced medium between the TRSA and the stricter controls of the TCA.

TERMINAL CONTROL AREAS (TCAS)

Now we come to those chunks of airspace that were subjects of considerable controversy during the latter years of the '80s—the Terminal Control Areas. The source of controversy was not so much the existence of the TCAs but rather their design and the FAA pilot/equipment proposals in and around them. What with at least four midair collisions within or near a TCA and an increasing number of reported near-misses, the combined public and Congressional pressure on the FAA to take action was considerable.

In response, the FAA issued Notice of Proposed Rulemaking 88-2, which contained some 40 proposed airspace and rule changes. As hearings on 88-2 progressed, several of the changes were dropped and others modified as the result of strong general aviation objections. What has, and is emerging, is the product of give-and-take by the FAA and those representing general aviation interests, particularly the Aircraft Owners and Pilots Association (AOPA).

Why TCAs exist is best summed up by quoting FAA Handbook 7400.2, issued July 11, 1988:

> The TCA program was developed to reduce the midair collision potential in the congested airspace surrounding an airport with high density air traffic by providing an area in which all aircraft will be subject to certain operating rules and equipment regulations. The TCA operating rules afford a level of protection that is appropriate for the large number of aircraft and people served by this type of airport. The TCA equipment requirements provide the air traffic control system with an increased capability to provide aircraft separation service within the TCA. The criteria for considering a given terminal as a TCA

candidate are based on factors which include the number of aircraft and people using the airspace, the traffic density, and the type or nature of operations being conducted.

Prior to January 12, 1989, there were two classes, or *groups*, of TCAs: Group I designated the nine busiest terminal areas, and Group II, 14 others that met the minimum annual passenger enplanement and instrument operation criteria for TCA qualification. Effective January 12, 1989, the Group classifications were eliminated, so that now we have just "single-class" TCAs with no distinction that would intimate size, traffic volume, or passenger enplanements. To qualify for TCA consideration, the current minimum FAA criteria are:

- at least 650,000 passengers are enplaned annually; or

- the primary airport has at least 150,000 annual instrument operations.

The Current TCAs

Early in 1989, there were 23 TCAs. The nine largest (formerly classified as Group I) were located at the major high density airports:

Atlanta	Dallas	New York (LaGuardia, Kennedy, and Newark)
Boston	Los Angeles	San Francisco
Chicago	Miami	Washington, D.C. (National and Andrews AFB)

The other 14 (once designated as Group IIs) were:

Cleveland	Kansas City	Pittsburgh
Denver	Las Vegas	Seattle
Detroit	Minneapolis	St. Louis
Honolulu	New Orleans	San Diego
Houston	Philadelphia	

However, nine additional airports whose activity meets the minimum TCA criteria have been nominated:

Baltimore	Memphis	Salt Lake City
Charlotte	Orlando	Houston-Hobby
Tampa	Phoenix	Washington-Dulles

If all goes as planned, these TCAs will be activated sometime in 1990.

Identifying a TCA

If you refer to any Sectional that has a TCA, one of the first features that will catch your eye is a large blue-band rectangle surrounding the TCA. The square (FIG. 6-8) represents the geographical area depicted on another chart, called a *VFR Terminal Area Chart* (TAC). This chart provides an enlarged and more detailed depiction of the area outlined by the square. Anyone nearing or intending to enter a TCA should definitely have a current issue of the TAC on board.

On the Sectional, the TCA lies within the rectangle and is easily spotted by the concentric blue circles surrounding the primary airport(s). These may be perfect circles, but more likely than not, there will be some irregularities to accommodate traffic at other nearby airports and/or IFR operations at the primary field.

The Sectional has another identifying feature. Outside the big blue rectangle is a small rectangular box with the name of the TCA on the top line, plus recommendations that pilots use the VFR Terminal Area Chart for "greater detail and clarity of information." (See FIG. 6-9.) And there is the always-reliable *A/FD* as another source of data and reference.

So, identifying a TCA should be no problem. As with the ARSA, however, the Sectional plan view does not give a complete picture of the TCA structure.

The TCA Structure

The typical description of a TCA is that it resembles an upside-down wedding cake, with the core surrounding the primary airport from the surface to the TCA's ceiling. The various levels, layers, or shelves (they're all synonymous), then extend laterally from the core at 3 to 10 nautical mile increments (typically), with each layer having a prescribed altitude floor. All levels, however, rise to the same common ceiling in a particular TCA.

Figure 6-10 illustrates the basic structure. What this figure shows is that this TCA extends from the surface to 8000 feet (80/Surface) at the core. Moving out one level, the floor is 2000 feet MSL with the same 8000-foot MSL ceiling (80/20). Farther out, the TCA altitudes are from 3000 to 8000 feet (80/30), and so on. Thus when operating below any of the floors, you're out of the TCA and out of any positive control by ATC (unless, of course, you happen to be within a satellite airport's ATA or ARSA). It's another story, though, within the TCA itself. Here is where the rules and regulations enter the picture.

Pilot and Equipment Requirements

Pilot Requirements. To land or take off at the 12 primary airports within the 9 busiest (former Group I) TCAs, the pilot must have at least a private license.

Fig. 6-8. *The area within the wide (blue) border on a Sectional is covered in greater detail on a larger-scale VFR Terminal Area Chart.*

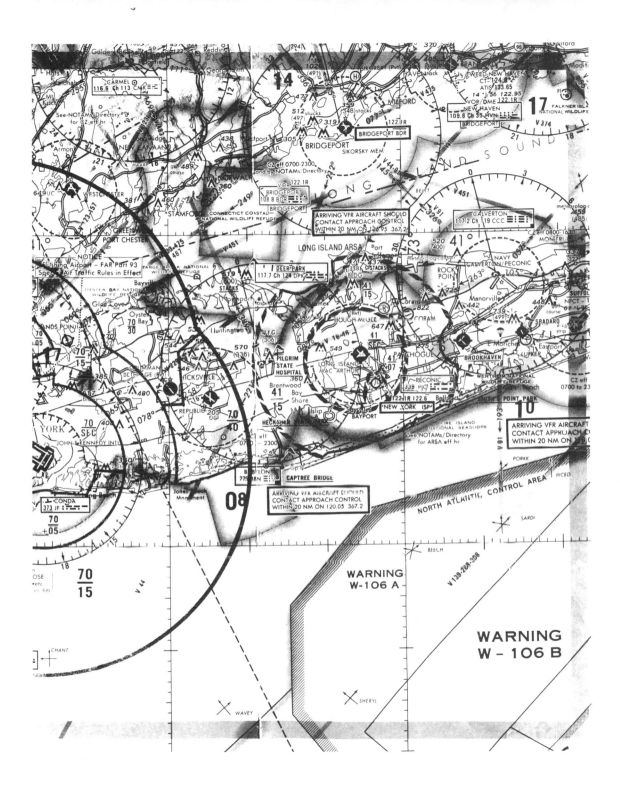

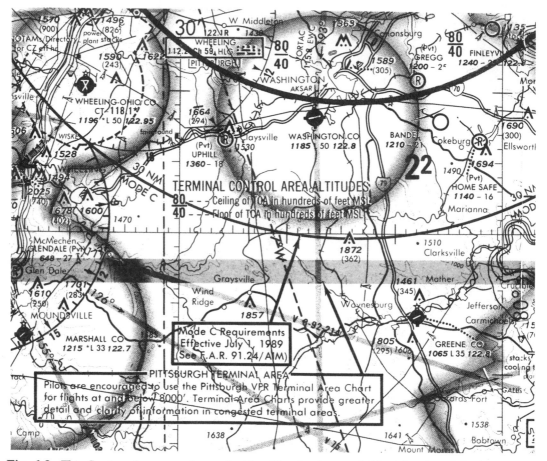

Fig. 6-9. *This Sectional excerpt shows the identification box and (blue) border of the Pittsburgh terminal area. The thin (blue) arc indicates the 30 nautical mile radius from Greater Pittsburgh International, within which Mode C transponders are required from the surface to 10,000 feet MSL, effective July 1, 1989.*

However, if a student has received ground and flight instruction for (and in) a TCA and has obtained the proper instructor logbook endorsement(s) within the preceding 90 days (see FAR 61.95), that student may:

- fly solo through that specific TCA, and

- take off and land solo at an airport within that TCA (if instruction took place at that specific airport), except at those 12 busiest airports that completely prohibit solo student operations.

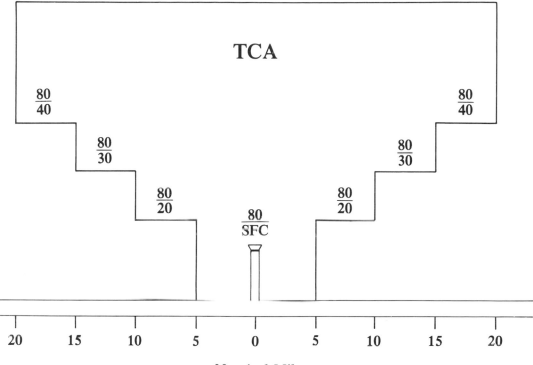

Nautical Miles

Fig. 6-10. *A typical TCA configuration. Dimensions vary from one TCA to another.*

Equipment Requirements. Unless otherwise authorized by ATC, the aircraft must be equipped with an operable VOR or TACAN (Tactical Air Navigation) receiver (except helicopters prior to July 1, 1989), an operable two-way radio capable of communicating with ATC on the terminal frequencies, and an operable transponder with altitude-reporting capabilities (Mode C or Mode S).

Effective July 1, 1989. all aircraft operating within 30 nautical miles of a TCA primary airport *must* have a Mode C transponder and it *must* be turned on, including the altitude-reporting function (FIGS. 6-9 and 6-11). It makes no difference whether you're going into the TCA or not. It's required even if you're shooting touch-and-gos at a grass strip 25 miles out from the TCA airport, well under any TCA floor.

Something else that FIG. 6-12 illustrates: Let's say the TCA ceiling is 8000 feet and you're crossing over the top at 9500 feet. Even though you're above—not in—the TCA, you are still required to have the transponder on and in the altitude-reporting mode. This requirement extends up to 10,000 feet MSL. (Above

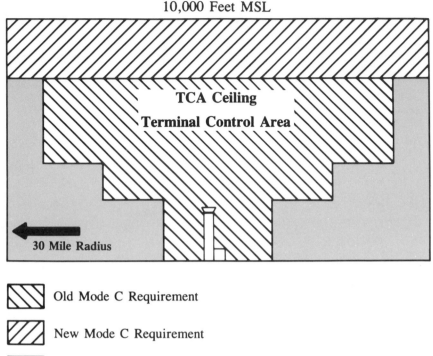

10,000 Feet MSL

TCA Ceiling

Terminal Control Area

30 Mile Radius

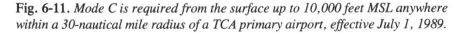

Old Mode C Requirement

New Mode C Requirement

Aircraft Without Electrical Systems
Ar Exceptions to the Requirement

Fig. 6-11. *Mode C is required from the surface up to 10,000 feet MSL anywhere within a 30-nautical mile radius of a TCA primary airport, effective July 1, 1989.*

that altitude Mode C is required everywhere, except at and above 2500 feet AGL in mountainous areas.)

Why the ruling? Because departing turbine aircraft can easily climb above the TCA ceiling while still within its lateral limits. So it's important for ATC, specifically Departure Control, to know what VFR traffic is up there and at what altitude. Only with that data will ATC be able to maintain the proper IFR/VFR aircraft separation.

Entering a TCA

If you want to land at a TCA primary airport or transit a portion of the TCA to save time and fuel, one basic rule applies: You *must* be specifically and verbally cleared into the TCA by Approach Control before entering the TCA at any level.

Approach controllers stress this point again and again. What frequently happens is that the pilot calls Approach well outside the TCA. Approach responds. The pilot gives his position and makes his intentions known. Approach tells the pilot to squawk a certain transponder code and then to ident. The pilot squawks and idents. Approach comes back with "Radar contact." Now the problem: The pilot interprets "Radar contact" as approval to enter the TCA. Here's where misunderstandings have arisen. The "Pilot/Controller Glossary" in the *Airman's Information Manual*, under the heading of *Radar Contact*, states:

> "2.   the term Radar Contact used to inform the controller that the aircraft is identified and approval is granted for the aircraft to enter the receiving controller's airspace."

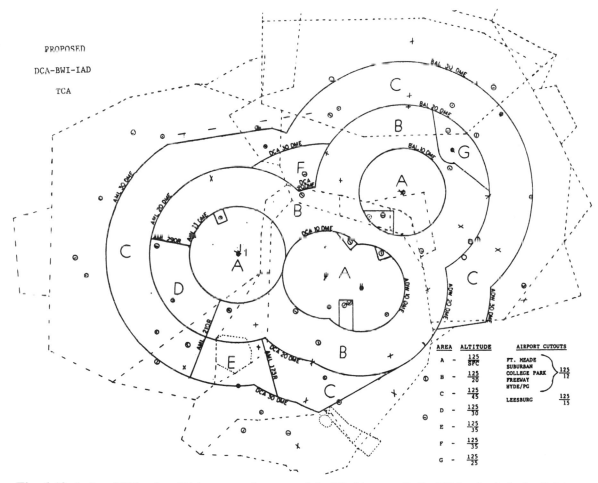

Fig. 6-12. *In late 1988, when FAA proposed to expand the Washington, D.C., TCA to include the Baltimore and Dulles airports, this was the preliminary design they came up with. Not exactly the epitome of simplification.*

What they're talking about is a controller-to-controller communication, not controller-to-pilot. Pilots reading this "definition" have undoubtedly interpreted it to mean that they have been cleared into the TCA as soon as a controller calls them and announces "Radar contact." Such is not the case. Until you distinctly hear, "Cleared to enter the TCA," "Cleared into the TCA," or "Cleared through the TCA" (plus what other instructions Approach may give you), you *must* remain outside that controlled airspace. Circle, slow down, practice some loops, do whatever you have to do. Just don't go where you haven't been invited. It's illegal and can result in your being fined, grounded, and cited for the violation. The offense will be on your record—for your insurance carrier to see!

But forget the punishment for the moment. Whether intentional or inadvertent, violating the TCA is just plain dangerous. You're in a controlled traffic environment with high-speed turbine aircraft buzzing around you in arrival, transiting, or departure postures. It's Approach Control's job to see that all aircraft are properly separated, but if you barge in unannounced or without clearance, you could be the source of all sorts of traffic problems, up to, and potentially including, the dreaded midair conflict.

Admittedly, though, willful violation of a TCA is rare. The prime cause is lack of knowledge or lack of preparation. Legally entering a TCA under VFR is no trick—if you've done the necessary homework, including answering at least these questions:

- Do I have at least a private pilot license? If not, and I'm flying solo as a student, have I received the proper TCA training and logbook endorsement(s)?

- Do I have a VOR receiver that works?

- What are the TCA lateral and vertical limits?

- How far out and at what checkpoint should I make the initial call to Approach Control?

- What are the radio frequencies—ATIS, Approach, Tower, Ground Control? And is my radio capable of using those frequencies?

- How should the initial call be worded? What should I say and in what sequence?

- What am I going to do if I am not immediately cleared into the TCA?

- What will I do if I haven't understood an instruction?

- Have I familiarized myself with the airport layout, including the runways and the upwind, downwind, and base-leg headings for each runway?

- What action will I take if I can't get into the TCA at all? Will I have enough fuel to go around it or get to an alternate airport?

- Is my transponder working? Am I familiar with the terminology associated with its use? Has it been turned to the ALT position?

Don't wait until you can taste the icing on the proverbial TCA cake. If you want to enter the TCA, give yourself plenty of time to make contact and receive the controller's instructions. Approach controllers recommend an absolute minimum of 10 miles from the TCA shelf you're planning to enter. Better still, 20 or 30 miles out. Approach's radar will still easily pick you up. Even at a relatively modest 110 knots of airspeed, it won't take you long to eat up those few miles.

How should the call go, and what could you expect to hear? Perhaps something like this:

You: Kansas City Approach, Cherokee Eight Five One November.

App: *Cherokee Eight Five One Five November, Kansas City Approach, go ahead.*

You: Approach, Cherokee Eight Five One Five November is over Lake Perry at five thousand five hundred, landing International with Bravo.

App: *Cherokee One Five November, squawk zero two six three and ident.*

You: Roger, zero two six three. Cherokee One Five November. (Now push the IDENT button just once.)

In a moment, Approach may come back with:

App: *Cherokee One Five November, radar contact.*

Are you cleared into the TCA? Again, *no.* Wait until you hear:

App: *Cherokee One Five November, cleared into the TCA.*

Included in this message may be instructions on headings to turn to, altitude changes, or advisories of other aircraft—or they may come later. Whatever the case, from this point on, Approach will guide you into and within the TCA until you near the ATA. At that point, Approach will tell you to contact the tower for landing instructions.

Departing a TCA

With only a couple of exceptions, departing a TCA primary airport is the reverse process, and the same as leaving an ARSA.

First, monitor ATIS.

Second, call Clearance Delivery, stating your intentions. You'll receive initial departure headings, altitude(s), squawk code, and Departure Control frequency.

Third, call Ground Control for taxi clearance.

Fourth, call the tower for takeoff permission.

Fifth, contact Departure when tower so advises.

Sixth, follow Departure's instructions until you are clear of the TCA and Departure advises you that "radar service is terminated," that you are free to dial-in whatever frequency you wish, and to "Squawk one two zero zero" (or he may say, "squawk VFR," which means the same thing).

Alternately, you might hear this:

Dep: *Cherokee One Five November, you are leaving the TCA. Resume own navigation. Remain this frequency for advisories. Squawk one two zero zero.*

What's Departure telling you? First, that you've left the lateral or vertical limits of the TCA and are free to change headings or altitudes as you wish. Next, the controller is saying, without saying it, that you're still in Departure's airspace and will be for another 15 miles or so. He thus wants you to continue to monitor his frequency, to "stay with him," in the event advisories of other traffic in your line of flight become necessary.

Finally, when you're clear of Departure's area of responsibility, the controller will call you once more and tell you to change to whatever radio frequency you wish. It will be a short call, no more than:

Dep: *Cherokee One Five November, you're leaving my area. Radar service terminated. Frequency change approved. Good Day.*

Now you can tune to another tower, a Flight Service Station, call Center for VFR advisories, or, presumably, but not wisely, turn the radio off completely. The choice at this point is yours, as Approach will not provide traffic advisories once radar service is terminated.

Transiting a TCA

The procedures for transiting a TCA are the same as entering for landing. There's nothing new to be said, other than the fact that you will be with Approach the entire time.

Whether you'll receive transiting clearance will depend on the volume of traffic in the TCA at the time. Every controller I talked with stated that he would gladly help a VFR pilot get through the TCA, workload permitting, but it may not be a straight line. For reasons of IFR approach and departure procedures and the runway(s) in use, he might have to route you a few miles out of the way.

Or you could be asked to change altitudes. Regardless of the deviations, however, your journey will be a shorter one than if you avoid the TCA altogether because of procedural uncertainty or fear of entering a territory presumably reserved for the "big" boys. If the TCA is crowded, Approach will tell you. Then circumnavigation is your only choice. Otherwise, you'll get all the help you need. So saith those responsible for traffic control in this airspace.

Remaining VFR

Whatever the reason for entering either a TCA or an ARSA, if you go VFR, you have the responsibility to adhere to all VFR regulations. If there are clouds around, Approach may give you vectors and altitude changes, all the while advising you to "remain VFR." On the other hand, a controller could unknowingly vector you too close to a cloud bank, causing you to violate the VFR cloud separation minimums. If that should happen, it's your responsibility to advise the controller accordingly. Yes, you're under ATC control, but that does not relieve you of the responsibility to maintain VFR at all times.

Related to this is the possibility that, in the TCA or ARSA, ATC will assign you a non-VFR altitude—say 4000 feet going eastbound or 5500 feet westbound. That's his prerogative, but once you hear "resume own navigation" or "maintain VFR altitude," it means that you are to climb or descend to the appropriate VFR altitude.

More TCA Changes

A couple of further TCA changes are being considered. For one, the configuration of most TCAs can be confusing, what with varying floors and numbers of rings surrounding the primary airport. In the Kansas City TCA, for example, a segment of one extreme outer ring has an altitude floor of 5000 feet MSL, but the floor of the next ring inward is 3000 feet MSL. Thus if you're just entering underneath that outer ring at, say, 4800 feet MSL (to stay below the TCA) and are headed directly for the airport, you have a maximum of 5 nautical miles to lose 2000 feet to get below the 3000-foot floor of the adjacent ring. At a no-wind 110-knot airspeed, that gives you only 2 minutes and 44 seconds to drop 2000 feet. Such an altitude change, with so little time, makes it easy to violate the TCA, albeit completely unintentionally.

The FAA has said that, "Simplification of the TCA airspace configuration is a prime requisite. Vertical and lateral limits should be standardized and, to the extent practicable, be designed to retain all published instrument procedures once their flight track enters the TCA. The number of subareas should be kept to a minimum."

To that, we say Amen, but take a look at FIG. 6-8 before you get too excited.

As a second recommendation, the FAA has suggested that just three rings surround a TCA primary airport. The first would have a 10 nautical mile radius from the airport and rise from the surface to the upper TCA limits, proposed to be 12,500 feet MSL. The second ring would extend 20 miles out from the airport, with a floor of 2800 to 3000 feet AGL and the same 12,500-foot upper ceiling. The outward limits of the third ring is proposed to be 30 miles from the airport and the floor 5000 to 6000 feet AGL.

Changes are thus in the wind, and, as pilots, we have to be alert to what they are or will be. For now, though, there was no alternative but to discuss TCAs and other air traffic control systems as they exist at the time of this writing, which we have attempted to do.

Conclusion

TCAs do scare off the ill-prepared or the unknowledgeable, which is understandable. If not ready to cope with the airspace, it's better to be scared off than to drive into the area, replete with unjustified self-confidence. The consequences, to put it mildly, could be serious.

Do pilots do this? Unfortunately, yes. In one example an Approach controller cited, a Cessna 210 departed a satellite airport under, but not in, a TCA. The aircraft showed up on Approach's radar just east of the primary airport and well within the TCA. It had never contacted Approach and was not Mode C equipped, so Approach had no idea at what altitude it was flying.

Meanwhile, the controller had vectored a descending Boeing 727 towards its downwind leg, and, as the controller put it, "For some reason—I don't know why—I told the 727 to level off at 5000 feet, advising the pilot that I had traffic out there, wasn't talking to it, and didn't know its altitude. The 727 captain came back in a second, advising that the traffic was dead ahead at 4500 feet."

Intuition? Premonition? The controller didn't know. But he did now that had he allowed the 727 to continue its descent, the likelihood of a 727/210 conflict was excellent.

To track down the 210, the controller called the satellite airport tower, explained what had happened, and wanted to know the aircraft's N-number. The tower had the information, and, by chance, the 210 reestablished radio contact with the satellite tower. The end result was that the pilot of this errant aircraft had a few not-very-pleasant chats with FAA personnel.

Yes, some pilots do barge in where only the prepared should not fear to tread.

On the other hand, do controllers really want to play cops-and-robbers? Are they like motorcycle patrolmen, hiding behind sign boards in hopes of trapping highway speeders? Perhaps a few, but of those I interviewed and talked with, many of whom were pilots themselves, not one said he or she wanted to nail a pilot for a really minor infraction. Playing the bad guy is not in the makeup of most of those folks who are dedicated to serving the flying public but with safety the overriding consideration.

Don't let these comments, however, give the wrong impression. The FAA is very firm about violations. They will be reported and controllers have little leeway in deciding whether to report a minor violation or merely informally warn the offender. The fact is: Be guilty of an offense, and then be prepared for the consequences. We say again, though, that most controllers are not sadists who enjoy hurting the very people they exist to serve.

SAY GOODBYE TO TERMINAL RADAR SERVICE AREAS (TRSAs)

We come now to that vanishing breed of controlled structures—the TRSAs. Not only are they rapidly disappearing, but the rules relative to operating within them minimize their value as a traffic controlling element. The reason for so saying is, as I mentioned earlier, pilot participation in a TRSA is optional. The pilot can request or reject the services the controller is prepared to offer. Vanishing though they are, a few will exist around the country until approximately 1992, so a discussion of terminal area control wouldn't be complete without a brief TRSA summary.

Identifying a TRSA

A TRSA appears on the Sectional as series of magenta circles surrounding the primary airport. Some TRSAs are similar in design to TCAs, others more like ARSAs. Figure 6-13 illustrates the Macon, Georgia, TRSA, one of the larger TCA-like TRSAs. Excluding the irregular configuration in the immediate vicinity of the Macon airport and Warner Robins AFB, the circles fan outward in 5-nautical-mile increments. Similar to the TCA are the floor and ceiling altitude designations for each TRSA level. 100/SFC, 100/15, 100/20, and 100/25.

For frequency determination, the table on the reverse side of the Sectional legend lists the frequencies to use, depending on altitude and location (FIG. 6-14). The other source, of course, is the *Airport/Facility Directory*. As FIG. 6-15 shows, "Stage III SVC" is available by contacting Approach Control. Whether you've checked the Sectional or not, if the *A/FD* states "Stage III SVC," you know the primary airport has a TRSA.

Pilot and Equipment Requirements

Like the ARSA, there are no minimum pilot requirements. Operating in a TRSA is for all—student on up.

Equipment-wise, only the two-way radio, which you must have to operate in the ATA anyway, is necessary to take advantage of the TRSA.

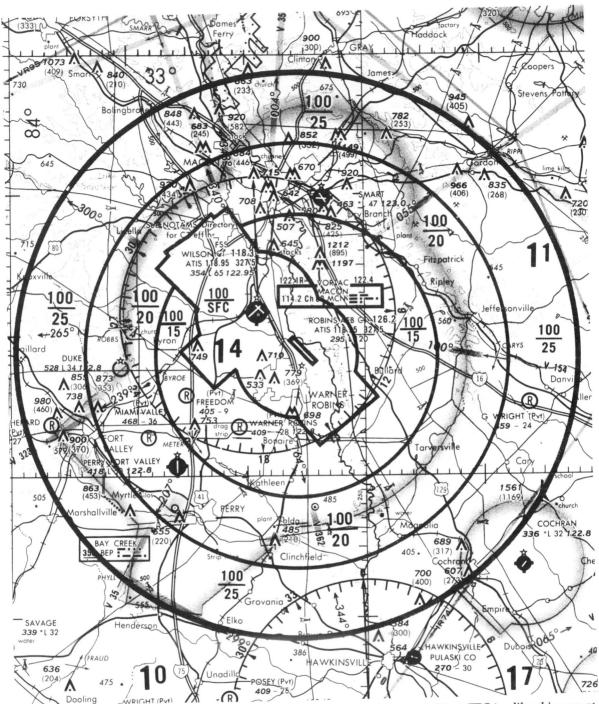

Fig. 6-13. *Solid magenta circles readily identify a TRSA on the Sectional. Most TRSAs, like this one at Macon, Georgia, will become ARSAs in the near future, but some TRSAs will disappear, not to be replaced. At the latter locations, Stage III radar service will no longer be offered.*

TCA, TRSA, AND SELECTED RADAR APPROACH CONTROL FREQUENCIES

ATLANTA TCA	EAST OF V97 NORTH OF V18 119.3 OR 381.6
	SOUTH OF V18 119.8 OR 343.6
	WEST OF V97 NORTH OF V18 121.0 OR 385.5
ASHEVILLE TRSA	124.65 351.8 (160°-339°)
	125.8 226.8 (340°-159°)
AUGUSTA TRSA	119.15 231.1 (350°-169°)
	126.8 270.3 (170°-349°)
BIRMINGHAM TRSA	132.2 385.6 (050°-230°)
	124.5 338.2 (231°-049°)
CHARLOTTE TRSA	126.15 316.7 (360°-179°)
	120.5 257.2 (180°-359°)
CHATTANOOGA TRSA	125.1 379.1 (016°-195°)
	119.2 321.2 (196°-015°)
COLUMBIA TRSA	124.9 285.6 (290°-109°)
	118.2 338.2 (110°-289°)
COLUMBUS TRSA	126.0 226.4 (001°-150°)
	126.55 278.5 (151°-240°)
	125.5 388.0 (241°-360°)
GREER TRSA	118.8 385.4 (WEST)
	119.4 350.2 (EAST)
HUNTSVILLE TRSA	125.6 354.1 (359°-179°)
	118.05 239.0 (180°-358°)
KNOXVILLE TRSA	123.9 353.6 (225°-044°)
	118.0 360.8 (045°-224°)
MACON TRSA	119.6 388.2 (130°-329° ABOVE 5000 FT)
	124.2 279.8 (330°-129° ABOVE 5000 FT)
	124.8 324.3 (ALL SECTORS 5000 FT AND BELOW)
MONTGOMERY TRSA	124.0 319.9 (SOUTH)
	125.3 369.2 (NORTH)
NASHVILLE TRSA	124.0 360.7 (016°-196°)
	120.6 388.0 (197°-015°)
SAVANNAH TRSA	120.4 388.8 (270°-010°)
	125.3 387.1 (011°-109°)
	118.4 354.0 (110°-269°)
LAWSON AAF RADAR	119.05 226.6

Fig. 6-14. *The Atlanta Sectional indicates the Approach Control frequencies to be used when entering the Macon TRSA, if you desire radar service.*

LEWIS B. WILSON (MCN) 9 S UTC-5(-4DT) 32°41′34″N 83°38′58″W **ATLANTA**
354 B 34 **FUEL** 100, JET A TPA—1154(800) ARFF Index B **H-5D, 4H, L-20E**
RWY 05-23: H6501X150 (ASPH-CONC-GRVD) S-80, D-128, DT-237 HIRL **IAP**
  RWY 05: SSALR. Trees. RWY 23: REIL. VASI(V4L)—GA 3.0°TCH 45′. Railroad. Rgt tfc.
RWY 13-31: H5001X150 (ASPH-CONC) S-44, D-65, DT-110 MIRL
  RWY 13: REIL. VASI(V4L) GA 3.0°TCH 45′ Rgt tfc. Trees.
  RWY 31: REIL. VASI(V4L)—GA 3.0°TCH 45′. Pole.
AIRPORT REMARKS: Attended continuously. ACTIVATE VASI Rwy 31—CTAF. Svc avbl 24hrs Sun-Thur, 0900-0300Z‡
  Fri and Sat; after hrs Fri and Sat, call arpt manager 912-788-3760. Control Zone effective continuously.
COMMUNICATIONS: CTAF 118.3 ATIS 118.95 (1100-0500Z‡) UNICOM 122.95
  MACON FSS. (MCN) on arpt. 122.4, 122.2, 122.1R. TF 800-WX-BRIEF. NOTAM FILE MCN.
Ⓡ **MACON APP/DEP CON** 119.6 (130°-329°) 124.2 (330°-129°) 124.8 (5000′ and below) (1100-0500Z‡)
  ATLANTA CENTER APP/DEP CON 133.1 (0500-1100Z‡)
  MACON TOWER 118.3 (1200-0300Z‡) GND CON 121.65
  STAGE III SVC ctc APP CON 124.8 20 NM out.
RADIO AIDS TO NAVIGATION: NOTAM FILE MCN. VHF/DF ctc MACON FSS.
  MACON (H) VORTAC 114.2 MCN Chan 89 32°41′28″N 83°38′50″W at fld. 350/01E
  SOFKE NDB (LOM) 200 MC 32°38′43″N 83°42′48″W 051° 3.6 NM to fld.
  ILS 109.5 I-MCN Rwy 05 LOM SOFKE NDB
  ASR

Fig. 6-15. *The "Stage III SVC" in the A/FD identifies the Macon TRSA surrounding the Lewis B. Wilson airport.*

125

Operating Requirements in the TRSA

Here is where the traffic-controlling value of a TRSA becomes questionable. *Stage III Service* means that Approach will provide separation between all IFR aircraft and participating VFR aircraft. The word *participating* correctly implies that the VFR pilot can choose to establish radio contact with Approach and receive vectors and advisories or disregard the availability of the service. Whether arriving, departing, or transiting, the option is his. Furthermore, unlike in an ARSA or TCA, the pilot has the right to request radar service after entering the TRSA, if he so wishes. And, Approach must honor the request.

Approaching a TRSA

The procedures here are simple. If you want Stage III, contact Approach well outside the TRSA limits and give the usual information, followed by "Request Stage Three." Approach will take it from there, leading you up to the ATA.

If you don't want radar service, don't call Approach. Just contact the tower 10 to 15 miles out—as though the airport had only an ATA with no TRSA, ARSA, or TCA.

Departing a TRSA

Departing a TRSA is similar to a TCA or ARSA departure, *if* you want Stage III. Most TRSAs have Clearance Delivery, so it's merely a matter of listening to the ATIS, calling Clearance, giving the same basic information of aircraft N-number, the fact that you're VFR, your destination, desired altitude, and then requesting Stage III service.

On the other hand, if you choose not to use the service, go directly to Ground Control for taxi instructions, concluding with the statement "Negative Stage Three."

Transiting a TRSA

If transiting a TRSA and you opt for Stage III, the call to Approach is almost the same as when entering the area. The only difference is that you would also include your next point of landing, followed by "Request Stage Three Service."

If you don't want the service, don't call anybody. You're on your own to see-and-avoid. Failing to avail yourself of Stage III, however, whether arriving, departing, or transiting, does seem shortsighted. As in any busy terminal area, it's just good insurance and common sense to have somebody down there sort of watching over you and alerting you to some of the possible airborne obstacles in your path. As with all the other controlling agencies, you've paid for the service through your annual donations to Uncle Sam, so why not reap a little benefit from your "investment?" Again, it's good insurance and common sense.

Conclusion

Where TRSAs exist today, they will soon be replaced by ARSAs—if the primary airport meets the minimum ARSA qualifying criteria. At the less busy airports, the TRSA will be eliminated and nothing will replace it. Only the ATA will remain. Things may change, but those are the current FAA plans.

DESIGNATED AIRPORT AREAS

Before we leave the subject, another example of things to come is what the FAA calls the *Designated Airport Areas* or "Appendix D" airport areas (referring to FAR Part 91 Appendix D). These are areas surrounding certain airports that, at the moment, don't have the volume of activity to justify an ARSA. At the time of writing, only two airports fall under this category—Logan International, Billings, Montana, and Hector International, Fargo, North Dakota. The effective date of the Designated Airport ruling is December 30, 1990.

The principal requirement is an operating Mode C transponder from the surface up to 10,000 feet MSL within a 10-nautical-mile radius of the airport (FIG. 6-16). Unlike an ARSA, however, no radio contact is required to operate in the airspace outside the ATA. Within the ATA, the normal communication rules apply.

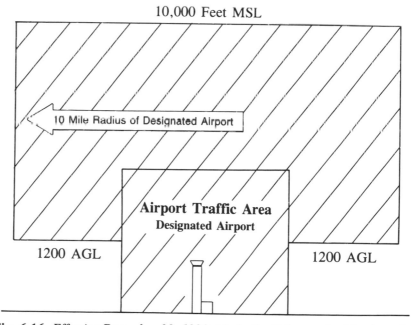

10,000 Feet MSL

10 Mile Radius of Designated Airport

Airport Traffic Area
Designated Airport

1200 AGL   1200 AGL

Fig. 6-16. *Effective December 30, 1990, Mode C will be required in the striped area shown, surrounding certain airports designated in FAR Part 91, Appendix D.*

EXCEPTIONS TO MODE C REQUIREMENTS

The FAA makes it clear that exceptions to Mode C regulations can be made on a case-by-case basis by the controlling ATC facility. Such exceptions may include crop-dusting operations, aerial photography, medical emergencies, and the like. Ultralights continue to be exempt from Mode C requirements.

CONCLUSION

The intent of this chapter has been to try to outline the principles and operating requirements of the ATA, ARSA, TCA, and TRSA environments. Some aspects of importance in understanding the air traffic control system have intentionally, but temporarily, been omitted—aspects as how the Approach/Departure Control operation functions, its coordination with the tower cab and Center, and an overview of the radar and computer equipment which makes the system function. Those are for the remaining chapters.

Is knowledge of the terminal areas absolutely essential? No, not if, as VFR pilots, we stay clear of the ARSAs, the TCAs, and never go into a tower-controlled airport. Otherwise, knowledge is essential. Too many of us, however, avoid these controlled areas because of uncertainty and probably at least a modicum of fear. Others, with unbridled cockiness, or even worse, dangerous ignorance, drive onward into forbidden territory unannounced. They screw up the radio communications; they ask questions that a little preparation would make needless; they fail to admit that they don't understand an instruction; they forget to turn on their transponder; they don't have Mode C but still take up air time trying to get into the TCA on a routine, nonemergency flight; and the offenses could go on.

Maybe it's the quality of instruction we received or didn't receive, but the cause is really secondary. It's what we do or don't do that matters. Flying in and around these terminal areas requires no unusual level of brilliance or extensive experience. It does demand knowledge, however, coupled with some practice. The combination is likely to result in a level of piloting skill that permits us to sally forth safely and with justified confidence in whatever airspace environment we might find ourselves.

7

Approach/Departure Control

ALTHOUGH I'VE ALREADY REFERRED TO APPROACH AND DEPARTURE CONTROL on several occasions and have discussed certain aspects of its role in terminal traffic control, some additional observations are in order. A couple of points may be repetitious, but the intent of the chapter is to tie things together and elaborate on what Approach Control does and how it does it. (For simplicity's sake, I'll refer to the function merely as "Approach.")

THE ROLE OF APPROACH CONTROL

Picture any major terminal, such as a Chicago or an Atlanta, but with only a control tower with the basic tower cab. Then imagine the scene if a couple of controllers in that tower were solely responsible for separating and sequencing all the arriving, departing, and transiting traffic within a 35- or 40-mile radius of the airport. Conservatively stated, the scene would be chaotic.

Enter then the role of Approach Control—the facility that does the separating and sequencing within its assigned airspace, except for the ATAs surrounding the primary airport and any satellite fields in the area. In essence, Approach, with its computers and radar equipment, is the bridge between the outside world and the tower for all arriving and departing aircraft. It does what no busy tower alone could do with any degree of order or safety.

WHERE IS THE APPROACH CONTROL FACILITY LOCATED?

With regard to the physical location of Approach Control, five possibilities exist:

- Approach may be physically in the airport tower structure—either in the tower cab (TRACAB) or, at busier terminals, on one of the floors below it (TRACON).

- It may be separate from the tower, but still on the airport, and provide Approach service to the airport as though it were located in the tower.

- The function may not be physically on the airport but, rather, at a larger nearby terminal.

- The service may be provided by the Air Route Traffic Control Center in whose area the airport is located.

- It may be provided by a Center down to or above the minimum altitude at which its radar can capture the image of the aircraft. Below that altitude, the controller uses "manual," or nonradar, procedures to separate and sequence IFR traffic.

With these five possibilities, how do you know what airports have what? The *Airport/Facility Directory* is the best determining source (FIGS. 7-1 through 7-5).

Do the TRACON controllers have any view of the outside world as they fulfill their responsibilities? No. Their job is to control all traffic in their airspace (beyond the ATA) by radar and radar alone. The room, or work area, is dark, with only the radarscopes and lighted computer buttons providing most of the illumination. Figure 7-6 is a floor plan layout of a typical TRACON.

QUESTIONS AND ANSWERS

Now for a bit more detail. What follows are some of the questions asked of Approach Control specialists—and their answers. The intent of the questions was to clarify certain issues that VFR, and perhaps IFR, pilots might have wondered about.

Q. Do you have any advance information on a VFR flight plan aircraft that would be entering your airspace?
A. *Not unless the pilot has been receiving traffic advisories from Center and had been handed off to Approach for transiting or landing purposes. We'd know about that aircraft because we had accepted the handoff. Otherwise, we have no prior information. IFR, of course, is a different matter.*

LEXINGTON

§   **BLUE GRASS**   (LEX)   4.3 W   UTC-5(-4DT)   38°02'12"N 84°36'21"W   CINCINNATI
     980   B   S4   FUEL 100LL, JET A   OX 1, 2   ARFF Index C   H-4H, L-22E
     RWY 04-22: H7003X150 (ASPH-GRVD)   S-140, D-169, DT-275   HIRL   0.4% up NE   IAP
       RWY 04: SSALR. VASI(V4L)—GA 2.8°TCH 60.0'.
       RWY 22: REIL. VASI(V4L)—GA 3.0°TCH 51'. Thld dsplcd 55'. Pole.
     RWY 08-26: H3501X150 (ASPH-CONC)   S-12.5, D-51, DT-97   MIRL
       RWY 08: Silo.   RWY 26: Tree.
     AIRPORT REMARKS: Attended continuously. Flocks of birds in vicinity of arpt from 1 hour before sunrise until 1 hour after
       sunset. When twr closed CFR facility monitors 119.1. When twr closed MIRL Rwy 08–26 unavailable. ACTIVATE
       SSALR Rwy 04 and HIRL Rwy 04–22—119.1.
     COMMUNICATIONS: CTAF 119.1   **ATIS** 126.3   **UNICOM** 122.95
       LOUISVILLE FSS (LOU) TF 1–800–WX–BRIEF. NOTAM FILE LEX.
       LEXINGTON RCO 122.1R 112.6T (LOUISVILLE FSS)
      (R) **LEXINGTON APP/DEP CON** 120.75 (221°-039°) 120.15 (040°-220°) 125.0 (1100-0500Z‡)
       INDIANAPOLIS CENTER APP/DEP CON 127.0. (0500-1100Z‡)
       LEXINGTON TOWER 119.1 (1100-0500Z‡)   **GND CON** 121.9   **CLNC DEL** 132.35
       ARSA ctc **APP CON**
     RADIO AIDS TO NAVIGATION: NOTAM FILE LEX.
       LEXINGTON (L) VORTAC 112.6   HYK   Chan 73   37°57'59"N 84°28'21"W   304°7.6 NM to fld. 1040/00E.
       BLAYD NDB (MHW/LOM) 242   LE   37°59'13"N 84°39'37"W   045°3.3 NM to fld.
       ILS 110.1 I-LEX Rwy 04 LOM BLAYD NDB. ILS unmonitored when twr closed. Glide slope unusable blo 1220'.
       ILS 110.5 I-GNJ Rwy 22 Localizer unusable above 4000' beyond 20° right of course. Glide slope unusable byd 5'
         either side of localizer course, unusable below 1220'. ILS unmonitored when twr closed.
       ASR (1130-0500Z‡)

Fig. 7-1. *The* (R) *indicates that the Lexington APP/CON is on the airport and is either a* TRACON *or a* TRACAB. *At night, when the tower and Approach are closed, pilots contact Indianapolis Center for Approach services.*

---

§   **PANAMA CITY-BAY CO**   (PFN)   3 NW   UTC-6(-5DT)   30°12'43"N 85°40'58"W   NEW ORLEANS
     21   B   S4   FUEL 100, JET A   OX 1, 2   LRA   ARFF Index B   H-5D, L-18F
     RWY 14-32: H6314X150 (ASPH-GRVD)   S-100, D-174, DT-300   HIRL   IAP
       RWY 14: MALSR.   RWY 32: REIL. VASI(V4L)—GA 3.0°TCH 50'. Trees.
     RWY 05-23: H4000X150 (ASPH)   S-40, D-70, DT-120   MIRL
       RWY 05: VASI(V4L). Trees.   RWY 23: VASI(V4L)—GA 3.0° TCH 39'. Trees
     AIRPORT REMARKS: Attended 1330-0130Z‡. Nights call (904) 763-6751. ACTIVATE MALSR Rwy 14
       (0500-1200Z‡)—CTAF. Helicopter towing cables below 500' bordering SW arpt tfc area and adjacent coastal
       waters. Extensive Helicopter operations from ramp. Acft arriving/departing S.E.-N.W. use caution due to intensive
       military jets transiting arpt tfc area 1500' and above on apch to Tyndall A.F.B. Flight Notification Service (ADCUS)
       available. Control Zone effective 1100-0400Z‡.
     WEATHER DATA SOURCES: LAWRS (904)763-8101.
     COMMUNICATIONS: CTAF 120.5   **ATIS** 128.3 (1200-0400Z‡)   **UNICOM** 122.95
       TALLAHASSEE FSS (TLH) LC 785-6631. NOTAM FILE PFN.
       RCO 122.1R 114.3T (TALLAHASSEE FSS)
      (R) **TYNDALL APP/DEP CON** 119.1 below 4000' 119.75 above 4000'
       TOWER 120.5 (1200-0400Z‡)   **GND CON** 121.7
     RADIO AIDS TO NAVIGATION: NOTAM FILE PFN.
       (L) VORTAC 114.3   PFN   Chan 90   30°12'58"N 85°40'52"W   at fld. 10/00W.
       LYNNE NDB (LOM) 278   PF   30°19'35"N 85°46'57"W   142°8.1 NM to fld.
       ILS 110.5 I-PFN Rwy 14 BC unusable LOM LYNNE NDB (ILS unmonitored when twr closed).
       ASR

Fig. 7-2. *An example of a* RAPCON, *with the Tyndall Air Force Base providing APP/DEP CON service to the Panama City-Bay County Airport.*

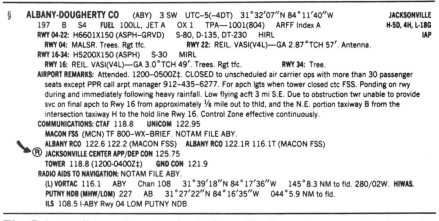

§   **FULTON CO ARPT-BROWN FLD**   (FTY) 6.1 W UTC–5(–4DT) 33°46'45"N 84°31'17"W   **ATLANTA**
    841 B S4   **FUEL** 100, 100LL, 115, JET A, B   OX 1, 2, 3, 4   LRA   **H-6F, 4H, L-20E, A**
    RWY 08R-26L: H5796X100 (ASPH-GRVD)   S-105, D-121, DT-198   HIRL   **IAP**
      RWY 08R: MALSR. Trees. Rgt tfc.   RWY 26L: REIL. VASI(V4L)—GA 3.0°TCH 52.4'. Trees.
    RWY 14-32: H4158X100 (ASPH)   S-30   MIRL
      RWY 14: REIL. VASI(V2L)—GA 4.0° TCH 52'. Trees.   RWY 32: REIL. VASI(V2L)—GA 4.0°TCH 51.9'. Thld
        dsplcd 200'. Tower.
    RWY 08L-26R: H2801X60 (ASPH)   S-35, D-45, DT-72   (VFR light acft only).
      RWY 08L: Twr.   RWY 26R: Tree. Rgt tfc.
    AIRPORT REMARKS: Attended continuously. Unlgtd 1207' pole 2.3 NM W. of arpt. Rwy 08L–26R clsd indefinitely. Rwy
      32 VASI out of svc indefinitely. Flight Notification Service (ADCUS) available.
    COMMUNICATIONS: CTAF 118.5   **ATIS** 119.0 (1100-0500Z‡)   **UNICOM** 122.95
      ATLANTA FSS (ATL) on arpt. 122.6 122.45 122.2. 404–691–2240. NOTAM FILE FTY.
  ® **ATLANTA APP/DEP CON** 121.0
      COUNTY TOWER 118.5 (Below 3000') 120.7 (1100-0500Z‡)   **GND CON** 121.7 **CLNC DEL** 123.7
    RADIO AIDS TO NAVIGATION: NOTAM FILE FTY. VHF/DF ctc ATLANTA FSS
      ATLANTA (H) VORTAC 116.9   ATL   Chan 116   33°37'44"N 84°26'07"W   334°10.0 NM to fld. 1000/00E.
        NOTAM FILE ATL.
      FLANC NDB (MHW/LOM) 344   FT   33°45'44"N 84°38'21"W   082°5.5 NM to fld.
      ILS 109.1 I-FTY Rwy 08R LOM FLANC NDB (G.S. unusable when twr not operating)
      ASR
      COMM/NAVAID REMARKS: DF unusable at 40 NM 350°-035° below 5000', 035°-050° below 3500', 050°-075°
      below 4000', 075°-150° below 4500', 150°-175° below 5000', 175°-265° below 3500', 265°-295° below
      4000'.

Fig. 7-3. *Atlanta APP/DEP CON provides the service to Fulton County, which is about 15 miles from Atlanta's Hartsfield Airport.*

§   **ALBANY-DOUGHERTY CO**   (ABY) 3 SW UTC–5(–4DT) 31°32'07"N 84°11'40"W   **JACKSONVILLE**
    197 B S4   **FUEL** 100LL, JET A   OX 1   TPA—1001(804)   ARFF Index A   **H-5D, 4H, L-18G**
    RWY 04-22: H6601X150 (ASPH-GRVD)   S-80, D-135, DT-230   HIRL   **IAP**
      RWY 04: MALSR. Trees. Rgt tfc.   RWY 22: REIL. VASI(V4L)—GA 2.87°TCH 57'. Antenna.
    RWY 16-34: H5200X150 (ASPH)   S-30   MIRL
      RWY 16: REIL. VASI(V4L)—GA 3.0°TCH 49'. Trees. Rgt tfc.   RWY 34: Tree.
    AIRPORT REMARKS: Attended. 1200-0500Z‡. CLOSED to unscheduled air carrier ops with more than 30 passenger
      seats except PPR call arpt manager 912–435–6277. For apch lgts when tower closed ctc FSS. Ponding on rwy
      during and immediately following heavy rainfall. Low flying acft 3 mi S.E. Due to obstruction twr unable to provide
      svc on final apch to Rwy 16 from approximately ⅛ mile out to thld, and the N.E. portion taxiway B from the
      intersection taxiway H to the hold line Rwy 16. Control Zone effective continuously.
    COMMUNICATIONS: CTAF 118.8   **UNICOM** 122.95
      MACON FSS (MCN) TF 800–WX–BRIEF. NOTAM FILE ABY.
      ALBANY RCO 122.6 122.2 (MACON FSS)   **ALBANY RCO** 122.1R 116.1T (MACON FSS)
  ® **JACKSONVILLE CENTER APP/DEP CON** 125.75
      TOWER 118.8 (1200-0400Z‡)   **GND CON** 121.9
    RADIO AIDS TO NAVIGATION: NOTAM FILE ABY.
      (L) VORTAC 116.1   ABY   Chan 108   31°39'18"N 84°17'36"W   145°8.3 NM to fld. 280/02W. **HIWAS.**
      PUTNY NDB (MHW/LOM) 227   AB   31°27'22"N 84°16'35"W   044°5.9 NM to fld.
      ILS 108.5 I-ABY Rwy 04 LOM PUTNY NDB

Fig. 7-4. *At Albany, Georgia, the Jacksonville Center is responsible for radar Approach/Departure Control.*

GAGE-SHATTUCK (GAG) 2 SW UTC-6(-5DT) 36°17'45"N 99°46'30"W
2223 B
RWY 17-35: H5435X150 (ASPH) S-30, D-45 LIRL .8% up S.
   RWY 17: Road.
RWY 04-22: H2700X150 (ASPH) S-12.5
AIRPORT REMARKS: Unattended. ACTIVATE LIRL Rwy 17-35—123.0. Arpt CLOSED to jet acft over 12,500 lbs.
   CAUTION: RWY 17-35 and RWY 04-22 condition not monitored. Visual inspection prior to ldg or tkf. RWY 17-35
   LIRL maybe unreliable. Control Zone effective (1300-0300Z‡).
COMMUNICATIONS: CTAF 122.9
   MC ALESTER FSS (MLC) Toll free call, dial 1-800-WX-BRIEF. NOTAM FILE GAG.
   RCO 122.55 (MC ALESTER FSS)
   KANSAS CITY CENTER APP/DEP CON 126.95
RADIO AIDS TO NAVIGATION: NOTAM FILE GAG. VHF/DF ctc MC ALESTER FSS.
   (H) VORTACW 115.6 GAG Chan 103 36°20'37"N 99°52'47"W 109°5.7 NM to fld. 2430/10E.

WICHITA
H-2H, 3A, L-6G
IAP

Fig. 7-5. *Because Gage is about 115 nautical miles from the nearest radar site, Kansas City Center can only provide radar APP/DEP CON down to about 7000 feet AGL. Below that, service is "manual," or nonradar. The absence of an* (R) *indicates that radar service is limited or not available.*

Q. Is there any way a pilot can determine what frequency he should use to establish initial contact with Approach? This assumes, of course, that there's been no handoff or previous contact with Center.

A. *Yes and no. The frequency published in the A/FD or on the Sectional is the one to try first, but once contact is made, the controller may ask the pilot to tune to a different frequency.*

Q. Why is that?

A. *It could depend on the runways in use. This will vary from terminal to terminal, but let's say we're using Runway 01 or 19. Approach might then have one controller handling all traffic east of the runway and another handling the traffic to the west. Today, you call on the published frequency of 119.0 and there's no problem. However, tomorrow, we're using Runways 09 or 27. The east controller today is now handling the traffic south of 09/27 and the west controller is handling that to the north—both on frequencies different from those published. Unless you're very familiar with the way Approach works at a given terminal, you won't know about the change. The answer, then, is to use the published frequency. If that's not the right one, we'll advise you.*

Q. For VFR traffic transiting the TCA, do you have a preferred altitude?

A. *At some terminals, there is a preferred, or perhaps required, altitude corridor, but that's not universally true. Much depends on the runways in use, the flow of IFR traffic, and IFR traffic at satellite airports for which Approach is responsible.*

Q. Another question on transiting a TCA: I'm coming in VFR from the east and want to go through the TCA to the west. I've been monitoring the east frequency for several miles, and there seems to be little traffic or activity. When I make

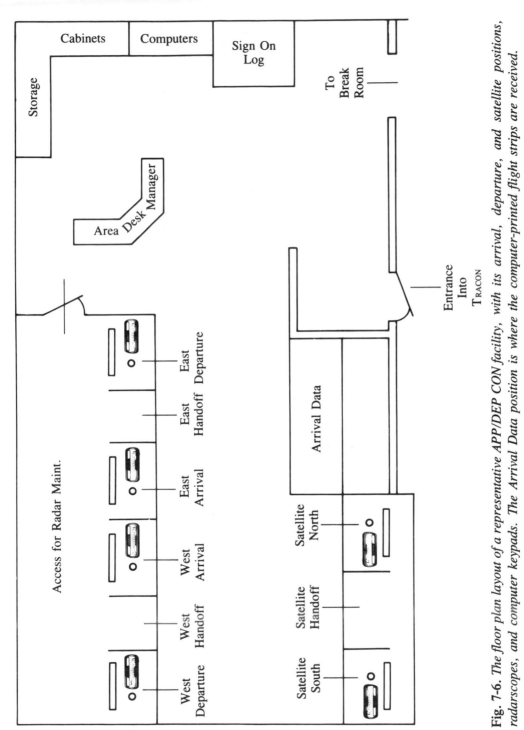

Fig. 7-6. *The floor plan layout of a representative APP/DEP CON facility, with its arrival, departure, and satellite positions, radarscopes, and computer keypads. The Arrival Data position is where the computer-printed flight strips are received.*

my first call and request clearance to the west, the request is denied "because of workload." How can that be? The controller obviously isn't that busy.

A. *No, he or she may not be, but what you're unlikely to know is the volume of activity the west controller is handling. At the time of your call, he could be too occupied with IFR traffic to accommodate a VFR transit. The east controller knows what's going on and would have to refuse your TCA entry request.*

Q. In another vein, I'm practicing instrument approaches to a satellite airport in your airspace. Is the controller I'm talking to also handling the primary airport traffic?

A. *It's unlikely. Usually there is a satellite controller who is responsible for just the satellite operations, including practice approaches as well as bona fide IFR traffic.*

Q. The controllers are assigned to specific geographical sectors, right?

A. *Right. Again, however, the volume of traffic at a terminal can make a difference, as do the runways in use. At this location, we have three sectors: east and west, or north and south, and satellite. The last covers eight airports in our area, including three with VFR towers, one that's a part-time military tower, and four that are uncontrolled.*

Q. I have departed either the primary airport or one of the satellites, VFR, and have received advisories from Approach. I request a handoff to Center for enroute advisories. What do you do when I make the request?

A. *You've already told us your route of flight, and we know what position, or sector, at Center handles IFR and VFR traffic in that geographical area. It's then just a matter of activating what we call an "override" phone that connects us directly with that sector controller. We'll ask if he can handle a VFR flight. His workload permitting, he'll say "Yes," so we'll give him your aircraft type, N-number, present position, altitude, first point of landing, and squawk. Meanwhile, he's manually filling out a VFR flight strip on you. Once the information has been relayed, we'll tell you to contact Center on such-and-such frequency. All you do now is get on the air, identify yourself with aircraft type and N-number, verify your present altitude, if climbing, and the desired altitude, or, if you've reached your cruising altitude, merely verify what it is. The call is simple: "(Blank) Center, Cherokee Eight Five One Five November is with you at five thousand, climbing to seven thousand five hundred." Don't say any more. Center already has the other pertinent information.*

Q. I imagine it's the same for arrivals when Center hands me off to you folks.

A. *Exactly the same.*

Q. What if Center is too busy to give me advisories?

A. *The sector controller will tell me, I'll tell you, advise you that radar service is terminated, ask you squawk One Two Zero Zero, and bid you good day. You're on your own now to see-and-avoid.*

Q. What if I'm VFR and want to land at the primary airport in a TCA, whether I've been using Center or not. Can you refuse my request for advisories?

A. *If you're in Approach Control's airspace but not in the TCA, and our workload is heavy, the answer is yes. Once I've cleared you into the TCA, however, it's my job to separate you from IFR traffic, advise you of other possible VFR traffic, and vector you to the airport.*

Q. What if I'm going to land at a satellite that is under but not in the TCA and want advisories. Would you give them to me?

A. *That's strictly a matter of workload. If I can, I will. Otherwise, stay out of the TCA and contact the tower at the satellite. If it's an uncontrolled field, self-announce your position and intentions 10 to 15 miles out.*

Q. On a cross-country, using Center for advisories, my route takes me near an Approach Control airport. Maybe it's an ARSA or a TCA, but I'm going to go around or above the area, regardless of what it is, and I'm not going to land there. Why, then, does Center tell me to contact Approach? I may be 30 miles away from the primary airport.

A. *It's because you'll be entering that Approach Control's airspace, and it's now Approach's responsibility, not Center's, to give you advisories. Again, though, if Approach is too busy, the sector controller may not be able to accept the handoff. Center will then tell you that radar service is terminated and to squawk 1200. If you want advisories down the road, you'll have reestablish contact with Center.*

Q. Are these handoffs also handled by override phones?

A. *For VFRs, yes. On an IFR flight plan, however, everything is computerized, and the transfer of control is more or less automatic. That's not the best use of the term, but it's reasonably descriptive of what happens.*

Q. Speaking of "automatic," I've heard a lot about something called a *slewball*. What is it?

A. *First, picture a baseball with all but the top 10 percent sliced off and thrown away. The remaining 10 percent is a rounded movable dome set in each controller's console. Then picture a video game where you can move a pointer, an arrow, or a symbol to a certain position by manipulating a control of some sort (FIG. 7-7). The slewball is the control we manipulate, and the symbol in our unit is simply a letter, such as a "W" for a West controller, "E" for East, "C" for Center, "H" for Handoff, and so on. When we want to make some computerized change to an identified aircraft in the area, we move the slewball until the letter is placed on the radarscope symbol of that aircraft. Then, by punching certain*

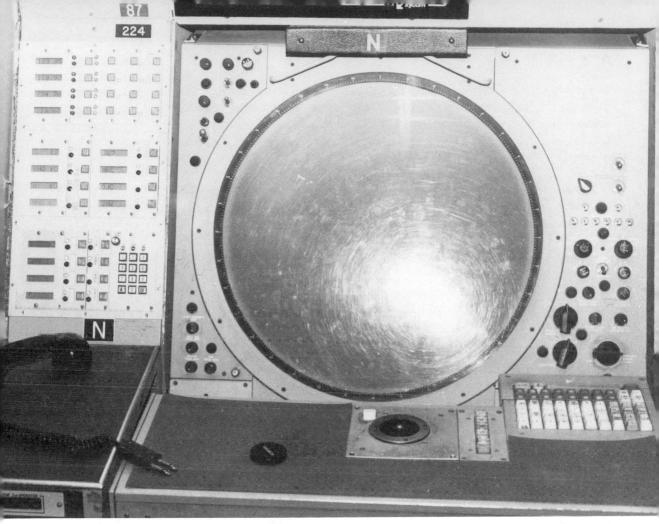

Fig. 7-7. *The slewball is at the six o'clock position, immediately below the radarscope. Various lighted computer-entry keys are at the right of the console. The telephone handset shown is not normally used by on-duty controllers. (Nor is the photographer's lens cap!)*

computer buttons, we can change the aircraft's transponder code, initiate a handoff to Center, or do anything else we wish that involves the computer.

Q. How does this sort of handoff go?

A. *Like this—but keep in mind we're talking only about IFR handoffs. VFRs are done by phone. Let's say an aircraft is departing the TCA to the northeast. Our scope shows the aircraft's N-number, its altitude, and ground speed. The "E," of course, indicates that the east controller is handling the aircraft. This constitutes the data block. Now to the handoff process itself.*

Four sectors at our Center handle all departures, arrivals, and transits within our immediate area. These are positions 40, 42, 46, and 48 in the Center complex. Position 40 handles the northeast sector—which our controllers automatically know. When the aircraft nears the outer limits of our airspace, the east controller slews the "E" up to the aircraft's symbol, hits the "C" for "Center" button, and then the "Enter" button on the computer console. As he does this, the entire data block appears and blinks on Sector 40's radarscope. When that controller accepts, or "buys," the handoff by punching a computer button on his console, the data block in Approach blinks, and the "E" changes to a "C". After the "C" appears, we then call the pilot and advise, "Cherokee Eight Five One Five November, contact (Blank) Center on 125.25 (or whatever the frequency might be). Good day." We'll keep 15 November on our scope, though, until he actually crosses the line into Center's airspace.

That's all there is to it. It's an automatic handoff, assuming Sector 40 accepts it. If the controller can't do so immediately, we will have to hold the aircraft in our airspace. No IFR aircraft can go from one controlled airspace to another without the approval of the receiving sector or facility.

Q. A question about those things called "flight strips." Would you decode this one for me? (FIG. 7-8)

A. *Sure. The aircraft N-number is obvious, as is the type—a PA28. For those unfamiliar with it, one of a series of letters follows the slash to indicate the type or types of avionic equipment aboard the aircraft. In this case, the "A" means that 15 November has a DME (Distance Measuring Equipment") and a transponder with altitude-reporting capabilities. The "613" is merely the computer identification number. Moving over a column, "4626" is the transponder code given the pilot to squawk. "P1620" indicates the proposed departure time, and "40" is the requested 4000-foot altitude. "MCI" is the departure point, and "TOPEK" is the "gate" through which the aircraft will be vectored out of our airspace. The balance indicates the route of flight to its termination at MKC.*

Q. A second question, then: Who originates these strips? How do they end up in Approach?

A. *They start at a Flight Service Station. When the pilot files an IFR flight plan, the FSS enters the information in its computer. That computer then "talks" to the central core, or* host *computer in Center, which interprets the data, processes*

Fig. 7-8. *An example of a computer-generated IFR flight progress strip, originated at the AFSS, automatically sent to Center's computer, which then transmitted it to Approach Control 30 minutes before the planned departure of 1620.*

the flight strip, and sends it to the appropriate Approach Control facility. Approach receives the printed strip from its computer 30 minutes before the proposed departure time. That time is valid for two hours, unless the pilot is delayed and contacts Approach, the tower, or at an uncontrolled airport, the Flight Service Station to request an updated departure.

Q. Is there anything like this for a VFR flight plan?
A. *No. A VFR flight plan is just between the FSS at which it was filed and the FSS in whose area the terminating airport is located.*

Q. I'm flying IFR and want to land at an airport in your airspace that has, let's say, a VOR but only a VFR tower—that is, it has no radar, no BRITE. I've heard many pilots complain that it often takes a lot of time for Approach to set them up and turn them over to the tower for final landing clearance. Now here's a satellite field without much traffic, but the delays often seem unnecessarily long. Why is that?
A. *That's the disadvantage of a strictly VFR tower. Before we can let you pass the outer marker on an instrument approach, we must know that the aircraft ahead of you is actually on the ground. So to space things properly, we have to have a six-mile separation between aircraft, rather than the normal three miles where the tower has BRITE radar. You're right. A lot of pilots do complain about the delays, but they may not understand that we must have the spacing so that the VFR tower can give us a down time before we can switch the next aircraft in line to the tower frequency—and we must make that switch before the aircraft reaches the outer marker.*

Q. So it's a matter of maintaining the proper spacing until you get that down time
A. *That's exactly what it is.*

Q. Towers are rated by Levels—Level 1 the least busy, up to Level 5, the busiest. What determines your Level, for instance?
A. *Levels are determined by the number of IFR aircraft Approach handles on a per-hour basis. We're a Level 4, which requires a count of at least 60 handlings per hour. Our average is 64, thus qualifying for that rating. A Level 5 terminal must handle 100 per hour, and a Level 3 is in the 40 range.*

Q. That's strictly IFR aircraft? VFRs don't count?
A. *Right. IFR only.*

Q. Do Approach controllers ever work the tower?
A. *Yes, if they have been tower-certificated. Here, we rotate day to day. We can do that because we're all tower- and radar-certificated. That's not true everywhere, though. Many tower controllers have not gone through the radar training and certification process, so they're limited to strictly tower duty.*

Q. Which do you think is the more stressful—tower or Approach?

A. *I'd say Approach. You're working a lot more traffic in a relatively confined airspace. Because of the volume, you have to be always alert to where the traffic is, whether it's following your instructions, the proximity of one aircraft to another, and so on. The same is true in the tower, but to a lesser extent. Yes, if I had to choose, I'd say there is more pressure in Approach. Being able to work both positions, though, varies the job and makes it a lot more interesting.*

CONCLUSION

Those were some of the questions asked to get a better feel of what goes on behind the scenes. Coupled with the observations and comments of various controllers cited in the last chapter, their responses here did shed further light on how things work in those dark and windowless facilities.

Suffice it to say, the Approach/Departure Control function is an essential element in the whole ATC system, regulating the safe and efficient flow of traffic in and around our busiest airports. As I said at the start, chaos would indeed reign were it not for this vital link in the ATC chain.

8

Flight Service Stations

IT'S TIME TO LEAVE THE ENVIRONMENT OF THE IMMEDIATE AIRPORT AND venture into the out-country. As we do, two facilities enter the picture—Flight Service Stations (FSSs) and Air Route Traffic Control Centers. Let's look first at Flight Service because of the role it plays in planning and embarking on a cross-country excursion of any duration.

FSS FUNCTIONS

The FAA states that three major components comprise the air traffic control system: enroute air traffic control; terminal air traffic control; and Flight Service Stations. If we're considering the basic ATC components, the FAA is right. Literally, however, it's wrong. Flight Service Stations are an essential element of the system, but they do not *control* traffic in any way. If their role could be reduced to three principal functions, they would probably be "to inform," "to advise," and "to search."

To inform: A given FSS has a wealth of data immediately available to help the IFR or VFR pilot intelligently plan his flight. Everything is there: local, enroute, and destination weather, winds and temperatures aloft, icing, cloud levels, visibilities, forecasted conditions, outlooks, NOTAMs, military operations—and the list goes on.

To advise: Here is where the FSS is not a controlling agency. It cannot order a VFR pilot not to takeoff or operate in IFR conditions or enter an active Military

Operations Area. It can suggest a course of action to adopt or avoid, such as, "VFR is not recommended," but that's all. It's the pilot's decision to go or not go. With the experience the FSS specialist has in his field, however, coupled with the data available to him, it behooves a pilot to heed his counsel. There are enough pilots who didn't, and aren't around today to regret their indiscretion.

To search: This is a role with which many of us are perhaps not thoroughly familiar. We'll go through the sequence of events later, but let's just say for now that when a pilot on a VFR flight plan fails to close out a flight plan within 30 minutes of his estimated arrival, the FSS takes the first steps to locate the aircraft. No, no one from a Flight Service Station literally goes out and searches for the missing plane, but its people do inititate and participate in what could be an exhaustive as well as expensive operation.

To put a little meat on these somewhat bare bones, the services that make up the three functions could be summarized this way:

- Accepting and closing flight plans

- Conducting preflight weather briefings

- Enroute communicating with VFR pilots

- Assisting pilots in distress

- Disseminating weather information

- Publicizing NOTAMs

- Working with search-and-rescue units in locating missing aircraft

- Monitoring air navigation radio aids

FSS CONSOLIDATION

Back in 1985, there were 294 FSSs across the country. In 1988, the number had dropped to around 200. By mid-1994, only 61 will serve the aviation public.

What's happening is just one facet of an extensive FAA National Airspace System (NAS) Plan designed to advance the whole ATC system to meet the needs of the 1990s, up to the year 2000. In the case of the FSSs, the plan is to automate and consolidate all stations into 61 highly sophisticated facilities, each capable of serving a large geographical area. FIGURE 8-1 depicts the eventual locations of these *Automated Flight Service Stations* (AFSSs), although a few sites haven't been finally determined.

Consolidation does have some drawbacks, most notably the loss of in-person briefings (other than at those 61 airports where an AFSS is on the property). Nothing can replace the advantages of seeing for oneself the radar screens, the

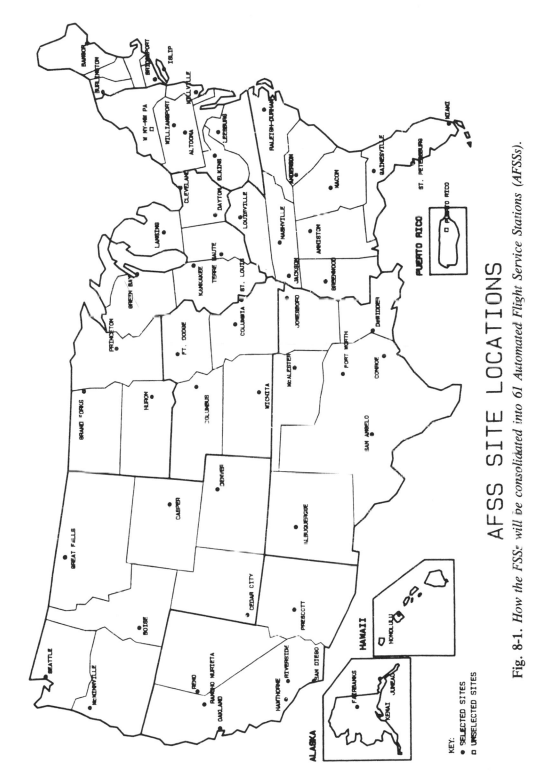

AFSS SITE LOCATIONS

Fig. 8-1. How the FSSs will be consolidated into 61 Automated Flight Service Stations (AFSSs).

charts, the tables, and so on, and discussing conditions face-to-face with a specialist.

However, the pluses are many, including:

- greatly improved automation and computer capabilities that would be cost-prohibitive if 200 or 300 small FSSs were to be so equipped

- faster flight plan filing

- more complete and more real-time weather data

- with the "Model 1" computer, instant weather reports of conditions 25 miles either side of an extended cross-country route, such as from New York to St. Louis

- color radar graphics, similar to but more detailed than those used in TV weather broadcasts

- automatic radar warnings of approaching significant weather

- fewer FSS specialists, meaning lower personnel costs

The minuses are thus few; the pluses many. Still, there have been complaints. With the telephone the only means for most of us to talk to an AFSS, busy signals and waiting times have been sources of pilot irritation. Trying to reach the Macon, Georgia, AFSS once took over 25 minutes just to get a line through to the station. On the other hand, the Columbia, Missouri, AFSS reports an average wait, or answering time, of 27 seconds, and the maximum 7 to 9 minutes.

Of course, the wait depends on the weather conditions and also on the callers. When everything is socked in, all of the briefers are naturally busy. Pilots who don't know what they want, who aren't prepared for the sequence of data they will be given, or who request a briefing on a 10- or 12-leg trip, quite obviously tie up the lines and cause excessive, as well as unnecessary, delays to other callers.

With any new system, there are always start-up problems. The AFSS consolidation is no exception, but the initial birth pangs are being resolved, and a far superior system is rapidly taking shape.

A TYPICAL AFSS: Positions and Staffing

The Columbia, Missouri, AFSS is typical of the majority of consolidated stations. Some are smaller, some larger, but this facility ranks about 15th in activity and is equipped with all of the automated hardware available today. To get an idea of its layout, which is also typical, FIGS. 8-2 and 8-3 may help.

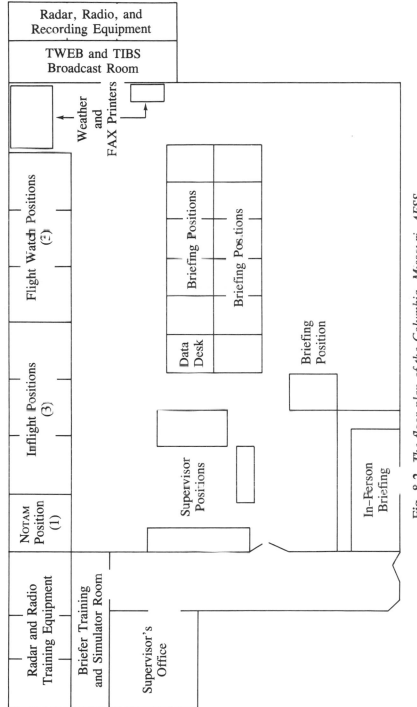

Fig. 8-2. *The floor plan of the Columbia, Missouri, AFSS.*

Fig. 8-3. *A view of some of the telephone briefing positions, looking from the vicinity of the in-person briefing area.*

The positions available for staffing are:

- 13 Briefing
- 3 Flight Watch
- 3 Inflight
- 1 NOTAM update
- 2 Data (to correctly phrase arriving data for computer input)
- 1 Broadcast (Transcribed Weather Broadcasts [TWEBs] and Transcribed Information Briefing Service [TIBS]). TIBS, by the way, is the new acronym, replacing PATWAS—"Pilots Automatic Telephone Weather Answering Service."
- 2 Supervisory

The total personnel headcount at Columbia is 65, and includes

48 Specialists	3 Training Specialists
7 Supervisors	1 Quality Assurance Specialist

1 Assistant Manager	1 Chief
1 Training Manager	1 Administrative Assistant
1 Area Manager	1 Secretary

The peak staffing, usually from 0800 to 1600 local time, is 17 specialists, plus staff members, with an average of about 12 specialists on duty at the same time. That doesn't sound like a lot of people, especially considering that the AFSS is responsible for two-thirds of Missouri and two very aviation-active counties in Kansas. However, automation, plus sophisticated computerization, make the difference. I've been in a number of nonautomated FSSs that had only a relatively small area of responsibility, yet a staffing of 10 to 15 specialists and supervisors was not unusual.

ROAMING THROUGH THE AFSS

With the general layout in mind, let's walk through the AFSS, again remembering that what we see is typical of almost all AFSSs. Also, as we take this tour, suggestions will be offered for pilots using the various services.

The NOTAM Desk

The specialist at this position is responsible for recording and updating all NOTAMs and entering them in the computer so that they are available to the briefers.

Inflight

The *inflight specialist* is the one you reach when you contact the AFSS by radio to open, amend, or close a flight plan, request a weather update, file a flight plane while enroute (not a recommended procedure), or make a position report.

Figure 8-4 shows a series of lights—48 in all. While there are some duplications, each light represents a radio frequency on which you can call the inflight specialist. Including the few duplications (those where two radio outlets use the same frequency but are geographically miles apart), this panel could handle up to 48 frequencies.

"Well, so what?" you say. The "so what" is that when you call in, the light representing the frequency you're using blinks, but it blinks *only* while you're talking. The instant you release the mike button, the blinking stops. Perhaps the specialist heard your call, but if he's otherwise occupied and didn't see the blinking, he'll have no way of knowing on which frequency he should reply. So you get no response.

Fig. 8-4. *These 48 lights represent a maximum of 48 frequencies the inflight position(s) has to monitor.*

The point is this—a point specialists stressed time after time: When you call, state the frequency you're using and your actual, or approximate, geographical location.

For example, you're at or over St. Joseph, Missouri, about 140 miles northwest of Columbia. The St. Joe Remote Communications Outlet (RCO) frequency to the AFSS is 122.3. Sedalia, Missouri, 45 miles west of Columbia, also has a 122.3 RCO. If you call in and merely say, "Columbia Radio, Cherokee Eight Five One Five November," the specialist, who may be talking to another aircraft, is unlikely to spot the blinking light and will have no way of knowing what frequency you're on.

But you do better the next time. Your call goes, "Columbia Radio, Cherokee Eight Five One Five November, on 122.3." That's more helpful, but are you at St. Joe or Sedalia? The specialist still can't tell, if he didn't see the blinking light.

So try it one more time: "Columbia Radio, Cherokee Eight Five One Five November, on 122.3 at St.Joe." Now, even if he missed the light, he'll know which transmitter to activate to acknowledge your call.

The format, then, is "Blank Radio" (it's always "Radio"—not "Flight Service" in these calls), aircraft type, N-number, frequency, and location. Now you'll get a response.

I said a moment ago that you could file a flight plan while enroute by contacting the inflight position. That's true, but again, it's not a recommended procedure. It takes up air time and possibly blocks out others who are trying to get a call through.

As an example, while observing the one Columbia specialist on duty at the time, I noted that he spent at least 10 minutes briefing an airborne pilot who then wanted to file an IFR flight plan. Both requests were thoughtless and most likely unnecessary. These were details the pilot should have handled on the ground. Meanwhile, the specialist wasn't available to respond to other calls that were coming in.

Another point worth noting: You're on a VFR cross-country, with or without a filed flight plan. And you have or haven't been in contact with a Center for enroute traffic advisories. Whatever the combination, you'd like to be sure that someone down there knows where you are and has an immediately retrievable record of your call. So you get on the air to the nearest AFSS and make a brief position report: "Jonesboro Radio, Cherokee Eight Five One Five November position report. Over Walnut Ridge at 1510, VFR to Tupelo."

Now, if a problem arises and you go down before having time to dial 7700 or contact another facility, the search for you that the AFSS initiates will be limited to the territory between Walnut Ridge and Tupelo. That one position report could be the lifesaver, should you end up in Farmer Brown's cow pasture.

Being in contact with a Center as you cruise along is an excellent practice, but Center exists primarily for IFR operations and is not designed to keep an enroute progress check of VFR aircraft. The AFSS does, however, if you periodically call in. Like insurance, you may never need it, but that one call is a small price to pay for the additional coverage it provides.

A final feature of the inflight position: VHF Direction Finder (DF) units that come into play when a pilot is lost and wants help in establishing his position. The one in FIG. 8-5 is an older vacuum-tube DF, while FIG. 8-6 pictures a digital DF. These will soon be replaced, however, by a fully computerized system.

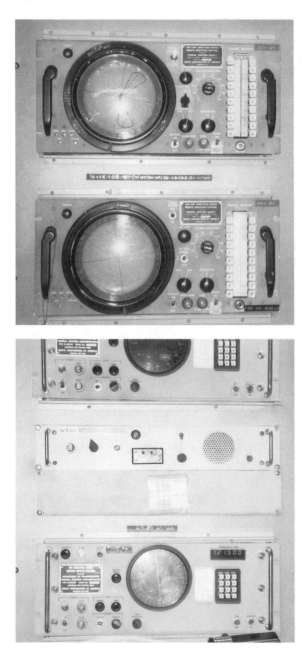

Fig. 8-5. *This is the older, vacuum-tube Direction Finder and strobe.*

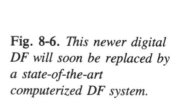

Fig. 8-6. *This newer digital DF will soon be replaced by a state-of-the-art computerized DF system.*

What happens is this: When you establish radio contact with "inflight" and announce your predicament, the specialist will ask you to transmit a signal on your frequency by keying the mike continuously for five to 10 seconds, concluding with your aircraft N-number.

150

As you do this, the two DF strobes search for the point of transmission, just as the ADF (Automatic Direction Finding) needle in the aircraft searches for a transmitting NDB (Non-Directional Beacon) on the ground. The point at which the two strobes intersect identifies the aircraft's position. The position is then manually plotted on a Sectional chart and its location reported to the pilot. If the pilot then requests, the specialist will give him headings to fly until he is reoriented.

The two DF outlets (FIG. 8-7) of course, have to be separated geographically to permit a triangulation. If both were located at the same site, they would merely point to the direction of the aircraft but not establish its position along that line. A *DF fix* is possible only when the two outlets are far enough apart to permit the strobes to intersect.

A *DF fix* ("Tell me where I am") or a *DF Steer* ("Tell me where I am and lead me to the airport") are just two more of the services the AFSS provides— and so far, we've only discussed one position.

Flight Watch

Moving along, the next positions are *Flight Watch*, often referred to as "EFAS"—Enroute Flight Advisory Service. You're cruising down an airway and would like an updated, detailed report on the weather ahead. If you've been getting advisories from Center, contact the controller with whom you've been talking and advise him that you're temporarily leaving his frequency to call Flight Watch (FIG. 8-8). (That, by the way, is a procedure always to keep in mind. Never leave one facility to go to another without informing the first facility. Otherwise, while you're gone, that controller might try to reach you.)

With Center advised, tune to 122.0, the common low-altitude Flight Watch frequency across the country. Then call the nearest AFSS, addressing it by name and including your aircraft identification as well as the VOR closest to your position: "Denver Flight Watch, Cherokee Eight Five One Five November, Pueblo VOR". If you're not sure which AFSS is responsible for the area you're in, address the call just to "Flight Watch", again indicating the VOR station you are near; "Flight Watch, Cherokee Eight Five One Five November, Durango VOR". Once contact has been established, go ahead with your message.

I say "message," because, indeed, that's what it might be. Flight Watch gives information, but it also wants information from pilots. I'm speaking here, of course, of PIREPs (Pilot Reports). Charts, maps, and radar graphics are useful; nothing, however, replaces reports of actual real-time conditions that pilots are experiencing. Flight Watch will communicate PIREPs it has received and asks that we offer one in return.

Fig. 8-8. *The Flight Watch specialist, with his array of weather charts and data.*

What makes up a PIREP?

- Type of aircraft
- Position
- Time (UTC—not local)
- Conditions you are reporting, as clouds, visibility, precipitation, icing, turbulence, etc.
- Whether in or out of clouds
- Altitude
- Duration of conditions you are reporting

Fig. 8-7. *A technician performs maintenance on a VHF Direction Finder antenna.* (FAA)

Be sure to report the conditions in accordance with the approved definitions in the *AIM*, Chapter 6. For instance, turbulence in a Cessna 152 might seem severe, but by definition, be only moderate or light. Misuse of terms because of unfamiliarity with them can easily mislead others to whom the PIREP is subsequently relayed.

Perhaps a question has already come to mind. If an AFSS has an inflight position, why call Flight Watch, or vice versa? For one, inflight, as we've seen, has responsibilities other than just reporting weather, and the weather he has is not as complete or detailed as Flight Watch's. Weather is Flight Watch Specialist's sole responsibility. He has nothing to do with flight plans, position reports, or the like. He's thus much more likely to be available for the specific weather-related information you want. He is also more thoroughly trained in meteorology than those manning the inflight positions, so he is better equipped to read, interpret, and determine potential weather conditions than inflight. Inflight can certainly be of help, but Flight Watch is the AFSS's specialist in short-range and real-time weather.

Briefing

The next function is briefing. The briefing positions are located in the center of the room (refer back to FIG. 8-3). Here are the people you talk to when you telephone the AFSS. With each position equipped with a computer screen, keyboard, and radar display (FIG. 8-9), the specialist has a wealth of data at his fingertips, including local conditions where you are, enroute and destination weather, ceilings, visibility, winds and temperatures aloft, icing information, forecasts, PIREPs, NOTAMs—just about anything you could want to plan a flight.

At this point, a few words about preparation before calling the AFSS and the sequence of information you can expect to receive are in order.

First, the matter of preparation. Many specialists have commented on the lack of information pilots initially supply and/or the disorganization of the information. The briefer, or specialist, will give you what you ask for, but he can't read your mind. If you're in Albuquerque and want the weather in Salt Lake City, that's what you'll get, but no more, unless you request it. The FAA's latest pamphlet, *How To Get A Good Weather Briefing* (FAA-P-8740-30B), recommends the following sequence of information that you should volunteer at the outset of the call:

1. Qualifications, as student, private, commercial, and if you are instrument-rated.

2. Type of flight—VFR or IFR.

3. Aircraft N-number, or your name, if you're not sure what plane you'll be flying.

Fig. 8-9. *Two briefing positions.*

4. Aircraft type.

5. Departure point.

6. Route of flight.

7. Destination or first point of landing.

8. Proposed altitude(s).

9. Estimated departure and enroute times (ETD and ETE).

10. Type of briefing desired: Standard; Abbreviated; Outlook.

A Standard briefing is just what it says. The specialist will give you all the data pertinent to your route of flight and proposed altitude. If you've had a Standard briefing and only want an update or certain specific information, ask for an Abbreviated briefing. The Outlook should be requested when your departure is six hours or more from the time of the briefing. In this case, however, call back and get a Standard or Abbreviated update on the current conditions.

Assuming you've asked for a Standard briefing, the specialist will give you the information in this sequence:

1. Adverse weather conditions.

2. A synopsis of existing fronts and other weather systems along your line of flight. If conditions are obviously unfavorable, based on items 1 and 2, the briefer will probably state, "VFR is not recommended." Otherwise, or if you still want more information, he'll continue.

3. A summary of current weather along the route of flight, based on surface observations, radar observations, and PIREPs.

4. A summary of forecasted enroute weather.

5. Detailed forecasted destination weather.

6. A summary of forecasted winds at your proposed altitude range, and if requested, temperature information.

7. NOTAMs that could affect your flight.

8. Additional information, such as active MOAs or MTRs in your line of flight, or information in response to your questions.

As a suggestion, before calling an AFSS, put these main headings on a piece of paper, leaving space between each for notes:

1. Significant weather

2. Enroute weather

3. Destination weather

4. Winds/temperatures

5. NOTAMs

6. Other

Now you'll know what's coming and in what order—you'll just fill in the blanks.

Filing the Flight Plan. Before the days of FSS consolidation, it was recommended that you get the briefing, hang up the phone, replot the flight as necessary, based on the briefing, and then call back to file the flight plan. That advice was, and generally is, logical in those nonautomated FSSs.

It's a different story, however, with the AFSSs. As you're giving the briefer the initial information of VFR or IFR, aircraft type and N-number, and so on, he is entering that data in the computer. Unless the weather he reports will materially affect your route of flight, ask the briefer to file the flight plan. As you give the balance of the information required on a flight plan form, speak slowly enough and clearly enough, as one AFSS manager put it, "so that the specialist writing/typing the info can 'absorb and digest' it." Doing as the manager suggests saves time, especially if the specialist doesn't have to ask you to repeat data that he wasn't able to understand or that you said too rapidly.

Afterward, and based on the briefing, do whatever replotting is necessary. If your route, altitude, or enroute or estimated arrival times are going to change to any measurable degree, just correct it when you radio the AFSS to open the flight plan. This way, you save another telephone call, possibly a wait, and you won't be duplicating information that the original briefer had already entered in the computer.

Another means of filing a flight plan offered by the AFSSs is *Fast File*. When making the initial telephone contact, a recording will read off the menus of service available, including Fast File, and the subsequent number to dial. When you do, all that's necessary is to give the data in the exact sequence of the Flight Plan form. Everything is recorded and stored in the AFSS's computer, ready for reference when you make the radio call, requesting that the flight plan be opened.

A suggestion made by the McAlester, Oklahoma, AFSS is worth noting. In essence, the comment was that Fast File is heavily used in areas with large volumes of traffic and when the AFSS is very busy. In areas of lower traffic or on less busy days, the preferred method is to establish contact with a specialist so that he can copy the flight plan directly, ask questions that he might need to ask, and determine where the caller can be reached over the next few minutes should a discrepancy of some sort be discovered.

Going back to what I said earlier, the AFSS is not a controlling agency. If the briefer observes that "VFR is not recommended," the decision to go or not go is yours. The fact that the recommendation was made, however, is recorded as part of the briefing, just in case. . . . The briefer has done his job, but if you want to fly in the face of knowledgeable advice, well, it's your neck.

As somewhat of an aside, when you or I receive a briefing or file a flight plan, we're not competing with the air carriers. Almost all airlines have their own weather sources and dispatchers, and their flight plans are filed directly with the originating Center. Even more, flight plans for daily scheduled flights are stored in Center's computer and retrieved prior to the scheduled flight departure. In essence, then, the service we're discussing is for general aviation IFR and VFR operations—so let's use it.

Closing the Flight Plan. Failure to close a flight plan after landing is one of the more common and costly pilot oversights. Admittedly, it's an easy thing to forget. You're tired after a few hours in the air; friends, family, or business associates are waiting for you; you're in a hurry to get one of the last rental cars;

you're a student and your instructor is anxious to hear how things went on your first cross-country; you just want the airplane tied down or hangared so you can get home. Whatever, you forget that final responsibility. The last line on the flight plan form says, in capital letters, "CLOSE FLIGHT PLAN WITH _____FSS ON ARRIVAL."

To minimize the chance for oversight, immediately radio the nearest AFSS, if possible reach it on the ground, when you come to a halt on the ramp. Otherwise, make a mental note to pick up a phone as soon as you're in the terminal or FBO's shop, and simply dial the nation-wide number: 1-800-WX BRIEF. Dont's let outside interferences distract you. The results could be costly. Which leads to . . .

What Happens When a Flight Plan is Not Closed. The following is the sequence of events when you file a flight plan but don't close it out:

1. On departure, you call AFSS "A" to open the flight plan.
2. The inflight specialist sends the flight plan to the AFSS which is responsible for the area in which your destination airport is located. Let's call it AFSS "B". All that is transmitted is your aircraft type, N-number, destination, and ETA.
3. You land at your destination, or some other airport, and fail to close out the flight plan with any FSS.
4. Thirty minutes after your ETA, the computer in AFSS "B" flashes the flight plan data sent by AFSS "A", indicating you are overdue and haven't closed the flight plan.
5. AFSS "B" sends a query to AFSS "A" to determine if you had actually departed or been delayed.
6. AFSS "A" calls your departure airport to verify your actual departure.
7. Since you did depart, AFSS "A" so notifies "B", and sends to "B" the balance of your flight plan information—route of flight, fuel on board, number of passengers, your name and address, and so on.
8. "B" calls the tower or FBO and your intended destination to see if you landed.
9. If so, and your aircraft is located, end of search. Let's assume, however, that you landed at a different airport than originally intended, or that neither you nor your plane can be located at your planned destination. The search then goes on.
10. One hour after your ETA, AFSS "B" initiates an INREQ (Information Requested). This goes to all FAA facilities along your route of flight, including Center and towers to see if any facility had heard from you. If one has, the search can be focused on the territory between your last reporting point and destination. A copy of the INREQ is also usually sent to the applicable search-and-rescue unit, alerting it to the possibility of a downed aircraft.

11. If there has been no recorded or immediately available evidence of any enroute contact, all AFSSs along the route of flight begin telephoning every airport 50 miles either side of the route.
12. If these actions draw a blank, an ALNOT (Alert Notice) is sent to every FAA facility along your route.
13. Each facility does further checking, such as playing back tapes to find a record of radio contact with you. The search-and-rescue unit also alerts the Civil Air Patrol. The Air Force may enter the investigation, contacting family or business associates to determine if they have heard from you or if you had indicated any possible route deviation before departing. All FSSs in the area broadcast over the VORs each hour that an aircraft has been lost and asks pilots to monitor 121.5 (the emergency frequency) for an activated emergency locator transmitter (ELT).
14. The physical search begins.

See what problems can be caused by a simple oversight? In one case, hardly exceptional, an AFSS made over 100 phone calls to airports along a pilot's route before he was located safely at an airport other than his planned destination. His only excuse? He just forgot.

All of this only emphasizes the value of making periodic position reports to an AFSS. If you should have a problem, the search is narrowed to the area between last reporting point and your destination.

Today's aircraft are dependable beasts, but things do go wrong. How much better to keep people down there informed of your progress than to fly merrily along and perhaps flounder for hours in an obscure corn field while others are searching thousands of square miles for a small speck on the ground.

Filing to the First Stop. You've got a six-hour journey ahead of you, but plan to make a pit stop about midway. Should you file a flight plan to the final destination, or to the midpoint airport? The answer is rather apparent: File to the next point of landing, no matter how many legs the trip may have.

Say you leave Point A at 1200 and file to your destination, Point C, with an ETA of 1800 hours. Thirty minutes out, the prop grinds down to windmilling status, you hit a furrow in the forced landing, and end up on your back. It's now 1230, but it will be 1830 before the AFSS at Point C even starts asking questions about you. The more intensive wheels of inquiry won't begin to roll until 1900. That's 6 ½ hours trapped upside down in a bent aircraft.

If you had filed to the midway point, Point B, with a 1500 ETA, the search would have started at 1530—a full three hours earlier. Also, the search efforts would be limited to the area between Points A and B, thus further enhancing the chances of rescue and survival.

Caution and wisdom do contribute to pilot longevity.

Transcribed Services

The next stop on the tour of the AFSS is the small room (FIG. 8-10) where two transcribed services are recorded: Transcribed Weather Broadcasts (TWEBs) and Telephone Information Briefing Service (TIBS).

TWEBs. These are continuous broadcasts, on certain VORs, that summarize the current weather over a 400-mile radius of the VOR. VORs broadcasting TWEBs are indicated by a small square in the lower right corner of the VOR

Fig. 8-10. *The area for TWEB and TIBS recordings, referred to as the "broadcast room." This position can also be used for briefing purposes when conditions require additional telephone personnel.*

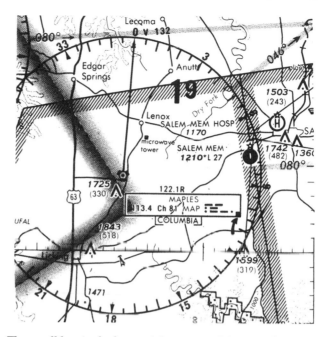

Fig. 8-11. *The small box in the lower right corner of the identification box indicates that TWEBs are broadcast over the VOR.*

identification box (FIG. 8-11). At some locations you can call the recording by telephone. Phone numbers are listed in the back of the *A/FD*.

TIBS. This AFSS service is similar to what has been known as PATWAS (Pilots Automatic Telephone Weather Answering Service) at the nonautomated FSSs, but covers many more geographical areas.

To be more specific, once the caller has reached the AFSS and listened to the recorded menu of service available, he dials 201, the universal number to access TIBS. Another recording then tells the caller what subsequent 200-series number to dial for the desired information. Those numbers range from 202 to 224, although all may not be currently in use. What the caller will hear is a transcript of the meteorological conditions within a 50-mile radius of the location in which he is interested. For example, at the Columbia FSS, by dialing the following numbers, except 202, 203, 211, 214, and 215, the weather data at the following locations will be summarized:

202 Weather synopsis	206 Springfield
203 Thunderstorm activity	207 Joplin
204 Columbia	208 Cape Girardeau
205 Kansas City	209 St. Louis

Under the PATWAS system, the caller is limited to the conditions within a 50nm radius of the FSS location. TIBS, however, offers a much wider range of locations, plus other pertinent data, simply by dialing the applicable number(s).

Despite the benefits of TIBS, it should not be a substitute for a standard briefing. Everything may be fine at departure and destination points, but what about the great in-between? TIBS won't really tell you that. What about VORs that may be out, runway construction at the enroute airports, active MOAs on the route of flight? TIBS provides area weather information and can be helpful in arriving at a go no-go decision. If things look good, fine. But get the details from a briefing specialist.

Fig. 8-12. *The desk where pilots get in-person briefings.*

In-Person Briefing

The final stop on the AFSS tour is the *in-person briefing* position (FIG. 8-12). Here the pilot can see first-hand the weather radar displays, the computerized forecasts, winds aloft printouts, and all of the information the telephone briefer provides. This type of briefing can be more instructive, particularly when conditions are marginal or questionable. It's sometimes difficult to visualize things over the telephone. However, this advantage is being lost with consolidation, except for those operating where an AFSS is located.

CONCLUSION

If one term could sum up the value of Flight Service to the VFR pilot, it would probably be "insurance." Indeed, the services available are optional. We don't have to get a briefing; we don't have to file a flight plan; we don't have to make periodic position reports; we don't have to get weather updates from Flight Watch; we don't have to offer PIREPs; and except for FAA test purposes, we don't have to know anything about Flight Service, what it does, or what it offers.

But isn't that a little shortsighted? Here's a facility with a wealth of information at its disposal and one that could literally be a lifesaver in an emergency. There are those among us, however, who don't know what services are available, or how to use them. And there are those who consider themselves above the need for briefings, filing a flight plan, and the rest. Perhaps—just perhaps—this chapter has persuaded the nonusers that taking advantage of Flight Service is simply common sense.

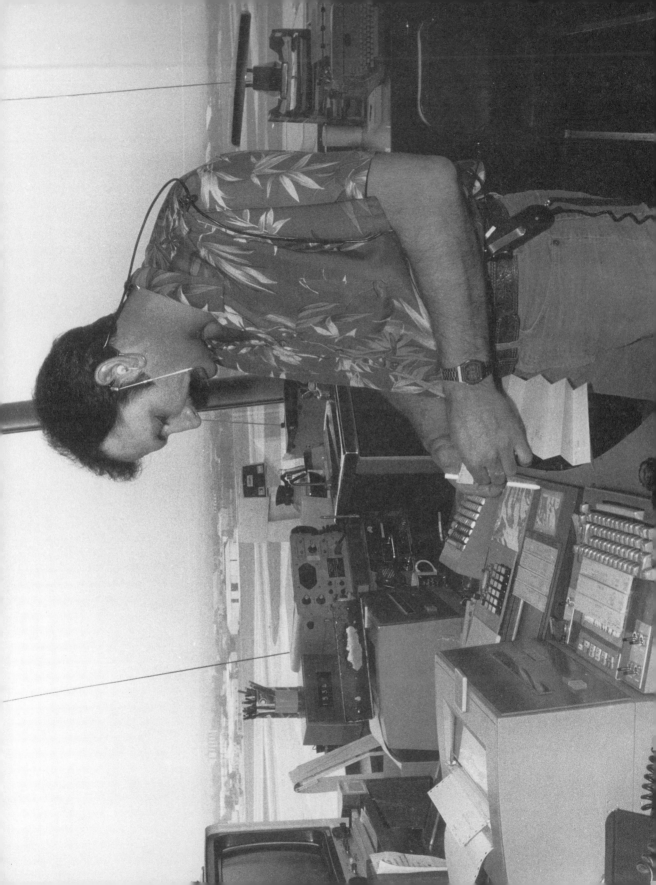

9

The Air Route
Traffic Control Center

W E'VE LEFT THE IMMEDIATE AIRPORT VICINITY AND ARE OFF TO A DISTANT destination. Well, it may not be "distant," but it's a cross-country excursion of some sort. We now have at our disposal one more FAA facility to help us along the way: The Air Route Traffic Control Center (ARTCC).

In one respect, "at our disposal" is somewhat of a misstatement, because "Center" exists primarily for IFR, not VFR, operations. Its first responsibility is to control IFR flight plan aircraft, ensure proper separation, monitor the aircraft's fix-to-fix and point-to-point progress, issue advisories, and sequence the aircraft both enroute and into the terminal environment. Thus, in marginal weather conditions or when the volume of IFR traffic is heavy, Center may have no time to provide advisory services to pilots operating under VFR. Those are considered to be additional services and are at the discretion of the individual controller, depending on his workload.

Barring such situations, Center can play an important role in enhancing the safety of VFR flight. Advising us of other traffic in our vicinity, alerting us if we should inadvertently (or perhaps carelessly) venture into an active MOA, offering vectors around potentially severe weather conditions, leading us to an airport in an emergency—these are just a few examples of the help Center is capable of providing.

Unfortunately, though, many VFR pilots are reluctant to request the services that are available. The reasons are various: The concept that Center is only for the big boys who drive the wide-bodies or the high-time IFR pros; lack of knowledge of what Center does and how it functions; afraid of being a nuisance to controllers who have enough to do without worrying about a Cessna 152 or Cherokee 140; uncertainty of how to communicate with the facility; reluctance to get on the air and perhaps display ignorance, make mistakes, or sound sort of stupid.

Whatever the case, whatever the cause, it's too bad, because Center not only will but *wants* to help the VFR pilot, whenever its workload permits. Controllers across the country have so stated and the FAA so encourages that help. Accordingly, a review of what a Center is, what it does, and how the VFR pilot can avail himself of the available service might diminish this reluctance.

CENTER LOCATIONS AND AIRSPACE RESPONSIBILITIES

Currently, 20 Centers blanket the continental United States, plus one each in Alaska, San Juan, Honolulu, and Guam. Those within the "48" are:

Albuquerque	Houston	Minneapolis
Atlanta	Indianapolis	New York
Boston	Jacksonville	Oakland
Chicago	Kansas City	Salt Lake City
Cleveland	Los Angeles	Seattle
Denver	Memphis	Washington
Fort Worth	Miami	

FIGURE 9-1 depicts all 24 Centers and the airspace for which each is responsible. As the figure indicates, any given Center has a fair piece of airspace to control, the typical Center being responsible for approximately 100,000 square miles or more. To service such an expanse, the geography is first divided into *areas*, and each area then subdivided into *sectors*, with two controllers and an assistant controller usually handling a sector.

A logical question is how a Center, physically located perhaps several hundred miles from an aircraft, can maintain radio contact and radar coverage. The answer, of course, is through many remoted air-ground radio outlets and a fewer number of remoted radar antennas that are connected to the Center via microwave links and landlines. The microwave signal is essentially the primary radar carrier, while landlines serve as backups in the event of a microwave outage.

FIGURE 9-2 illustrates the Kansas City Center airspace and the various sector boundaries, as well as the radio frequencies in the sectors. From left to right, the extreme western limit just touches the southeastern corner of Colorado, and the eastern limit reaches almost to Indiana. The square boxes designate the Remote Communications Air/Ground (RCAG) locations and their radio frequencies.

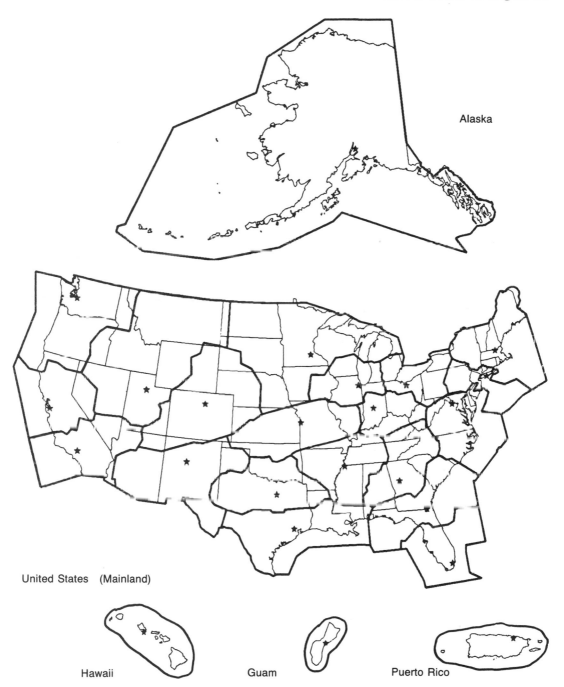

Alaska

United States   (Mainland)

Hawaii

Guam

Puerto Rico

Fig. 9-1. *Locations of the Air Route Traffic Control Centers (starred) and their geographical areas of responsibility.*

Figure 9-2 also illustrates the changing of frequencies as you move across the airspace. Going from sector to sector means that you're leaving one controller's area and entering that of another. As this occurs, the first controller will call you and advise you to change from his frequency to the one monitored by the next controller. This is the *handoff* process, which is very similar to the steps Approach takes when it transfers the monitoring of an aircraft from the terminal area to a Center. The only major difference is that one handoff is between facilities, while the other is between sector controllers, separated, perhaps, by only a few feet. (We'll get into the details of how this is done a little later, as well as brief examples of the correct communication procedures.)

Something else FIG. 9-2 illustrates: You'll note that several of the sectors have two or more frequencies back to Center. As the aircraft moves out of the range of one, the controller will, for example, tell the pilot to "Change to my frequency, 134.9." This simply means that the pilot will be talking to the same controller but on another frequency. The key to what's happening is the word *my*. Be alert to that, because it will have some effect on what you say when you make the change and re-establish radio contact. (This, too, we'll review at the proper time.)

HOW A CENTER IS ORGANIZED

Not all Centers are identical in physical organization, but the one in Kansas City (actually Olathe, Kansas, about 20 miles southwest of Kansas City, Missouri) is typical in terms of size, staffing, and layout. Figure 9-3 is its position layout, but it does require a bit of explanation.

At the extreme left, you'll see the letters "A" to "D." These identify the four rows of controller positions and their related radar/radio/telephone equipment.

The rows are then divided into geographic airspace areas, designated here as Flint Hills, Trails, Ozark, Prairie, and Rivers/Gateway.

The next breakdown is the division of areas into sectors, with each sector responsible for the control of high (HI) altitude traffic, 24,000 feet and up, or low (LO) altitude, 23,000 feet and down. You may recall in the Approach/Departure Control chapter that traffic out of the Kansas City TCA is handled by Sectors 40, 42, 46, and 48 at Center. These appear in Row C, with the geography each covers identified below the position boxes: IRK-LO, ANX-LO, BUM-LO, STJ-LO, and FOB-LO. IRK is the code for Kirksville, ANX— the Naploeon VOR, BUM—Butler, Mo., and STJ—St. Joseph. Sector 44 handles FOE—Forbes Air Force Base, about 60 miles to the west in Topeka, Kansas. The circles around the sector numbers designate the physical location of the radarscope, also called the *Planned Visual Display* (PVD).

The enlargement of a typical position in FIG. 9-4 explains the alphanumerics to a degree, but, again, some decoding is necessary.

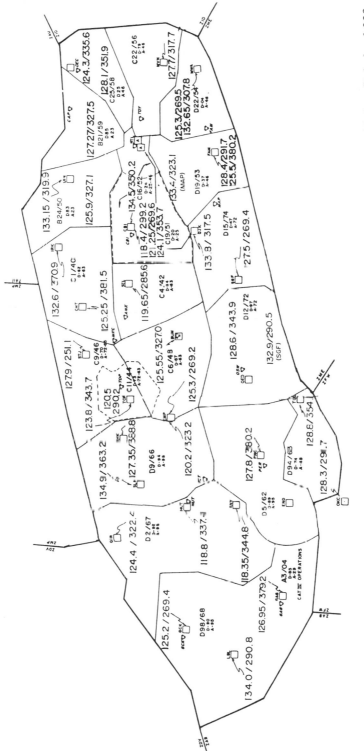

Fig. 9-2. This figure outlines the various sectors and their frequencies within Kansas City Center's airspace at and below flight level 230. The squares identify remote communication facilities. VOR locations are also represented by what appears to be small triangles.

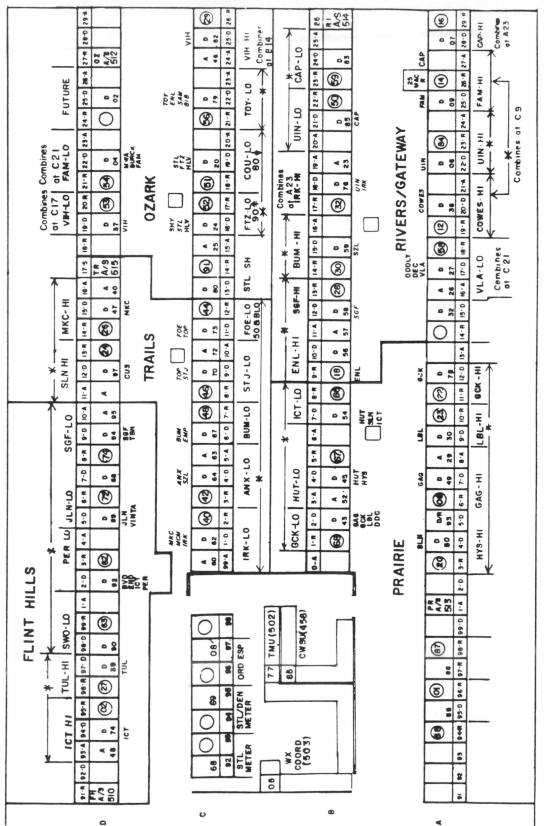

Fig. 9-3. The floor plan of a typical ARTCC.

The codes at the top, the Bay Header, represent the VORs—MKC, MCM, and IRK—in the sector.

"A" stands for an *air traffic assistant* (commonly referred to as the *A-Side*), who is basically in a learning capacity. He's been through the FAA's initial screening course at Oklahoma City, but has been assigned to the Center for further and intensive on-site training.

Among his tasks as a trainee is to remove the computer-processed IFR flight strips from the printers and hand-deliver the strips to the appropriate sector position. If a Flight Service Station wanted to correct or update a filed flight plan, the FSS would call the A-Side's telephone dial-code (60, in the IRK-LO sector), and the A-Side would manually amend the flight plan data.

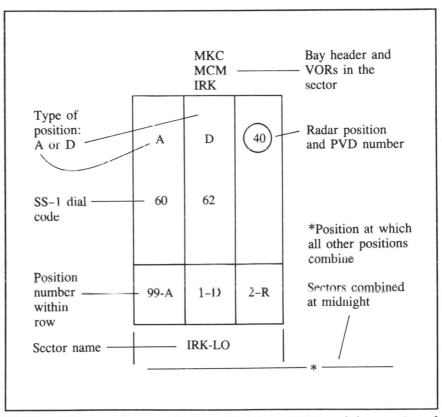

Fig. 9-4. *A blow-up of a controller's position from* FIG. 9-3, *and the meaning of the various numbers, symbols, and letters.*

In essence, the A-Side is an assistant to one or more sector controllers, although the layout chart shows one "A" and one "D" at almost every position. Actually, only one A-Side may serve up to six "Ds" and/or controllers who have reached the "full performance level" (FPLs), carrying out many of the duties that would otherwise divert the "Ds" and FPLs from their primary responsibility of air traffic control. The A-Side, however, never talks to an aircraft until he has completed a rigid formal training program at the Center and has demonstrated, through simulated exercises, the basic traffic-controlling skills. At that point, he is advanced to a D position.

"D" stands for a *developmental controller* (also called a *D-Side*)—one who may be on the radio and controlling the traffic within his sector. But, and an important "but", he or she does this in conjunction with an FPL controller or an instructor. Whichever it is, one of the FPLs is listening and watching the D, monitoring every word and action.

Not being radar-certificated at this stage, the D is often referred to as a *manual controller*. He or she is qualified, or in the process of being qualified, to handle IFR aircraft in nonradar conditions, such as when an aircraft is operating at an altitude below radar coverage. In these instances, the only means of separating and controlling the aircraft is verbally and by following a strict set of procedures that apply here and when an actual radar outage occurs. The type of control is thus referred to as *manual*, or *non-radar*, as opposed to *radar*.

The developmental is a former A-Side who has advanced to the more responsible position but has not yet attained the full performance level status. On average, it takes about three years, from start to finish, to reach that FPL level.

The "2-R" locates the position of the sector's radarscope—its PVD—and the FPL radar controller.

A further word should be said about the D position. Yes, this is where a developmental goes for on-the-job training, but it doesn't mean that a developmental is always at the position. On a given day, it could be an FPL, a radar-trained developmental, or a developmental fresh from the Center's on-site training program. The level of controller that mans the position is determined by need, staffing, or personnel scheduling.

The "SS-1 (Selective Signaling) DIAL CODE" is the direct-line number that a controller or outside facility, such as Approach, would use to reach a specific sector and its A or D specialist. In the illustration, to contact the A or D in Sector 40, the caller would merely dial 60 or 62, respectively, and be directly connected to the position.

"99-A" and "1-D" identify the position numbers in the row. For maintenance or a telephone outage, the problem would be reported as at Position 99-A or 1-D.

Finally, the horizontal line with the asterisk defines the sectors that are combined during the midnight shift when traffic is at its ebb.

One other set of functions not yet mentioned are those to the left between Rows B and C in FIG. 9-3. "STL METER," "STL/DEN METER," and "ORD ESP" ("ESP" means enroute spacing) are computerized displays of all aircraft that are going to land at St. Louis, Denver, and O'Hare. Rather than allowing 20 or 30 planes to deluge a given terminal at the same time, an orderly flow of arriving traffic is established by *metering*.

Based on terminal weather conditions, runways in use, or other local factors, the maximum number of arrivals per hour that the airport can accommodate is established. The Center computer then assigns each inbound flight a specific time by which it is to arrive over a given fix—one that is located well outside the terminal's Approach Control airspace. If the aircraft fails to arrive at the fix within the period two minutes before to two minutes after that assigned time, or it doesn't appear that it will, the sector controller handling the flight will instruct the pilot to speed up, slow down, or take what other action is necessary to slot the aircraft into the planned arrival pattern.

The metered displays of the aircraft for which that controller is responsible also appear on his sector PVD—but only those aircraft. He's thus expected to take unilateral action to maintain the precise time schedule of flights into the terminal area.

In the case of O'Hare, the Chicago Center handles that traffic, but Kansas City tries to ensure the proper enroute spacing of ORD-bound aircraft in its airspace so that there won't be an unnecessary build-up once the traffic is handed over to Chicago. The same principle applies to traffic going into Denver.

The overall coordination, however, is the responsibility of the *Traffic Management Unit* (TMU). These specialists are constantly monitoring the meters to ensure that the computer-generated spacing and timing are being met. When discrepancies occur, it's up to the TMU, through the sector controllers, to ensure compliance with the designed arrival flow.

The other function in this complex is the CWSU—*Center Weather Service Unit*. The Planned Visual Displays at the controllers' positions in a Center are all computer-generated. Thus, from a weather point of view, what the controller sees on his scope is only a series of lines, some close-set, some more widely separated, superimposed with an "H" (Heavy) to identify thunderstorm intensity. Unlike the terminal ARTS II or III radar that produces a much more realistic image of the weather, these lines alone are really of minimal help in guiding a pilot around or through conditions that might exist out there.

The CWSU, however, has a real radar picture of the weather, with the various degrees of thunderstorm activity in color. Using this and other available data, the CWSU briefs the controller supervisors twice a day on what's happening and what to expect. Then, if severe weather or turbulence develops between briefings, the CSWU issues a typed General Information (GI) message that goes to all position printers, alerting controllers to current disturbances, where they are, and the degree of reported intensity.

So that's the overall layout of a typical Center, illustrated in part by FIG. 9-5. Other Centers may have different layouts, but the functions are the same, and, basically, so is the hardware. I say "basically," because advances under the National Airspace System Plan are coming rapidly, and not all Centers receive the same new equipment at the same time.

USING CENTER'S SERVICES

What happens when we contact a Center for advisories, and why is it to the VFR pilot's advantage to utilize the services available? Let's review a few of

Fig. 9-5. *Looking down one row of controller positions.*

the procedures we should follow, as well as certain controller recommendations, particularly for VFR pilots.

Determining the Correct Center Frequency

- If you've filed a flight plan, ask the FSS specialist what the frequency is for your initial route of flight.

- If you forget or didn't ask the FSS, get the frequency from Clearance Delivery, Ground Control, or the tower.

- If departing an ARSA or TCA and are not handed off to Center, ask Departure Control.

- If you're enroute and want to establish contact with Center for the first time, merely radio the nearest FSS or Flight Watch, giving your aircraft identification, position, and altitude, and then make the request.

These alternatives are listed because it's not always easy to determine the correct frequency for the area you're in. The *A/FD* and Enroute Low Altitude Charts give a general idea, but, as the Kansas City Center sector-frequency chart illustrated, a given sector could have two or more frequencies. Furthermore, how many of us have a sector-frequency chart on board? It's not something routinely distributed to the public.

Calling Center for Advisories

Assume there has been no handoff from Approach or another Center. You decide enroute that you want traffic advisories, so you get on the mike and call a Center for the first time. A point controllers continually stress is do nothing more than establish contact in that initial call. Don't volunteer any information other than the aircraft type and N-number:

> Kansas City Center, Cherokee Eight Five One Five November.
> (Period!)

A couple of reasons for this: the controller may be listening to an aircraft on another frequency and won't hear your call, or if he's not on the air with someone else, once he hears your call, he'll be doing some things related to it before responding. For one, he'll take a quick glance at the flight strips before him to see if he has one with your N-number. If not (and he won't on a VFR flight), he'll reach for a blank flight strip and write down the N-number. That done, he'll acknowledge your call and will be ready to talk to you. Now is the time to give the rest of the information he needs and to make your request:

Ctr:	*Cherokee Eight Five One Five November, Kansas City Center. Go ahead.*
You:	Center, Cherokee Eight Five One Five November is over Butler at seven thousand five hundred, VFR to West Memphis. Request advisories.
Ctr:	*Cherokee One Five November, Roger. Squawk one seven zero one and ident.*
You:	Roger, one seven zero one. Cherokee One Five November.
Ctr:	*Cherokee One Five November, radar contact. Altimeter two niner three five.*
You:	Two niner three five. Cherokee One Five November.

From here on, Center will advise you of traffic that is or might be in your line of flight:

Ctr:	*Cherokee One Five November, traffic nine o'clock, three miles, a Cessna 172, altitude seven thousand five hundred.*
You:	Negative contact. Looking. Cherokee One Five November.

If, in a couple of minutes, you do spot the 172, tell Center:

You:	Center, Cherokee One Five November has the traffic.
Ctr:	*Cherokee One Five November, roger. Thank you.*

Controllers like such information. It's one less thing they have to worry about.

Another reason for establishing contact and waiting for the call to be acknowledged is that some pilots get on the mike and ramble on and on with unnecessary trivia, including the fact that they've got the dog in the rear seat. As the trivia flows, the controller has two IFR aircraft on a merging pattern, both at the same altitude. Watching them come closer and closer, his blood pressure rises, but he's helpless to do anything about the pending crisis. The rambler has the frequency tied up.

Another thing about requesting advisories: Give Center only your next point of landing, not necessarily your final destination. If you're on the first leg of a four-leg flight, where you're ultimately going is useless information to the controller. Where you're going to land first is what matters to him.

It's the old admonition, again: Know what you need to say, say it, and get off the mike.

Using Center's Services

A Word About Frequncies

Perhaps you've experienced this: You've been using a Center for advisories, or were merely eavesdropping. You hear the controller call another aircraft, but you hear no response.

What's happening is that he may have as many as six frequencies to work with. He thus could be hearing you on one, but receiving the second pilot on another. His transmissions, however, go out on all frequencies assigned to his position.

The Flight Strip

Okay, Center agrees to give you advisories. As you provide the necessary information, the controller is manually completing a flight strip that will look like FIG. 9-6.

To decode the strip, from left to right:

N91570	Aircraft N-number
C-182	Aircraft type
1705	Time of radio contact
VFR 55	A VFR flight at 5500 feet
R	Radar
ANX-SUS	Reporting point and destination: Napoleon VOR to Spirit of St. Louis airport
1701	The computer-generated transponder code
TC	Traffic Count (for Center's record of aircraft handled)

An IFR strip is another matter. Once the flight plan has been filed, the FSS computer sends the basic information to the Center computer, where it is stored until 30 minutes before flight departure. The computer then spits out that

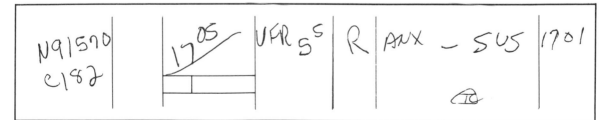

Fig. 9-6. *A VFR flight strip is handwritten as the pilot communicates his position, altitude, and first point of landing.*

177

information to the appropriate Center sector printer. One printer will serve up to about six sectors. The A-Side tears off the printed strip, takes it to the sector controller, inserts it in a plastic-like holder, and places the holder on a slanted rack, along with the other IFR and VFR strips, as in FIG. 9-7. Now, when the aircraft is handed off from Approach, from sector to sector, or from one Center to another, the controller responsible for the sector has the pertinent flight data right before him. Figure 9-8 is an example of an actual IFR strip, decoded as follows:

FLX152	FlexAir Flight 152
BA11/A	Type of aircraft, BAC111, equipped with DME and Mode C transponder
T380	True airspeed of 380 knots
G325	Ground speed of 325 knots
40	Sector 40
776	Computer identification number
02	The second strip for this flight
MCI	Departed Kansas City International
1508	Departure time (UTC)
15 19	Time aircraft should be over the SANTO fix (1519 UTC)
230	Assigned altitude: flight level 230 (approx. 23,000 feet)
MCI DSM J25 MCW MEINZ4 MSP	Route of flight from MCI to Minneapolis
°FLEXAIR	The call sign when the flight has a three-letter designation, as "FLX"
1737	Transponder code
ZCP	Minneapolis Center, the facility receiving the handoff from Kansas City Center

Radar Target Symbols

Unlike Approach Control, which has the ARTS II or III radar system that produces target symbols as well as alphanumeric data, Centers use the National Airspace System Stage A, or the Planned Visual Display we've already mentioned. With ARTS II or III, you'll recall, two systems function in unison—primary and

Fig. 9-7. *The A Side has done his job. The flight strips are "stuffed" and racked.*

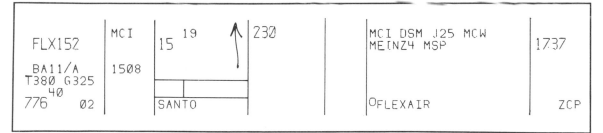

Fig. 9-8. *Unlike the hand-prepared VFR flight strip, this computer-generated IFR strip is based on data transmitted by the AFSS computer to the core computer at Center. The handwritten "up" arrow indicates a departing aircraft.*

secondary radar, or *broadband* and *narrowband*. It is the combination of the two that produces a particular aircraft symbol, depending on whether it is just a primary target without an operating transponder, one with Mode 3/A, one with Mode C, and so on.

The Center's enroute NAS Stage A relies on just the narrowband radar, where the signal goes out, hits the target, and the ''reply'' is then processed through the computer, which produces only a digital alphanumeric readout of the pertinent aircraft data. No ARTS III-type symbols (except for a small blip representing the aircraft) and no weather depiction, other than the lines and the superimposed ''H.''

To be more specific, FIG. 9-9 illustrates what the data blocks for an IFR and a VFR aircraft being tracked would look like on Center's radar system. Here is the IFR data block decoded:

Aircraft ID

  90 : Desired altitude—9000 feet

  ↑ : Climbing

  50 : Present Mode C altitude—5000 feet

 312 : Computer ID number, for computer storing or recall purposes

 150 : Ground speed in knots

The VFR data block is identical except that ''VFR'' replaces the desired cruising altitude. No transponder squawk code appears on either IFR or VFR aircraft in the Stage A system.

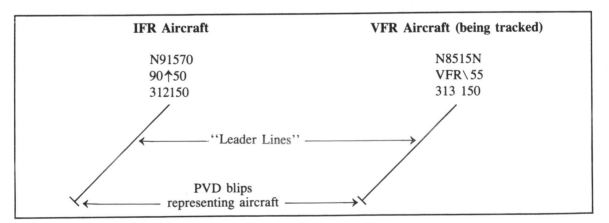

Fig. 9-9. *How IFR and VFR data blocks appear on Center's radarscope. The VFR aircraft is receiving advisories and is being tracked by radar.*

At some radar positions, the aircraft's future track over the next one, two, four, or eight minutes can be projected by turning a button on the radar console. A line then extends out from the blip, indicating the probable flight path. The immediate "history" of a flight can also be displayed, designated by a few short trailing lines (see Item 15 on FIG. 9-10).

The statement a moment ago that NAS Stage A radar does not transmit the ARTS-type target symbols is true. However, in addition to the data block information, it does produce certain computer-generated symbols, such as a triangle over a target when it is off course, or on a *free track*; a diamond when the target is on course and on time—a *flat track*, a + for a primary target; a square for a major airport; a right angle for a small airport; and others that identify types of targets and the current status of the aircraft it is tracking.

In addition, Stage A also projects the weather lines I mentioned earlier (Item 28 on FIG. 9-10). Again, the major difference between ARTS and NAS Stage A is that the latter produces digitized symbols as opposed to the various images generated by the ARTS primary and secondary radar.

The Handoff Process

Let's first take the case of a VFR handoff. You're coming to the limits of a controller's sector —say, Sector 40, and the next sector on your route is Sector 48. Before any transfer is made, Sector 40's controller calls Sector 48 on the override phone and asks if he can accept a VFR aircraft. Sector 48 says yes. Sector 40 rolls his slewball (just as in Approach Control) to the blip by your data block and punches the console HANDOFF button, with Sector "48."

As he does, your data block appears on 48's scope with an intermittent, or "time-sharing" flashing "H-48," meaning "Handoff to Sector 48." The flashing appears over the ground speed segment of the data block, showing first the ground speed and then the H-48. This continues until 48 accepts the handoff. To do this, the controller rolls his slewball over to your blip and enters your call sign or computer identification into the computer. The computer accepts the handoff, the flashing stops on both his and 40's scopes, and the 40 controller can now erase the data block from his screen. The A-Side then walks your flight strip to Sector 48, puts it on the slanted rack, and the handoff is complete.

At this point, or perhaps a moment or two before, Sector 40 will call you and tell you to change to one of Sector 48's frequencies—let's say 125.3. The call sequences would then go like this:

Ctr:	*Cherokee One Five November, contact Kansas City Center on one two five point three.*
You:	Roger, one two five point three. Cherokee One Five November.

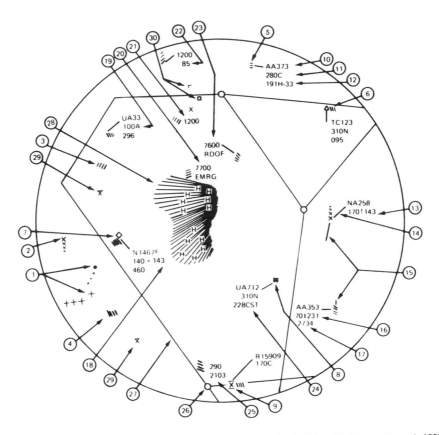

Target Symbols

1 Uncorrelated primary radar target + ●

2 *Correlated primary radar target X

3 Uncorrelated beacon target /

4 Correlated beacon target \

5 Identing beacon target ≡
   (*Correlated means the association
   of radar data with the computer projected track of an identified aircraft)

Position Symbols

6 Free track (No flight plan tracking) △

7 Flat track (flight plan tracking) ◇

8 Coast (Beacon target lost) #

9 Present Position Hold ⊠

Data Block Information

10 *Aircraft Identification

11 *Assigned Altitude FL280, mode C altitude
   same or within ±200' of asgnd altitude

12 *Computer ID #191, Handoff is to Sector 33
   (0-33 would mean handoff accepted)
   (*Nr's 10, 11, 12 constitute a "full data
   block")

13 Assigned altitude 17,000', aircraft is
    climbing, mode C readout was 14,300
    when last beacon interrogation was
    received

14 Leader line connecting target symbol
    and data block

15 Track velocity and direction vector
    line (Projected ahead of target)

16 Assigned altitude 7000, aircraft is
    descending, last mode C readout (or
    last reported altitude was 100'
    above FL230

17 Transponder code shows in full data block
    only when different than assigned code

18 Aircraft is 300' above assigned
    altitude

19 Reported altitude (No mode C readout)
    same as assigned. An "N" would indi-
    cate no reported altitude)

20 Transponder set on emergency code 7700
    (EMRG flashes to attract attention)

21 Transponder code 1200 (VFR) with no
    mode C

22 Code 1200 (VFR) with mode C and last
    altitude readout

23 Transponder set on Radio Failure code
    7600, (RDOF flashes)

24 Computer ID #228, CST indicates target is
    in Coast status

25 Assigned altitude FL290, transponder
    code (These two items constitute a
    "limited data block")

Other symbols

26 Navigational Aid

27 Airway or jet route

28 Outline of weather returns based on
    primary radar . H's represent
    areas of high density precipitation
    which might be thunderstorms. Radial
    lines indicate lower density precipi-
    tation.

29 Obstruction

30 Airports Major: □ , Small: ⌐

Fig. 9-10. *The NAS Stage A controllers display in the full automation mode.*

Make the frequency change and then re-establish contact:

> **You:**   Kansas City Center, Cherokee Eight Five One Five November is with you, level at seven thousand five hundred.
>
> **Ctr:**   *Cherokee One Five November, roger. Altimeter three zero one five.*
>
> **You:**   Three zero one five. Cherokee One Five November.

That's all there is to it. From here on, keep the radio tuned to that frequency, listen for your call sign, and acknowledge all advisories.

And so it goes, from sector to sector, Center to Center, Center to Approach, Approach to Center. Each VFR handoff is preceded by an inter- or intrafacility direct phone call to determine whether the next sector or facility can handle a VFR operation. If it's impossible because of workload, the controller with whom you've been in contact will make that clear:

> *Cherokee One Five November, radar service terminated. Frequency change approved. Squawk one two zero zero.*

There can be some variations in all of this. For example, you're cruising along in the 3000 to 4000-foot range. Depending on your position, that could be too low for Center's remoted radar to pick you up. You'd then be told that radar service was terminated but that you might try to establish contact again a few miles down the road.

Another variation: Some Centers prefer to enter VFR aircraft in their computer rather than handwriting the flight strips. If the Center you're leaving uses handwritten strips, the controller will not hand you off but tell you that radar service is terminated and to contact the next Center on a particular frequency. If you still want advisories, you will have to go through the initial radio contact procedures all over again.

The handoff process is thus not necessarily uniform everywhere, nor is it something automatically accorded every VFR operation. Controller workload is the deciding factor.

An IFR handoff is a little different:

- There is no phone contact between controllers.

- It can be accomplished by the computer, which automatically hands the aircraft off from one sector or Center to another.

- It can also be accomplished in a manner similar to a VFR handoff, except for the controller-to-controller phone contact. Using Sectors 40 and 48 again, the 40 controller puts his slewball on the aircraft's blip, hits the ENTER button and "48." The blip and data block now appear on 48's scope, along with the intermittently flashing "H-48." Sector 48 puts his slewball on the blip, hits his ENTER button, plus "O," the symbol indicating that the handoff has been accepted. As he does, the flashing on both scopes stop, 40 sees the "O," and the handoff is complete. When the aircraft nears the limits of 40's sector, he erases the blip and data block from his scope.

- No IFR aircraft can enter one controller's sector or area until he or she has bought the handoff. Nor can an aircraft re-enter a sector or area that it has left without the first controller's approval. The separation of IFR aircraft is too critical to allow unapproved flight deviations. None of this applies to VFR aircraft.

- The flight strips are computer-generated, not handwritten, and are automatically sent to the appropriate sector or facility printer 30 minutes before the flight is estimated to enter that airspace. The A-Side then removes the strip from the printer, takes it to proper sector, and inserts it in the holder.

Figure 9-11 is an example of several racked flight strips. Those to the left represent IFR flight plans, but the aircraft have not yet left the Tulsa, Wichita, Ponca City, Bartlesville, and Enid airports. On the right are aircraft in flight and still within Kansas City's control.

ADVANTAGES FOR THE VFR PILOT

Yes, the ARTCCs do exist to monitor and separate IFR traffic. At the same time, however, knowing what their services are, plus knowing how to take advantage of them, can be of tremendous benefit to the VFR pilot. Let's consider just a few of the things Center can do.

Routine Advisories

It's comforting to know that someone down there is aware of your existence, has you on radar, and is monitoring your progress across his airspace. It's also comforting—but should never be relaxing—to know that you're likely to be advised of some of the traffic that could impinge on your line of flight, or that questionable weather might lie ahead. And it's nice to know, should you be venturing into an active MOA, that you could well be informed of the F-14s involved in aerobatic maneuvers—or that there's a flock of B-52s barreling along the Military Training Route you happen to be paralleling.

Those are only samples of what a Center can do to enhance safety. That should not, however, nurture complacency. Lots of VFR aircraft are out there, with and without transponders, with and without Mode C, in contact with Center or not. These targets may appear as only small blips on the radarscope, their altitudes unknown to all but their drivers. Whether VFR—or, indeed, IFR in clear skies—safety begins in the cockpit. Regardless of help from the ground, it's up to us to see and get out of the way of objects that could bring everything to a tragic climax.

Weather Problems

A situation one controller cited is a good example of how a Center can be of considerable help when weather causes inflight problems.

It seems that a VFR pilot got a weather briefing early one morning for a flight from City A to City C. Conditions were reported favorable, so off he went,

Fig. 9-11. *The IFR flight strips for yet-to-depart aircraft are on the left. Those for enroute aircraft are on the right.*

but did not file a flight plan. Enroute to City C, he stopped at City B for about three hours and then headed out again.

Midway between B and C, he ran into snow showers, poor visibility, and the potential of icing. Becoming more than concerned, he contacted a nearby FSS (one that was still operating before it was consolidated), and explained his predicament. The FSS, in turn, called Center to see if it could help get the guy to safety. By this time, he was down to about 3100 feet, and below Center's radar coverage. With instructions to the pilot, Center was able to determine the aircraft's position by establishing a fix off two VORs.

Meanwhile, the weather at City C had deteriorated, making continued flight in that direction even more hazardous. Getting the pilot to an alternative airport (we'll call that City D) near his present location was the only option. He could have retraced his steps back to clearer weather, but the potential of icing made it critical to get on the ground as soon as possible.

Another problem arose, however: The pilot was in the immediate vicinity of a Restricted Area, where the military was shooting off cannons. Now there were two threats. Center called the military, however, had them shut down the range, and then successfully guided the pilot to the lighted runway threshold of City D's no-tower airport.

Center filed an "Aircraft Assist" report on the incident, and, in checking back, found that the only weather briefing the pilot had had was at his point of origin, some seven or eight hours earlier. None had been recorded at City B, where he was on the ground for three hours or more.

Two obvious lessons here: One, get *current* weather briefings. Conditions can, and do, change rapidly, and forecasts do not always become reality. Two, if you get in trouble, don't wait until things become critical before contacting a Center. A crisis may well be avoided if Center is brought into the picture early enough.

As a Center area manager put it, "Give us a chance to help you before you really need help. Even if things look great right now, a short call is all that's necessary: 'Kansas City Center, Mooney One Two Three Four Alpha, over Emporia at six thousand five hundred to Dallas. What's the weather a hundred miles ahead?' We might tell you that there are severe storms south of Wichita, or whatever. Don't be afraid to call us, but do it before an emergency develops."

What the manager said doesn't mean you should rely on Center as your primary source for weather information. The FS⌐ is the first and best source—but Center can and will help when help is needed.

Emergencies—Mechanical and Otherwise

Here's another reason to use Center, or at least monitor its frequencies, as dramatized by an experienced controller: "Ginny up front suddenly breaks loose and spurts oil all over the windshield. You're frantically trying to read charts to find the nearest airport, keep the airplane level, see where you're going, and scour the terrain below for a place to put down the dying bird. And, if you still have time, squawk 7700.

"If you had been in contact with me, I'd know exactly where you were, and I would know the closest airport to your position. I *know* my sector. That's my job. I could lead you to the airport and perhaps save your hide. At the very worst, had you been talking to me and couldn't reach the airport, I'd know where you went down and could start the rescue operations immediately."

The benefits of at least tuning to a Center frequency are apparent. Even if you have not been getting advisories, you can get on the air in a hurry with the "Mayday" call when the situation gets tight. That universal distress code gets immediate attention.

The same controller told about a student he helped who, on his first cross-country, was hopelessly lost, with his fuel dwindling. He knew that he had crossed a certain VOR 30 or 40 minutes previously, but disorientation, coupled with growing panic, had set in.

To the student's credit, he had the presence of mind to call Center. The controller, who was also a pilot, in a calm and friendly tone, vectored the pilot toward the nearest airport, and, in the process, put him over a four-lane highway that led to the town where the airport was located. As the controller said, "It was a very narrow runway, but it was 20 miles long." The student landed with no more than 15 minutes of fuel in the tank.

Before signing off, the controller told the student to call him on the phone as soon as he could. (You can picture the student's emotions when he heard that edict!) When the call came through, though, the controller told the student that he had done exactly the right thing. He had kept his head and asked Center for help in an emergency. The controller's only request was that the student tell his instructor what had happened.

The controller concluded the story by saying that handling the student took about 20 minutes, basically tying up the frequency during that time. Meanwhile, he had a bunch of air carrier operations he was watching but contacting only when necessary. The air carrier pilots, however, were listening to the dialogue. As the controller put it, he'd have had 25 pilots on his neck if he hadn't devoted his almost complete attention to one lost neophyte in a Cessna 152.

Perhaps these incidents at least partly illustrate the value a Center can be to those of us who fly VFR. Perhaps they also hint at the sensitivity so common to the vast majority of those manning the headsets in the Center complex. They want to help; they're there to help; and they will help—be it a routine flight or an emergency. The routine is on a workload-permitting basis; the emergency receives instant attention.

Position Reporting and Center

You've filed a VFR flight plan and are using Center for enroute advisories. At some point, Center becomes too busy to handle you, you lose contact, or you voluntarily terminate contact yourself. Whatever the case, you subsequently have an emergency and go down. One hour after your flight plan has expired, the Alert Notice (ALNOT) goes out, and Center receives a copy of it. In this situation, how much help will Center be?

Frankly, it's questionable. For one, as I said in the Flight Service chapter, Center keeps no written record of radio contacts with VFR aircraft. It has only the flight strip for those aircraft that had requested advisories. When it receives the ALNOT, one of Center's first actions is to go through the VFR flight strips to see if yours shows up—as it would in the case at hand. Another is to ask the controller who last handled you if he remembers you and any communications that would shed light on your possible whereabouts or what might have happened. Finally, if necessary, a specialist in the quality assurance office will review the tape recording of all radio communications during the period you were in contact with Center, to determine the time of your last transmission. This might require several hours, and, should the ALNOT come during the night, the review wouldn't take place until morning, when a specialist in the process is on duty. Meanwhile, you could be down and injured for hours before anyone finds you. Hopefully, your emergency locator transmitter (ELT) is working.

Relying solely on Center for position reports is better than contacting no one inflight, but it's not the best way to keep ATC advised of your whereabouts. Some pilots have even tried to make these reports when they haven't previously been in contact with Center at all—an almost totally futile gesture, because the only record of the call would be just a brief moment on the tape. Not even a flight strip.

No, for reporting purposes, the facility is Flight Service, not Center. There, every position or flight progress report is not only tape recorded, but also written down. With the data almost immediately available, any FSS is far better equipped to initiate a rapid search-and-rescue mission—and in a smaller geographic area.

RECOMMENDATIONS FOR VFR PILOTS

I asked several Center controllers and managers what VFR pilots do, or don't do, that bugs them or causes them problems. The following are a few of their comments as well as recommendations.

Radio Skills

This we've discussed enough, but knowledgeable use of the radio kept cropping up again and again. The basic points, almost direct quotes, were:

- Monitor the frequency and listen before you start talking. Don't pick up the mike and jump in until you're sure that the frequency is clear.

Otherwise, only squeals and squawks will drift through our headset. Two people can't talk on the same frequency at the same time.

- Depending on the nature of the call, know what you should say, plan how you're going to say it, say it, and get off the air. Disconnected messages, rambling, and inconsequential trivia drive us nuts. (This, as you've probably gathered, was one of the most-voiced criticisms of VFR pilots, but even the IFRs were not immune.)

- Don't leave a frequency without telling us. You want to call an FSS for some purpose? Fine, but first advise us that "Cherokee One Five November is leaving you temporarily to go to Flight Service." (This assumes, of course, that you've been getting advisories from a Center.) When the call to the FSS is completed, re-establish contact with, "Center, Cherokee One Five November is back with you."

- A lot of pilots who receive advisories get near their destination and start dial-twisting to reach the tower or a UNICOM frequency—but they never tell us what they're doing. Meanwhile, we can't raise them and don't know whether they've gone down, have radio trouble, or what. If you're leaving our frequency for any reason *please* tell us first, and then tell us when you're back with us.

- Call us before you get into trouble. We can probably help you. Otherwise, it might be too late.

- Don't be afraid to ask us for advisories. We're here to help, if our workload will let us.

Stay VFR

One situation cited: A VFR pilot who had been getting advisories called the controller at a certain point, saying, "Center, I won't need advisories any more. I'm out of the clouds."

"Gulp," said the controller.

Remember that Center's radar won't pick up cloud layers or formations unless there is thunderstorm activity in them. In this instance, the controller couldn't know that the VFR character was or had been in the soup. VFR means adhering to the visibility/cloud separation regulations, even when receiving advisories.

Report Altitude Changes

With or without Mode C, if you're getting advisories, Center has you pegged at your reported altitude. Being VFR, you have the freedom to climb or descend at your discretion, but do not do either until you have notified the controller.

"Center, Cherokee One Five November is leaving six thousand five hundred for eight thousand five hundred due to turbulence." When you reach the new altitude, although it's not mandatory, it's a good practice to confirm the fact with another short call: "Center, Cherokee One Five November level at eight thousand five hundred."

The reason for the first call, particularly, is that Center has you at a certain altitude and is giving you and other aircraft advisories based on that altitude. If you move up or down at will (which is still your right), you could be venturing into the flight paths of other traffic. With Mode C, your variations will be spotted, but even then, the controller may have a question. Are you really changing altitudes, or is the Mode C malfunctioning? Things do go haywire, which is one reason why controllers ask pilots to verify that they actually are at such-and-such an altitude. As one said, "I've seen Mode C report a Cessna 182 at 19,000 feet—a little unlikely for a 182."

Enroute Flight Plan Filing

Don't use Center for filing VFR or IFR flight plans. It's not designed to provide such a service, although I have heard it offered when a pilot has encountered, or was about to encounter, non-VFR weather conditions. It was a voluntary offer on the part of the controller, however, to help the pilot out of a potential predicament. Flight Service is the place to file—and even then, airfiling should be a last resort. It takes up a lot of the specialist's time.

Visits to a Center

This is something the FAA and controllers alike recommend highly. Do it as a group, do it on your own, or attend one of the FAA's "Operation Raincheck" sessions. Just be sure to make arrangements in advance.

Nothing can replace a personal tour to get the real feel of what goes on. Even one trip through the facility will answer a lot of questions and alleviate some of the concerns bugging a lot of pilots about requesting the services a Center offers.

CONCLUSION

While a personal visit to Center may not be feasible for pilots who live hundreds of miles from the nearest such facility, there are just as many pilots who are within an hour's drive of a Center but have never set foot on the property. Recognizing both realities, and the fact that a goodly number of pilots consider Center a somewhat mysterious institution, I've tried here to outline the organization of a typical Center, to explain how it functions, and to provide a few glimpses of what goes on behind the scenes, including what happens when a VFR pilot contacts the facility for advisories or for help. I hope that, if you were previously uncertain, you will now have a little more confidence in your ability to use and profit from the services a Center can provide. There's an old adage that "What we're not up on, we're down on." What we don't understand, we avoid. But, the adage works in reverse: "What we're up on, we're not down on."

There's nothing mysterious about a Center, and the folks there aren't ogres. Many are pilots who know very well what goes on in the skies above them. Pilots or not, they're more than willing to help guide you, maybe even save you. It's you, however, who must make the first contact. No one in that darkened room can.

10

ATC Specialists

You have to be able to think abstractly, especially at the Center.
You have to do first things first, establish priorities.
You have to have automatic recall.
You have to look at errors objectively and reconstruct situations.
You have to accept the responsibilities of the job.

THE FAA's *AIR TRAFFIC CONTROL SPECIALIST* (ATCS) BROCHURE, DESIGNED TO to acquaint potential applicants with what the job of an ATCS is all about, opens with this summary of what is required of an air traffic control specialist. They are not exaggerations, but the brochure could easily have added other traits or characteristics, such as the ability to learn rapidly, self-control under tension, communication skills, patience, flexibility, dependability, planning skills—to mention a few.

Having listened to, observed, and talked with many ATCSs, all of the above are realistic portrayals of what it takes to be a successful controller or FSS specialist. The job demands quality in both its hardware and its human resources.

No one questions the need for the most sophisticated equipment available. The National Airspace System Plan is designed to meet that need, is doing so now, and will continue to do so over the next decade. Regardless of the technical advances, however, it's the human resource that brings to life whatever benefits the hardware offers. Perhaps some day automation will be so perfected that we will no longer need people, other than technicians, in the Centers, towers, and Flight Service Stations. Perhaps some day the only resources in the system will be the threes M's—Machines, Materials, and Money—with the fourth M—Manpower—becoming obsolete. That's 21st century dreaming, though. Today, and in the foreseeable future, people will be the primary link between aircraft and the various ground-bound facilities.

So what about these people who play such a critical role in maintaining the finest air traffic control system in the world? What weds them to the job? How do they handle the stress the job is purported to produce? What screening and training do they undergo to prepare them for the tasks at hand? What sort of people are they? Recognizing the dangers of generalities, let's try to find some answers.

WHAT SORT OF PEOPLE ARE THEY?

Starting with the last question first, the traits and characteristics listed earlier give a pretty good idea of the sort of person we're talking about. The picture, however, is not complete.

Through the work of psychologists and behavioral scientists, we know quite a bit about what motivates people and some of their needs. As one example, Dr. David McClellan of Harvard developed, as the result of considerable research, a concept called the "need for achievement," or n/Ach, for short. Among the several traits of a person with a high n/Ach, at least two seem particularly characteristic of the ATCS: the need to solve problems, make decisions, and act on his or her own; and the need for concrete feedback on how he or she is doing.

Whether consciously aware of these so-called "needs" or not, it's unlikely that an ATCS would have even applied for the job if the n/Ach were not part of his makeup. Certainly, were it lacking, it is very unlikely that he could have completed even the initial phases of the training program. If ever a job demanded the ability to solve problems *now*, to make decisions *now*, and to act independently of others, this is it. Similarly, it's a job that provides almost immediate, concrete feedback on how well the individual is performing. Working as an ATCS is not for those who want to be told what to do and are satisfied with a vague, once-a-year "You're doing OK" performance appraisal. No, the possession of a high need for achievement seems most compatible with the psyche of the typical specialist or controller.

Taken to the extreme, of course, the need can be destructive—destructive in the sense that the individual wants to do everything by himself, jumps to solutions, makes hasty, not-thought-through decisions, and resists outside counsel or advice. Wanting feedback, he constantly brings to the attention of others, particularly supervisors, the things he has done well, the problems he has solved—and, in the process, drives everybody nuts. He is, in effect, the perfect example of an insecure attention-seeker.

Conversely, and in proper balance with the other traits listed, the need is not just a desirable characteristic; it is almost essential for anyone now in, or seeking a career in air traffic control. The industry is fortunate that it has such people manning the scopes and the radios.

THE TRAINING

Much could be said about the training these folks go through, but three words seem to sum it up: lengthy, tough, and thorough. Not only is it long, taking 2½ to 3 years to reach the full performance level (FPL), but the pressure to succeed is almost constant. And it is thorough, which accounts for its length.

It begins at the FAA's Academy in the Mike Monroney Aeronautical Center in Oklahoma City. There, for the first 12 to 16 weeks, the would-be specialist goes through a rigorous screening, academic, and laboratory regimen, designed primarily to determine whether the trainee has the potential even to be considered for an ATCS position.

Upon successful completion of the Academy screening program, the trainee (now called "a developmental") is interviewed by representatives from the various sites and then assigned to a tower, a Center, or a Flight Service Station. Several factors enter into the assignment decision, including personal desires, Academy grades, previous aviation-related experience, and where a staffing need exists.

Once at the assigned facility, the developmental begins with a series of "phases" or "steps" that takes him or her through the academic, laboratory (simulated exercises and problems), and on-the-job instruction essential for ultimate certification as an FPL. The following are brief outlines of the training format at the three ATC facilities: Center, tower/Approach Control, and the Automated Flight Service Station. There may be some minor local variations, but the FAA designs the basic programs and sets the instructional standards to which each facility must adhere.

Air Route Traffic Control Center

The nationwide program for an ARTCC developmental involves 13 phases, the first three being at the Academy (for some reason, there is no designated Phase IV). At the site, and in classes ideally composed of no more than six developmentals, the balance of the phases are:

> *Phase V*: Learning the Center's airspace area and the specialty to which the developmental has been assigned. "Specialty" or "area of specialization" refers to the division of the airspace into geographic areas, such as those illustrated in FIG. 9-3 (Trails, Ozark, Flint Hills, etc., at Kansas City Center). Each developmental is assigned to one of these areas, and that becomes known as his or her "specialty." Maximum time: 5 weeks.

> *Phase VI*: On-the-job training (OJT) in the area of specialization of duties assigned to the A-side position. Maximum time: 2 weeks.

> *Phases VII and VIII*: These two phases are combined and consist of 10 percent classroom and 90 percent laboratory (simulator) training,

where the developmental learns the duties of a *radar associate* (the "D" position mentioned in Chapter 9), including nonradar, "manual" control. Maximum time: 15 weeks.

Phase IX: OJT on two sectors in his or her specialty as a radar associate, helping the radar specialist, but in a learning capacity. Maximum time: 18 weeks.

Phase X: OJT at the balance of sectors in the area of specialization. Maximum time: 18 weeks.

Completion of Phases IX and X leads to certification of the developmental on all radar associate/nonradar positions in his/her specialty.

Phase XA: The developmental returns to the Academy's RTF (Radar Training Facility) for basic radar training before beginning Phase XI. The primary reason for the return is that the RTF training takes about three weeks, and the Center can't afford to limit the use of its own simulation equipment for basic training purposes only when the equipment is needed in the Phase VIII and Phase XI training. It's a question of the proper utilization of hardware resources. Maximum time: 3 weeks.

Phase XI: Classroom and laboratory training, learning to perform radar control duties on one sector of the assigned specialty. Maximum time: 3-4 weeks.

Phase XII: OJT as a radar controller on two sectors in the assigned area of specialization. Maximum time: 18 weeks.

Phase XIII: OJT to qualify the developmental to perform the full range of duties and attain certification on all radar positions in his or her area of specialization. If successful, the developmental becomes an FPL. Maximum time: 18 weeks.

Add the first 16 weeks at the Academy, and you have 136 weeks, or over 2½ years of constant screening and training before a Center developmental is certificated as an FPL and considered capable of functioning independently under only general supervision. Meanwhile, he or she has been tested, graded, watched, monitored, and critiqued throughout the entire period. It is, indeed, a tough and thorough process.

The Tower

After completing the 16 weeks' screening program at the Academy, those assigned to a tower remain at the Academy for four weeks of preliminary training before going to the site. At the site, whether an Approach or non-Approach tower, the training starts in the tower cab, and follows this sequence:

1. Training in the operation of flight data equipment, such as the FDIO (Flight Data Input/Output); the ATIS recording equipment, including recording the ATIS hourly data; marking and delivering instrument flight strips; and reading IFR clearances to pilots.

2. Functioning as a Ground Controller and coordinating ground traffic with the local controller.

3. Training as a local controller (the control of departing, arriving, and transiting traffic within the ATA). Also, if the tower has BRITE radar equipment, preliminary radar training is included in the program.

Average training time for these steps: 32 weeks.

For those bidding or assigned to Approach Control, the additional training includes these steps:

4. He or she returns to the Academy's Radar Training Facility (RTF) for basic radar training. Maximum time: 5 weeks.

5. Classroom training back at the site. Maximum time: 5 weeks.

6. OJT in Approach Control, always with an instructor or FPL watching and monitoring the actions and words of the trainee. Maximum time: 16 months.

Including the screening program at the Academy and these six steps, the average time required to reach the full performance level is approximately 2½ years.

Automated Flight Service Station

Finally, those assigned to an Automated Flight Service Station go through these training steps:

1. Classroom training in all of the following steps (2 through 8), including the equipment, before beginning any on-the-job training. Maximum time: 9 weeks.

2. Familiarization with the geographical area for which the AFSS is responsible. Maximum time: 4 to 6 weeks.

3. OJT: Broadcast—preparing and transcribing TWEBs and TIBS. Maximum time: 5 weeks.

4. OJT: NOTAM Coordinator—accepting and screening information coming in from all sources and entering same into the computer system. Maximum time: 2 weeks.

5. OJT: Flight Data—Preparing incoming data for computer entry. Maximum time: 7 weeks.

6. OJT: Preflight—Providing pilot telephone briefings. Maximum time: 12 weeks.

7. OJT: Inflight—Responding to aircraft radio calls. Maximum time: 11 weeks.

After successful completion of these seven steps, the developmental is certificated as an FPL. For those interested, Step 8 is available.

8. Flight Watch training back at the Academy, plus OJT at the site. This, however, is a bid position and not one for which all AFSS specialists are, or have to be, qualified. Time: 22 days at the Academy; 4 weeks OJT at the site.

The training time to become an AFSS FPL, including the initial Academy training, is thus approximately 15 months, excluding the additional Flight Watch training.

So, in a nutshell, those are the three training programs, beginning with the raw recruit up to FPL certification. We haven't attempted to review the training requirements for transferees, the recertification process for ATCSs who have not worked an operational position for a period of time, or the currency requirements for various management personnel. Those are all specially tailored programs, depending on the individual's experience and time away from an operational position—and to include such a discussion here would be superfluous to the central issue of how the beginner advances to the full performance level.

The one commonality for the would-be FPL is the initial Academy screening and training. From that point on, the program depends on the facility to which he or she is assigned and any local peculiarities that have to be addressed.

A second commonality is the fact that no developmental controls any traffic or communicates with any pilot, on the ground or in the air, at any stage of his or her training without an instructor or supervisor plugged in, listening to every word and observing every action. The nature of the job simply won't tolerate anything less than certificated professionalism at the scope or on the mike. In effect, the developmental is riding on the FPL's ticket. If the developmental makes a mistake, the trainer is responsible—a fact that puts even more pressure on the trainee when the FPL is perpetually looking over the developmental's shoulder. But, by the time the developmental has been through the wringer and is certificated as an FPL, the level of professionalism required is as assured as human effort can make it.

Despite its difficulty and the ever-present threat of elimination, only one criticism of the training seemed common: its length. That is being attacked, however, both at the Academy and in the field. With more and better equipment, plus some phase or step streamlining at the site, a shorter road to producing an FPL is in sight. Reducing time, however, does not mean sacrificing quality. Neither the FAA nor the industry would permit that.

HOW DO THEY FEEL ABOUT THEIR JOB?

When a number of ATCSs were asked how they felt about being a controller or a specialist, the responses were refreshingly constant. One said, without hesitation, "I love it, I'd do it for nothing." This from a veteran FPL. In explaining his feelings, he said, in part, that it was the sense of exhilaration, of satisfaction, of knowing that he had done a good job or a not-so-good job when the day was done.

Another equated it with playing a video game—and getting paid to play the game. Others voiced the sense of contributing to pilot, plane, and passenger well-being, whether through radar and radio or giving preflight briefings over the phone.

The elements of satisfaction and contribution emerged time after time. Perhaps I talked to the wrong people, but everyone I encountered (and there were many) voiced only genuine enthusiasm for the job. At the same time, that enthusiasm was evident as they discussed what they do and how they do it.

Not every day on the job is perfect, of course, nor is everything idyllic. However, in answer to the question, "If you could change anything about the job, what would it be?", the sole response from one group was, "I wish we could have more say in some of the decisions that management makes." In other words, greater lower-level involvement in the procedure and decision-making processes. This was hardly an unusual "wish." It's one I've heard thousands of times from employees and first-level supervisors in hundreds of private as well as public organizations.

To paint an overly rosy picture would be false and unwise. Every shop has its malcontents; every shop has its complainers; every shop has those who find the job not what they expected. Certainly, such personalities exist among the ATCSs. In the same vein, certain aspects of the working conditions can always be improved, including the equipment the people have to use.

Those realities recognized, it still seems that the vast majority of ATCSs are finding from the job many of the intangibles that make work worthwhile—challenge, recognition, contribution, opportunity (to do something of significance by their own standards), a sense of achievement, feedback, and overall satisfaction. A paycheck is important, but it's not the only thing people work for.

THE MATTER OF STRESS

The basic question put to many ATCSs was, "How stressful is the job? Has the media made more of it than is justified?"

The responses, of course, varied, but a common thread became evident: There can be stress, but it's a matter of how you handle it. Starting with the basic Academy screening, the ability to cope with stress is constantly tested, and only those who have demonstrated calmness and stability under fire make it to the FPL level. In fact, many ATCSs said that they experienced more continuing stress while in training than at any other time in their careers.

Along the same line, an article titled "Air Traffic Safety: Stress One Factor," which appeared in the August 1987 issue of *U.S. Medicine*, substantiated that thread. Written by Dr. William E. Collins of the FAA's Civil Aeromedical Institute (CAMI), the article states, "All of the CAMI studies indicated that, in general, ATCSs were psychologically highly suited to their occupation. That conclusion does not mean that controllers are emotionally immune to job (or other) crises, or that their working environments need not be improved. However, the conclusion is reassuring, since the job of the ATCS is a very responsible one with the direct, central issue being the safety of people."

As much as anything, conclusions reached on the basis of tests indicate, again quoting Collins, "that the ATCS's job was not uniquely stressful, and that it was not so much the job (i.e. handling the traffic) but the context in which the job was done that was significant"—meaning, in part, how management was interacting with its employees.

More and more, the emphasis seems to be shifting from the inherent stressfulness of the job to the overwork created by the volume of traffic the ATCSs must handle. As Collins says, "Flight delays have little to do with stress or with the current level of ATCS staffing, but have a lot to do with the need for more airports and runways (a 'concrete' problem) and the habitual scheduling by airlines of a significant number of flights at two or three choice times during the day." That was an observation voiced by many ATCSs.

None of this should imply that ATCSs are above stress. It does imply that the testing, screening, and training have, to the maximum extent possible, weeded out those who weren't able to handle the situations that accelerate the heart rate and inflate the blood pressure.

Undoubtedly, some ATCSs would scoff at CAMI's test results and verbalized conclusions. It does seem apparent, however, according to ATCSs and the aeromedical profession alike, that what stress exists is not caused by the inherent nature of the job but rather the overwork inspired by the volume of traffic in the skies today. If that's the case, in one respect, it's like any job: Tension and stress are entirely normal when you have more to do than you can skillfully and professionally handle.

In sum, ATCSs are where they are because they thrive on the challenge and the satisfaction the job provides. And they're there because they are psychologically equipped to meet the challenges that could be extremely stressful to others.

Does every ATCS fit that mold? Probably not. People have varying levels of tolerance. The vast majority of ATCSs, however, have to possess the measure of emotional stability that allows them to thrive on what they're doing.

DRUG TESTING

"Are you for it or against it?"

To that question, the almost unanimous response among controllers was, "I'm for it." Their only concerns were related to the accuracy of the tests. "I just don't want to have a test come back positive, when I *know* I haven't been on drugs." Who can argue with that stance?

The common comment, however, ran along the line that no one could do the job if he or she were a drug user. The job's demands simply won't tolerate clouded minds or emotional instabilities. If it takes testing to ensure against drug-induced aberrations, it's an unfortunate commentary on our times, but perhaps there's no other avenue available.

Again, there are undoubtedly a fair number of ATCSs who feel differently about the issue—and perhaps justifiably so. The claim of infringements on personal rights is a powerful counterargument. Despite that or other anti testing reasons, it does appear that the majority favor such a program, simply because of the serious nature of the occupation.

WORKING WITH VFR PILOTS

First and foremost, the biggest criticism of VFR pilots is radio technique. We've already beaten that subject to death, so enough said. A group of Center Controllers, however, did have a couple of other points or suggestions:

- Attend an FAA "Operation Raincheck" session. This, said one, should be mandatory for every VFR pilot.

- Practice with controllers when they're not busy. You can tell whether they are or not by just monitoring their frequency and by the current weather conditions. If you hear them turn down an enroute VFR advisory request, or if they're continually on the air with a bunch of IFR operations, you'll know what's going on. Even then, stay tuned and listen to the dialogues. That, in itself, is a learning and skill-sharpening experience.

- Helping the VFR pilot is part of their responsibility. They want to help, but you must do your part by knowing what to do, what to say, and keeping in communication with them when they are giving advisories.

- Finally, and to underscore these and similar comments, one FPL told me, "Don't put anything in the book that would discourage VFRs from using any Center services."

If you fly VFR around a tower-controlled airport, an ARSA, or a TCA, you have no choice. You must maintain radio contact with the tower or Approach Control. Center is the only traffic-controlling facility you're not required to use. If you have not had much experience operating in a controlled environment, just keep in mind that confidence will come with experience. Hopefully, the ARTCC chapter dimmed some of the apprehensions you might have had. The Center controllers emphasized their desire and their responsibility to help those of us who fly VFR, and a visit to a facility or a discussion with a controller would substantiate the sincerity of their words.

CONCLUSION

The FAA has several thousand controllers and FSS specialists in the ATC system. As in any amalgam of people, there are wide varieties of attitudes, personalities, abilities, character, and competence. Not all controllers are paragons of virtue and not all are models of excellence. That said, it's fair to conclude that those who have reached the full performance level have proven their merit and their mettle. Whether hired in pre- or post-strike days, they've been tested, probed, questioned, examined, and pressured to degrees not common in most professions. Those who stood up to the constant scrutiny made it and are on the job today. These are the ones you have been, or will be, talking to. The others dropped by the wayside, voluntarily or otherwise.

The Mikes, Marys, Jacks, and Jills in the FSSs, towers, and Centers are not superhumans; they're just well-balanced, well-trained folks who happen to possess certain uncommon traits that equip them for a most uncommon occupation.

On second thought, "occupation" seems a bit mundane; "profession" is more descriptive. A profession includes, in part, two elements: a science, and an art. The science is the body of knowledge pertaining to the profession that must be learned and mastered. The art is the ability to put the knowledge to work with skill, adeptness, vision, accuracy. Knowledge is the foundation, but it is of questionable value unless the practitioner possesses the skill to bring it to life.

In the broadest sense, the air traffic control specialist must be strong in both facets of professionalism—and it's safe to say the vast majority are. The record and the reputation of our air traffic control system are evidence enough. Yes, we have the doomsayers and the hypercritics among the media and the public who are continually waving red flags. When you consider, however, the volume of traffic that these folks handle each day, in fair weather and foul, in crowded as well as uncrowded skies, the record is remarkable by any standard. We have the finest human and hardware resources available—and both are only going to get better during the next decade.

Why such an assertion? Well, that leads us to the next chapter.

11

Where Do We
Go from Here?

BACK IN CHAPTER 1, WE TOOK A GLIMPSE AT THE BEGINNINGS OF A NATIONAL airspace system. The intervening chapters then focused on the system we have today and the facilities that make it work. To round out the picture, let's look briefly into the immediate future and summarize some of the plans that will take the industry into the 21st century. This look ahead is not a matter of stargazing, however. Instead, it's a review of what the FAA has committed itself to do to cope with the increasing demands on the airspace and the terminal and enroute environments. What follows, then, is based directly on the FAA's National Airspace System Plan (NASP) that came into being late in 1981.

Prior to 1980, there really was no plan. What technical and procedural improvements came about were largely designed to attack localized problems— existing or anticipated, rather than those of a systemwide nature. In the process, a patchwork quilt of equipment emerged, composed of varying characteristics and stages of development. As the FAA says, ''. . . the system of 1980 was expensive to operate and maintain, expansion capability was limited, and adaptability to changing requirements was difficult.''

Thus, sparked by equipment limitations, and certainly fueled by the air carrier Deregulation Act of 1978, a formal National Airspace System Plan was first established in December 1981. The Plan included a set of goals and actions to address problems classified as ''immediate'' (1981-1985), ''near-term'' (1985-1900), and ''long-term'' (1990-2000).

Since 1981, the FAA has issued a Congressionally-requested annual progress update, the most recent published in June 1988. The update, titled the *National Airspace System Plan*, is an inch-thick document that summarizes the status of 92 projects—some completed, some underway, some not yet in the start-up stage. All, however, are in concert with a systematic plan to meet the airspace and traffic control requirements of at least the next decade.

Plans and projects, however, first require a set of goals. The plans are then developed to bring the goals to reality. The FAA adhered to this sequence. The following were the FAA's goals and assumptions.

NASP GOALS

- Having a National Airspace System in place that meets the national aviation demand at the time it is required.

- Accommodating increasing demand in a way that allows airspace users to operate with a minimum of artificial constraints and with fuel efficiency.

- Reducing operational errors by 80 percent between 1984 and 1995. Techniques for more accurate classification and accounting have been developed.

- Reducing risks of midair and surface traffic collisions, landing and weather-related accidents, and collisions with the ground.

- Increasing air traffic controller and flight specialist productivity by a factor of at least two by the year 2000, compared with 1980. The productivity goal in the year 2000 is 10,982 operations per position per year.

- Reducing the technical staff required to maintain and operate the modernized and expanded system by one-third by the year 2000, compared with 1980. By the year 2000 the technical staff is expected to be 7,735.

- Maintaining the overall air traffic and airways facilities maintenance cost of field operations of the National Airspace System at the 1980 level, when adjusted for inflation, excluding the cost of modernization. Field operations include enroute and terminal air traffic control, Flight Service Stations, and field maintenance (1980 budgeted cost: $1.48 billion).

NASP ASSUMPTIONS

- Aviation demand will grow significantly during the next 20 years.

- Air carrier routes and services will reflect a better balance between trip frequency and cost than would be the case under a closely regulated system.

- The commuter airline industry will be affected by deregulation for several more years. Anticipated growth will require many years of adjustment before routes and schedules stabilize. The number of commuter operations is expected to decrease slightly over the period.

- Growth in business use of IFR-equipped general aviation aircraft will continue. Significant growth in turbopowered aircraft will result in increased operations above 12,500 feet. This growth is expected even though both fixed and variable costs of operating aircraft are increasing.

- The number of general aviation aircraft will decrease.

- System limitations on any class of users' right-of-access to the system should be imposed only when no other recourse is available to ensure the common good. Any such restrictions should be removed as soon as possible and not be considered a final solution. However, to gain access to the system, individual users must comply with conditions applicable to all classes of users and essential to the safety and efficiency of the system.

- Specific equipment may be required to operate in designated airspace.

- Individual user's preference for routes, runways, approaches, altitudes, etc., may not be honored if they will cause delays to other users or impair the safety of the system.

- No change to the system will be permitted to reduce safety or increase risk. A very high level of midair protection, including a backup ground independent airborne separation device, called traffic alert and collision avoidance system (TCAS) will be available. "See-and-be-seen" operations will continue.

- Major airports have limited expansion capability due to physical, environmental, airspace, runway, and/or landslide limitations. Few new large commercial service airports are anticipated. These factors will continue to impose capacity constraints at many large and medium hubs.

- A limited amount of additional capacity will be achieved through reduction in separation standards resulting from technological advances, through refinements in air traffic control (ATC) procedures, and through runway, terminal, and access improvements. Solution of wake vortex problems will reduce delays, but not eliminate them entirely. National policies on noise abatement will affect all of these assumptions.

- The airspace structure demands on participants will continue at several levels. There will be airspace in which no services are available and none are needed. The National Airspace Review has had positive impact on the airspace structure, and follow-on activity is, therefore, likely to affect this Plan.

- Fuel will be available. The only fuel constraint used in developing the demand forecast in this Plan is that of price.

- ATC services within the NAS will continue to be provided by a mix of civil (FAA) and military air traffic control facilities. The military approach controls, control towers, and other facilities will provide service to civilian and military aircraft alike.

THE NEED FOR A PLAN

The potential growth of both civil and military aviation has been well documented. Based on FAA figures and forecasts, in 1982, we had 237,500 air carrier, general aviation, and military aircraft using the airspace. In 1990, the estimate is 240,000, and by the year 2000, 249,000. The number of pilots will increase only 4.0 percent, going from 764,000 in '82 to 795,000 in 2000. Those with instrument ratings, however, will jump 15.2 percent (253,000 to 291,000), and they, of course, are the prime users of the Approach and Enroute facilities.

With a continually growing demand for services, equipment modernization and innovations are essential. The system in place today is, in many ways, behind the available technology. Too many things are still being done manually; some radar systems, such as the TPX-42, first installed in 1972, and the BRITE tower cab radar, are outdated or unreliable; vacuum-tube equipment is still around; ILS remains the principal instrument landing aid, although its genesis goes back to the 1930s. In sum, there's a lot of work to do and money to be spent to replace equipment that is unnecessarily labor-intensive, requires too much maintenance, and is archaic by current technological standards.

Facing growth and increasing demands on the system, the FAA had to take at least four broad actions: replace obsolete equipment, automate, consolidate facilities, and implement improved traffic control, navigation, and safety-enhancing systems. In the process, costs and manpower constraints were always serious considerations.

The 92 NASP projects I mentioned earlier can be broken down by facility or function, along with the number of projects already completed:

Facility/Function	Projects	Projects Completed
Enroute	16	3
Terminals	17	6
FSS and Weather	13	4
Ground-Air Communications	18	1

Interfacility Communications	9	3
Maintenance and Operating Support System	19	1
Totals	92	18

Theoretically, the aviation community should be interested in every NASP project because each, in its own way, impacts on the safety, the equipment, the operational requirements, and/or the costs associated with the Plan. For purposes here, however, to review in detail all of the completed or intended projects would be impractical. So, I'll just outline a few with which pilots can readily identify and that will have a direct or potential effect on them: Terminals, Flight Service Stations and Weather, and Enroute, plus those in the area of Ground-to-Air Communications.

TERMINALS

- Improved ATIS (Automatic Terminal Information Service) transmission and reception by updating existing electromagnetic recorders with solid-states. Completion: 1989.

- An improved tower communications system. Completion: 1998.

- Higher quality BRITE radar in the tower cab, along with BRITE installation at qualifying satellite towers that may or may not presently have the equipment. Completion: 1992.

- Upgrading and modernizing ATCTs and TRACONs, including constructing new towers (where necessary), adding tower operating positions, upgrading TRACABs to TRACONs, replacing old or unreliable heating, ventilating, and air conditioning systems. Completion: 1992.

- Consolidation of TRACON and TRACAB functions into the Air Route Traffic Control Centers. (More on this in the Enroute section.) Completion: 2000.

Other Terminal projects are: ARTS IIA enhancement—1990; ARTS IIA Interface with Mode S/ASR (Airport Surveillance Radar)—1991; Multichannel Voice Recorders—1992; TPX-42 radar replacement—1990.

FLIGHT SERVICE STATIONS AND WEATHER

- Continuing consolidation of FSSs into 61 Automated Flight Service Stations (AFSSs). Completion: 1994.

- A Hazardous Inflight Weather Advisory Service (HIWAS) transmitted over selected VOR stations, providing continuing weather advisories, including SIGMETs (Significant Meteorological Information), AIRMETs (Airman's

Meteorological Information), and PIREPs (Pilot Reports). HIWAS will replace the 3-minute TWEBs. VORs for HIWAS will be selected to avoid competition with VOR voice features used for AWOS (Automated Weather Observing Service). HIWAS reports will be prepared by FSS specialists, using solid-state recorders with a 4-minute capacity. Final equipment delivery: 1989.

- High-altitude Enroute Flight Advisory Service (EFAS) above 18,000 feet on discrete frequencies assigned to each ARTCC area. The lower altitude frequency of 122.0 for EFASs (or Flight Watch) will remain. Completion: 1989.

- Final development of the Flight Service Automation System (FSAS) as FSSs are consolidated. The FSAS allows users direct access to weather data and flight plan filing without the need for an AFSS specialist intervention. Completion date: 1994.

- The Automated Weather Observing Service (AWOS), a system that obtains critical aviation weather data, such as visibility, cloud height, temperature, dew point, winds, altimeter settings, and precipitation types, through automated sensors. The data is then processed and disseminated to pilots via a computer-synthesized voice over VOR/NDB or discrete VHF/UHF outlets. The plan is to install 160 AWOS systems at nontower airports in 1991, 233 in 1992, and 304 at tower airports in 1994. These will be funded by Facilities & Engineering under FAA or National Weather Service contracts. The Plan also estimates an additional 400 systems at nontower airports, funded under the Airport Improvement Program and acquired by airport managers or fixed-base operators. No completion date has been set for the 400 systems.

- An expansion of the Low Level Wind Shear Alert System (LLWAS). Two hundred and eleven systems are already in place, using six sensors—one at a midfield position and five around the periphery of the airport. A computer then processes the sensor information and displays wind shear conditions to controllers. Expansion plans include adding more sensors, improving the information/alert displays, and updating the six-sensor system at 110 sites. Completion: 1993.

Other FSS and weather projects, and final implementation dates, include: Central Weather Processor—1996; Weather Message Switching Center—1992; Aeronautical Data Link—1993; Integrated Communication Switching System—1992.

ENROUTE

- Consolidation of Approach Control facilities and functions (TRACONs and TRACABs) into the Air Route Traffic Control Centers. The combined units will then be known as Area Control Facilities (ACFs). Through this project, all Approach and Enroute Control functions will be handled by the ACFs, and the nation's 188 TRACONs/TRACABs will be merged into fewer than 30 ATC facilities. The tower cabs, however, will continue to function as they do today, but with advanced processing and display capabilities. Phase I, ACF Preconditioning Activities, begins in 1989, with a completion date of 1995. Phase II, Implementation, starts in 1996 and concludes in 2000.

- Improved enroute tracking with the final implementation of E-EARTS (Enhanced Enroute Automated Radar Tracking System), a radar enhancement that provides controllers with collision alerts (CAs) and minimum safe altitude warnings (MSAWs). In addition, E-EARTS increases radar coverage, thus enabling the controller to make more efficient use of the airspace and contribute to a reduction of aircraft fuel consumption. Completion: 1989.

- The creation of *sector suites* in enroute facilities, with each suite having displays of the position of aircraft in the sector, alphanumeric flight and weather data, NOTAMs, and air traffic planning data that will permit the controller to analyze the system for conflict-free, fuel-efficient flight paths. Electronic displays of flight data will eliminate the manual flight strip processing. With more data immediately available to the controller than in the current sector configuration, he or she will be better equipped to ensure safer, less costly flight operations. Implementation to start in 1993; Completion: 1995.

- Upgrading of the Traffic Management System (TMS) into a fully integrated national system through the Central Flow Control Facility in the FAA's Washington headquarters and the individual ARTCC Traffic Management Units (TMUs). The upgrading will improve traffic flow efficiency, minimize delays, expand services, and contribute to more effective aircraft departure sequencing, enroute spacing, and arrival sequencing. The entire project is to be completed in 1991.

Other Enroute projects and their completion dates are: New Flight Data Entry and Printout devices—1989; Direct Access Radar Channel (DARC) System—1990; Conflict Resolution Advisory (CRA) function—1991; Conflict

Alert IFR/VFR Mode C Intruder—1989; Voice Switching and Control System (VSCS)—1993; Automated En Route Air Traffic Control (AERA)—2000.

GROUND-TO-AIR SYSTEMS

- Improved VOR/DME reliability by replacing all VOR/DME and VORTAC tube-type equipment with solid-state systems (completed in 1985). Along with relocating certain VORs for operational reasons, as many as 70 new VOR/DME sites may be selected to meet identified needs. Conversion of VORs to Doppler VORs (DVORs) will be underway, but the projected number of conversions is unclear. Another step is to add DME at 46 VOR-only sites. All projects should be completed by 1994.

- Upgrading the ILS landing system by replacing tube-type components with solid-states in 263 systems and retrofitting the systems with Remote Maintenance Monitoring (RMM). A basic premise is to keep the ILS system operational during the transition period leading to the introduction of MLS (Microwave Landing System) in the late 1990s.

- The approach of MLS, which has been adopted by ICAO as the worldwide replacement of ILS. Tests began in 1988, but full implementation and the phase-out of ILS is a 1998-and-later project. ILS is a 50-year-old system, subject to signal fluctuations caused by terrain, structures, and weather. Furthermore, it is basically two-dimensional, allowing only a straight-in approach to the airport in accordance with glide slope and localizer signals. MLS, on the other hand, is not materially subject to terrain, weather, or structures, and it permits a multiple-curved approach and pilot-selected glide slope angles. Also, connected with MLS is precision distance measuring equipment (DME-P) that is compatible with conventional DMEs. Final implementation date: 2004.

- The ongoing upgrading of runway lighting.

- Replacing the tube-type Direction Finding system with solid-state equipment, plus adding equipment in areas where the present DF does not provide complete coverage. Completion: 1993.

- More and more signs of the advent of the Mode S transponder. As mentioned in Chapter 5, Mode S (selective address) permits direct interrogation of a given aircraft and, through a digital data link, the exchange of information between the aircraft and automated ATC functions. If the aircraft is electronically equipped (meaning with a computer keyboard, printer, and cathode ray tube), the pilot can request or receive information and data from an automated ATC function. All this is done through data links and automation, with no voice communications required.

210

Also, with Mode S, the Traffic Alert and Collision Avoidance System (TCAS) will come into being. The first Mode S systems, to be installed in 1990, will provide data link coverage down to 12,500 feet MSL. Starting in 1994, the next set of systems will extend the coverage down to 6000 feet MSL. By 1995, Mode S should be well established.

- An aviation weather program that will provide more extensive data (precipitation, wind velocity, and turbulence) to controllers. The project includes the development, procurement, testing, and installation of long-range Doppler weather radar for enroute purposes. The equipment is called NEXRAD (Next Generation Weather Radar). Implementation of enroute NEXRAD is scheduled for 1991, and 1992 for 17 selected terminal sites. Those at the terminals, however, will only be the forerunners of the Terminal Doppler Weather Radar (TDWR) that is currently being evaluated.

- The implementation of Terminal Doppler Weather Radar which detects microbusts, wind shifts, gust fronts, and precipitation. At least three air carrier accidents have been attributed to one or more of these weather phenomena in landing or takeoff postures. When TDWR becomes operational, it will replace NEXRAD at those terminals where NEXRAD had been installed. Forty-seven TDWR systems, plus options for up to 102, have been ordered, with implementation scheduled for 1993 and completion in 1997.

Other Ground-to-Air projects and completion dates include: Global Positioning Systems (GPS)—1997; Runway Visual Range (RVR) improvements—1994; Airport Surveillance Radar (ASR) program—1991; LORAN-C system—1991.

CONCLUSION

These, then, are most of the projects formulated by the FAA as early in 1981. Of the original 92, only 18 (20 percent) have been completed, so there's a lot of work still to be done. And it's costly but essential work if industry demands are to be met. In the long run though, economies are inevitable—economies in aircraft operations, fuel consumption, FAA ground personnel, ATC and FSS equipment, and equipment maintenance. And then there's the ever-present factor that supercedes all other considerations: safety. Undoubtedly, the NASP will change as innovations and technical improvements come on the scene, but those I've cited here are the principal actions currently on the drawing board that will lead us into the next century.

The public and the media have been clamoring rather vocally for FAA action on midair collisions, reported near-misses, weather delays, airport congestion, and so on. The updated National Airspace System Plan should put much of the criticism to rest. The FAA *is* doing something, but it takes time to revamp and modernize a system that had been allowed to grow willy-nilly during the years leading up to 1980.

The ball is not entirely in the FAA's court, however. It can't order air carriers to stop inundating airports with 5:00 P.M. departures or arrivals; it can't stop them from establishing traffic-choking hubs; it can't direct states or municipalities to add runways or build new airports; and it can't stop careless pilots from violating regulations, disregarding checklists, acting as though "it can't happen to me," or committing any of the other errors of omission or commission that often lead to tragedy.

On the other hand, it is the FAA's responsibility to do everything within its power to provide the industry with the necessary equipment, technology, and human resources that ensure a safe, efficient system. Coupled with its pilot operating rules and regulations, the FAA's NASP, when fully implemented, should do just that and, in the process, achieve the various goals listed earlier in this chapter.

In Conclusion ...

THE ONE THING THAT PROBABLY WON'T CHANGE IN THE FIELD OF AVIATION over the next dozen years is change itself. The NASP is ample indication of what lurks around the corner in equipment and automation. But change is not limited just to future hardware. Operating rules and regulations are in a state of flux as well. There's enough evidence of that with the new Mode C requirements, the restructuring of TCAs, more and more ARSAs, the "Designated Airport Area," the expansion of controlled airspace, the proposed reclassification of airspace— and how these will impact on all pilots, IFR as well as VFR. Automation is the trend of the future, and we've seen only the beginning of it, with the AFSSs as a prime example.

All of us who hold valid pilot licenses are going to have to be students of what change brings. If we don't keep up with the times, including new regulations and new equipment requirements, we'll be as out of date as a 1980 Sectional. It's not hard, once we get a private ticket, to become a little complacent—or overconfident—or just lazy. We've passed the tough tests, ground and flight, and perhaps have the tendency to rest on those laurels. There are those among us who level off at a certain learning altitude and never try to climb any higher.

Proficiency and currency take work. A lot of us are part-time pilots who probably average 75 to 100 hours a year—if we're lucky. In between, we've got a job to tend to, a family to care for, or an education to complete. Flying is an avocation, a hobby, for all but those who do it for business purposes. With all of the other concerns and responsibilities, it's easy to lose touch. Back when change was not as dramatic, what applied yesterday probably applied today. Then, if currency wasn't maintained, we weren't that much out of touch. A brief ground and flight review would bring us up to snuff.

But that was then—not today. Even a thorough biennial flight review may not be enough. With the way things are going, it would be difficult to absorb in a couple of hours of ground instruction all of the ''new'' that has or will come to pass.

The monkey for keeping current is on the pilot's back. That means reading all we can read about new and proposed rules, regulations, procedures, and equipment requirements that would affect us. It means attending FAA seminars or ''Operation Raincheck,'' or participating in the FAA's Pilot Proficiency Wings Program, or joining general aviation organizations such as the Aircraft Owners and Pilots Organization, the Civil Air Patrol, or state pilot associations. Or any combination thereof.

True, the majority of us are not professional pilots, in the sense that we fly for a living. And true, we probably have a raft of other interests and responsibilities. Neither fact, however, relieves us of the need to maintain informational currency as well as pilot proficiency. Once again, it's a matter of *knowledge* plus *skill* equaling *professionalism*, in whatever the field may be. Flying probably isn't the source of our paychecks, but that doesn't mean we can't be a professional pilot as far as knowledge and skill are concerned.

Admittedly, some of this sounds like preaching, but the very purpose of this book was to contribute to the general aviation pilot's knowledge and understanding of our airspace and air traffic control systems. I don't pretend to have described every function or facility in its most minute detail, or to have given examples and descriptions that are universal throughout the system. No two facilities are identical, nor do they function exactly the same. Despite relatively minor variations, there is a necessary commonality. If there weren't, we wouldn't have a ''national'' airspace system. Instead, it would resemble the patchwork of local and state regulations, or the period of nonregulation of the '20s and the '30s. What a mess that would be, as we move into the '90s!

So, if the preceding chapters have shed just a little more light on the subject, the purpose of the book will have been achieved. I doubt that this will be the last word on the subject of airspace and ATC, but until change warrants the printing of another edition, I wish you well in the world of flight.

Acronyms
and Abbreviations

AAS	Advanced Automation System or Airport Advisory Service
ACF	Area Control Facility
ADF	Automatic Direction Finding
ADIZ	Air Defense Identification Zone
AERA	Automated Enroute Air Traffic Control
A/FD	*Airport/Facility Directory*
AFSS	Automated Flight Service Station
A/G	Air-to-Ground
AGL	Above Ground Level
AIM	*Airman's Information Manual*
AIRMET	Airmen's Meteorological Information
ALNOT	Alert Notice
App	Approach Control
ARF	Airport Reservation Function
ARSA	Airport Radar Service Area
ARSR	Airport Route Surveillance Radar
ARTCC	Air Route Traffic Control Center
ARTS	Automated Radar Terminal System
ASDE	Automated Surface Detection Equipment
ASR	Airport Surveillance Radar

Acronyms and Abbreviations

AT	Air Traffic
ATA	Airport Traffic Area
ATC	Air Traffic Control
ATCAA	Air Traffic Control Assigned Airspace
ATCRBS	Air Traffic Control Radar Beacon System
ATCS	Air Traffic Control Specialist
ATCT	Air Traffic Control Tower
ATIS	Automatic Terminal Information Service
AWOS	Automated Weather Observing System
BRITE	Bright Radar Indicator Tower Equipment
CA	Conflict Alert
CAA	Civil Aeronautics Authority
CAB	Civil Aeronautics Board
CA/MSAW	Conflict Alert/Minimum Safe Altitude Warning
CARF	Central Altitude Reservation Function
CD	Clearance Delivery
Center	Air Route Traffic Control Center
CERAP	Combined Center Radar Approach Control
CL	Clearance (Delivery)
CONUS	Continental, Contiguous, or Conterminous United States
CRT	Cathode Ray Tube
CTAF	Common Traffic Advisory Frequency
CWSU	Center Weather Service Unit
CZ	Control Zone
"D"	"Developmental" controller or specialist
Dep	Departure Control
DF	Direction Finder
DLP	Data Link Processor
DME	Distance Measuring Equipment
DME/P	Precision Distance Measuring Equipment
DOD	Department of Defense
DOT	Department of Transportation
DUAT	Direct User Access Terminal
DVOR	Doppler Very High Frequency Omni-Directional Range
EARTS	Enroute Automated Radar Tracking System
EFAS	Enroute Flight Advisory Service
ELAC	Enroute Low Altitude Chart
ELT	Emergency Locator Transmitter
EPA	Environmental Protection Agency
ESP	Enroute Spacing Program
ETA	Estimated Time of Arrival
ETD	Estimated Time of Departure

216

ETE	Estimated Time Enroute
FAA	Federal Aviation Administration
FARs	Federal Aviation Regulations
FDEP	Flight Data Entry and Printout
FDIO	Flight Data Input/Output
FPL	Full Performance Level controller or specialist
FSAS	Flight Service Automation System
FSP	Flight Strip Printer
FSS	Flight Service Station
GC	Ground Control
GCA	Ground Control Approach
GOES	Geostationary Operational Environmental Satellite
HIWAS	Hazardous In-Flight Weather Advisory Service
HVAC	Heating, Ventilating, and Air Conditioning
IATA	International Air Transport Association
ICAN	International Convention for Air Navigation
ICAO	International Civil Aviation Organization
IFAPA	International Federation of Airline Pilots Association
IFR	Instrument Flight Rules
ILS	Instrument Landing System
IMC	Instrument Meteorological Conditions
INREQ	Request for Information
INPAID	Identification-Position-Altitude-Intentions (or) Destination
IR	Military Instrument Flight Training Route
ISSS	Initial Sector Suite Subsystem
IVRS	Interim Voice Response System
LLWAS	Low Level Wind Shear Alert System
LORAN	Long Range Navigation
MARSA	Military Assumes Responsibility for Separation of Aircraft
MLS	Microwave Landing System
MOA	Military Operations Area
Mode 3/A	Standard transponder without altitude-reporting capability
Mode C	Standard transponder with altitude-reporting capability
Mode S	Selectively addressable transponder with data link
MRU	Military Radar Unit
MSAW	Minimum Safe Altitude Warning
MSL	Mean Sea Level
MTR	Military Training Route
MULTICOM	nongovernment air-to-air radio communications frequency
NAR	National Airspace Review
NAS	National Airspace System
NASP	National Airspace System Plan

Acronyms and Abbreviations

NDB	Nondirectional Beacon
NEXRAD	Next Generation Weather Radar
NM	Nautical Miles
NOAA	National Oceanic and Atmospheric Administration
NOTAM	Notice To Airmen
NWS	National Weather Service
PAR	Precision Approach Radar
PATWAS	Pilots Automatic Telephone Weather Answering Service
PIREP	Pilot Report
PVD	Planned Visual Display
RAPCON	Radar Approach Control
RCAG	Remote Center Air/Ground Communications Facility
RCF	Remote Communications Facility
RCO	Remote Communications Outlet
RDT&E	Research, Development, Testing & Evaluation
RML	Radar Microwave Link
RMM	Remote Maintenance Monitoring
RNAV	Area Navigation
RTR	Remote Transmitter/Receiver
RVR	Runway Visual Range
SIGMET	Significant Meteorological Information
SM	Statute Miles
Squawk	Activate specific number code in the transponder
SUA	Special Use Airspace
SVFR	Special Visual Flight Rules
TA	Transition Area
TAC	Terminal Area Chart
TACAN	Tactical Air Navigation
TCA	Terminal Control Area
TCAS	Traffic Alert and Collision Avoidance System
TDWR	Terminal Doppler Weather Radar
TIBS	Transcribed Information Briefing Service
TML	Television Microwave Link
TMS	Traffic Management System
TMU	Traffic Management Unit
TPX	Military Beacon System
TRACAB	Terminal Radar Approach Control in the Tower Cab
TRACON	Terminal Radar Approach Control
TRSA	Terminal Radar Service Area
TWEB	Transcribed Weather Broadcast
UHF	ultra high frequency
UNICOM	non-government air/ground radio communications facility

Acronyms and Abbreviations

UTC	Coordinated Universal Time
VFR	Visual Flight Rules
VHF	very high frequency
VOR	VHF Omnidirectional Range
VOR/DME	VOR also equipped with DME
VORTAC	VOR co-located with TACAN
VR	Military VFR Training Route
VRS	Voice Response System

About the Author

Paul E. "Pete" Illman is the owner and president of Management Training, Inc., an international consulting firm specializing in training programs for business managers. Mr. Illman holds a commercial certificate with single- and multiengine ratings. A graduate of Harvard University, Mr. Illman was a B-25 instrument flight instructor in Albany, Georgia. Mr. Illman spent 30 years with Trans World Airlines, holding various positions, including Director of Customer Service Training and Director of Marketing Management Training.

Mr. Illman is a coauthor of *The Pilot's Radio Communications Handbook—3rd Edition* (TAB book #2445) and lives with his wife, Susan, in Prairie Village, Kansas.

Index